PERESTROIKA AND THE SOVIET PEOPLE

To the memory of
PETR PETROVICH SIUDA 1937 – 1990
and to the other participants of the strike in
Novocherkassk on June 1-2 1962

PERESTROIKA AND THE SOVIET PEOPLE

Rebirth of the Labour Movement

DAVID MANDEL

Montréal/NewYork

© **BLACK ROSE BOOKS 1991**
No part of this book may be reproduced or transmitted in any form by means, electronic or mechanical, including photocopying and recording, or by any information storage or retrieval, without written permission from the publisher, except for brief passages quoted by a reviewer in a newspaper or magazine.

BLACK ROSE BOOKS No. V164
Paperback ISBN: 1-895431-14-X
Hardcover ISBN: 1-895431-15-8

Canadian Cataloguing in Publication Data

Mandel, David, 1947 –
  Perestroika and the Soviet People

ISBN 1-895431-15-8 (bound) – ISBN 1-895431-14-X (pbk.)

  1. Perestroika.   2. Soviet Union—Economic conditions—1985–   .
3. Soviet Union—Politics and government—1985–   . I. Title.

DK286.M36   1991   947.085'4   C91-090495-2

Library of Congress Catalog No. 91-72984
Cover Design: Werner Arnold

Editorial Offices
BLACK ROSE BOOKS
3981 St-Laurent Boulevard
Suite 444
Montréal, Québec
H2W 1Y5 Canada

Mailing Address
BLACK ROSE BOOKS
P.O. Box 1258
Succ. Place du Parc
Montréal, Québec
H2W 2R3 Canada

BLACK ROSE BOOKS
340 Nagel Drive
Cheektowaga, New York
14225 USA

CONTENTS

Acknowledgements vi

Introduction 1

1. "Revolutionary Reform" In Soviet Factories: Restructuring Relations Between Workers and Managers 7

2. Perestroika and Women Workers 43

3. The Rebirth of the Soviet Labour Movement: The Coalminers' Strike of July 1989 51

4. Soviet Trade Unions at the Crossroads 79

5. "A Market Without Thorns": The Ideological Struggle for the Soviet Working Class 91

6. "Destatization" and the Struggle for Power in the Soviet Economy: A New Phase in the Labour Movement 117

7. The Strike Wave of March-April 1991 155

Acknowledgements

Many people, too numerous to name, have helped me in writing this book. Over the past years, I have been fortunate to discuss the issues treated here with Soviet workers in different branches and from different cities and towns. Among these, I probably learnt the most from Serezha Agapov, an autoworker and a good friend. Although we disagree on many things, we share the view that an active working class is the key to a genuinely democratic transformation of the Soviet Union and the only social force capable of blocking the "revolution from above" that is being attempted by the new/old élites. Although our acquaintance has been brief, I have also learnt much from Aleksandr Sergeev, a miner and one of the clearest minds in the Independent Miners' Union.

My discussions with Soviet intellectuals have generally been less fruitful. But fortunately, there were important exceptions. Three people to whom I owe a particular debt are economists Yurii Sukhotin, Viktor Dement'ev and the late Viktor Bogachev. The generous help they afforded me in coming to grips with the complex and quickly evolving political-economic reality has been invaluable. Possibly even more important has been the moral support I have received from the knowledge that there are socialists among the Soviet intelligentsia who believe, and can convincingly argue, that socialism is a realistic — indeed, *the* realistic — alternative for the Soviet Union. I have also benefited greatly from discussions with Nikolai Preobrazhenskii, Aleksandr Buzgalin, Andrei Kolganov, Vadim Rogovin, and Lena Gordeeva. Of course, I alone bear responsiblity for the views expressed in this book.

Among the people who have commented on various parts of this book, I would like to thank in particular Allen Fenichel, Leo Panitch, Dave Melnychuk, and Andrea Levy.

Most of all, I would like to express my gratitude to Sonia, my wife, who has graciously tolerated my extended absences from the household over the past years while I was doing research for this book.

This research was funded by a Social Science and Humanities Research Council Canada Scholarship.

INTRODUCTION

The essays in this volume were written between January 1989 and June 1991. All but the final one have been published earlier. They have been edited minimally with a view to avoiding repetition, but the original analyses have not been modified. This introduction, written two weeks after the abortive coup of August 19-21 1991 that led Gorbachev to call for the dissolution of the Communist Party, presents an appropriate occasion to look back and to evaluate the point of view that has informed this book.

This point of view is socialist. By this I mean simply that my point of departure was a concern for democracy in the most basic sense of the term: government for and by the people. Among other things, this means that the basic decisions about the economy, certainly the most fundamental sphere of social life, cannot be left in the private hands of a privileged minority. In contrast, it is just such a "revolution from above", one that would transform the mode of domination without eliminating domination, that was, and remains, the aim of the bureaucratic reformers who initiated perestroika. This aim is shared by their radical liberal sometime critics and sometime allies.

This point of view may surprise readers who are accustomed to the linking by our media and politicians of "democracy" with "market reform" (or more accurately, "capitalism" — the term that seems to arouse shame.) We are told that Western aid to the Soviet Union must be premised upon the progress of "democratic and market reform," as if there could not possibly be any contradiction between the two. But if democracy were a genuine concern (Western leaders do not insist on it very much elsewhere in the world, for example, in China, Guatemala or Kuwait), surely the people themselves, and not the developed capitalist states should decide what sort of economic reform corresponds best to their interests.

For this to occur, the people of the former Soviet Union would have to cease being passive objects of the state and become the collective subject of their own history. My decision to focus on the workers in these essays rested upon the hypothesis, itself based upon my reading of modern world and Russian/Soviet history, that the workers are the only social force with both the interest and the political potential for carrying through the consistent democratic transformation of the Soviet state and society.

Has this hypothesis been borne out? Yes and no. As usual, history has proven itself more cunning than any theory. The labour movement is today the main organized social force in Soviet society. The only other significant forces are the national movements, principally in the Soviet periphery, and the liberal movement. But it is difficult to qualify these as organized social forces. They are better described as élites with a basis in atomized masses who are moved more by symbol and emotion than rational calculation of interest. The labour movement has also proven itself the most consistently and radically democratic force in Soviet society. To that degree, the hypothesis has been supported.

On the other hand, the process of "class formation" has proven much more tortuous and drawn-out than I had anticipated. The organized labour movement today still embraces only a relatively small part of the working class. In retrospect, this is perhaps not surprising. The Soviet workers have only recently emerged from over 60 years of harsh political repression which had made independent organization impossible. The "Stalin revolution" (more precisely, counterrevolution), collectivization, mass immigration from the countryside, and the terror broke any living ties between this class and its historically brief, but rich and heroic past.

Perhaps even more important was the bureaucratic regime's ideological monopoly. Even the minority of people citizens who through great personal efforts succeeded in freeing themselves from it often remained decisively under its influence. "Critical thought" in the Soviet Union tended — and unfortunately still tends — to be a blanket rejection of everything emanating from official (or until recently, official) sources. Especially among the liberal intelligentsia, the Stalinist mode of thought still thrives and manifests itself in the eagerness to impose "harsh and unpopular measures" upon a reluctant population, whose mentality is said to be too much influenced by the past for it to understand its "real" interests. For the workers, the consequence of this ideological monopoly had been the identification of socialism with the old régime and, consequently, increasingly a rejection of socialism itself. To this extent, too, the reality has contradicted the hypothesis.

Of course, the repudiation of socialism has been greatly aided by a steamroller-like, anti-socialist propaganda campaign conducted by both the Communist and liberal mass media over the past few years. Nevertheless, this campaign could not have had the same impact had it not found a fertile social soil. Looking back, this too should not have been unexpected.

Almost 25 years ago, the great Marxist historian of the Soviet Union, Isaac Deutscher, wrote: "… The Soviet Union…seems to be burdened with a mass of accumulated disillusionment and even despair that in other historical circumstances might have been the driving force of a restoration. At times the Soviet Union appears to be fraught with the moral-psychological potentiality of restoration that cannot become a political actuality." This was written just before the onset of the "period of stagnation," that, perhaps even more than Stalin's terror, did so much to utterly discredit the régime.

In the above passage, Deutscher formulated the essential contradiction of the period treated in the present volume and which runs through each of its essays: in practice, the concrete aspirations, demands and actions of the Soviet workers today are compatible only with a democratic, socialist transformation of the society, but this transformation is blocked to a significant degree by the ideological rejection of, or inability to formulate, a socialist alternative. However, the other side of this contradiction is that the working class remains the major obstacle preventing "the moral-psychological potentiality of restoration from becoming a political actuality."

To this extent, then, the original hypothesis has been borne out. he future shape of Soviet society hangs on how this contradiction is resolved: either the new-old élites will resolve it in their favour, neutralizing and/or crushing the labour movement, or inversely, the labour movement will develop its own programme of socio-political transformation corresponding to popular interests and will prevent the efforts to limit democratization to "Western-style" competition among political élites, whose basic concern is to "maintain the confidence of the business community."

This question is today still very much open. The effect of the abortive coup of August 19-21, contrary to its portrayal in the media as little less than a revolution, has been to accelerate processes already well advanced in the Soviet Union. The coup revealed in dramatic, definitive fashion, the weakness of the conservative forces, every one of whose previous non-violent counter-offensives had also resulted in strengthening the liberals. It also consolidated the Gorbachev-Yeltsin alliance, that is, the alliance between reform bureaucrats and liberals, that had been re-established on April 23 by the "accord of ten." This accord had also marked Gorbachev's acceptance of the complete destruction of the old Union and an accelerated transition to capitalism.

The role attributed to Yeltsin and his liberal supporters in defeating the coup appears to be greatly exaggerated. Rarely has the world witnessed so ineptly organized and indecisively executed an attempt to seize power by people already standing at the head of the state. The coup's authors did not even assure the loyalty of the repressive apparatuses, the army, Ministry of Internal Affairs and even the KGB. Most of these forces, even had the new leaders decided to use them, did not support the coup.

On the other hand, neither was the coup defeated by popular mobilization, which was quite minimal. A crucial question is why. The crowd in front of the Russian Supreme Soviet may have reached 130,000 at its peak but most often did not exceed 20,000 to 30,000. Even the Moscow crowds celebrating the coup's defeat hardly surpassed the same 100,000 figure that has been cited for virtually every major pro-Yeltsin demonstration of the past year. What are the other 8,900,000 Muscovites thinking? And the tens of millions outside of Moscow? Why did workers, except in some coalmines and in some factories in Sverdlovsk (Yeltsin's old stomping ground), not respond to Yeltsin's call for a general strike? Should this be attributed to political fatigue and apathy, to a sense of political impotence, or to ambivalence about the coup as well as about the opposing Yeltsin camp? According to one report, workers in many Leningrad enterprises declared their readiness to strike…if the need arose. But in Moscow's factories, nothing much at all seems to have happened. Perhaps this wait-and-see attitude reflected a sense of the coup's weakness. After all, virtually the whole government, except for Gorbachev, kept working, and "normal life" (a relative term in the Soviet Union today) went on as usual.

These questions are crucial because the next months will see an attempt to speed up the market reform. The fact that the coup was defeated without a mobilization on the part of the workers surely strengthens the autonomy of Yeltsin and the liberals in this area: they are, for moment at least, less dependent upon working class and popular support and will soon have their own loyal bureaucracies, propaganda machines, and repressive forces firmly in place. In fact, the liberals are now in the process of carrying out their own coup, with scarcely more respect for democratic procedure than the defeated conservatives.

On the other hand, it will not be possible much longer for liberals to blame the deteriorating economic situation on the Communists and on the absence of "real" reform. There will no longer be conservative provocations to bolster the liberals' flagging popularity. The market reform will cease to be an abstract symbolic issue for workers (the promise of Western wages and living standards), enabling them to define more clearly their attitudes toward it on the basis of concrete experience with its functioning and consequences. It is also possible that the coup's defeat, despite the limited popular mobilization, will leave the population with an increased sense of its own strength and political efficacy, something that the past five years of economic decline have been unable to do.

Will the population remain an essentially passive spectator to the coming transformations, as has been the case so far in Eastern Europe? Or will it organize in defence of its interests and become the author of its own destiny? These are the key questions that will be answered by the new chapter in Soviet history opened by the failed coup.

September, 1991
Montréal

Chapter 1

"Revolutionary Reform" In Soviet Factories: Restructuring Relations Between Workers and Managers

On June 2, 1962, on the second day of their strike, the workers of the giant Novocherkassk Electric Locomotive Factory, joined by the rest of the worker population of this southern Russian town, set off for the city centre some 10 kilometers away. Peter Siuda, then a worker at the locomotive factory and one of the strike leaders who had been arrested early that morning, gives the following account of what followed, based on eye-witness reports. "Red flags and portraits of Lenin appeared in the columns. The demonstrators sang revolutionary songs. As they approached the bridge over the railway and the Tuzlov River, the demonstrators saw on the bridge a cordon of armed soldiers and two tanks. The column halted and fell silent. The revolutionary songs ceased. Then shouts rang out: 'Make way for the working class!' These shouts grew into a mass chant. With precision and tremendous force, they repeated: 'Make way for the working class!' The soldiers and tankmen did not try to stop the column but began to help the workers over the tanks. The massive current of humanity flowed around the cordon and over the tanks on the bridge. Spirits soared and the demonstrators again took up the revolutionary songs, louder than before, more forcefully, and in unison." [1]

"This wasn't the programmed celebration of people going to our May First demonstrations," comments Siuda. "These were free, unchained workers on the march. They were convinced of the justice of their cause. They were going to defend their rights. And, in the last analysis, they were going to their own Soviet government. I'm speaking of revolutionary songs, banners, portraits of Lenin. This was no game, no holiday spectacle directed from above. They believed. They were going to their Soviet government, to their party, in search of truth. They wanted to be heard and to discuss. And when they arrived, the city party commmittee was cordoned off by troops. No one came out. No one wanted to speak to them." In the chain of events that followed, the workers stormed and seized the party committee. When they learnt that there had been arrests, some headed down the street to the police station (adjoining the political police) and stormed it. The order to open fire was given here and at the party committee. To this day, the state has not revealed the number of workers, their family members and bystanders, all unarmed, killed in this massacre. Their grave-sites also remain a state secret.

In Siuda's account, several elements form the background to these events, which were a part of a larger wave of worker protest that swept the Soviet Union in this period.[2] "The Novocherkassk events were preceded in the 1950s by the processes of public revelation [exposing 'glasnost'] of the crimes of Stalinism, the debunking of the 'cult of the personality', the attempted humanization of socialism. The people believed in the genuineness of these processes... This democratization announced in the 1950 once again took in the people, gave the toilers hope that they could successfully conduct a dialogue with the authorities... But the party 'chiefs' and state leaders, while condemning the 'personality cult', left intact stalinism itself, the criminal party-state system,...the voluntarism of the 'chiefs', of the leaders and bureaucrats, the arbitrary rule of the élite and the absence of rights of the masses, the organs of repression, the KGB and MVD [Ministry of Internal Affairs], that remained outside of society's control."

At the same time, "in those years, wage rates were being arbitrarily lowered virtually every year. This allowed the bureaucrats to attain the high indicators of labour productivity and lowered production costs demanded by the central authorities, without the corresponding capital investments, increased mechanization and automation of production, or organizational changes and qualitative improvement of technological processes ... Beginning from January 1, 1962, at the locomotive factory, the campaign began anew to lower wage rates in all the shops. They were reduced by 30-35%. The last shop to have its rates lowered was the steel foundry, in May... Then on June 1, the central radio announced a sharp, "temporary" rise in the prices of meat, milk, eggs, and other food products."

The housing and food supply situation in Novocherkassk were particularly bad, "but even these circumstances would probably not have led to a strike, if a presumptuous bureaucrat bastard had not thrown into the 'powder keg' of popular indignation and dissatisfaction the spark of insult, of lordly impudence." On the morning of June 1, the workers were discussing the news of the price rise in their shops. They were especially angry in the steel foundry. Still, no one was talking about a strike. The director and party committee secretary came to talk to the workers. As they spoke, a woman went by carrying meat pies. Seeing this, the director turned to the workers: "If you don't have money for meat and sausage, then eat liver pies." This was the spark that set off the strike: "And the bastards are even laughing at us!" In a few minutes, the whole factory was shut down by a spontaneous movement that ended in the the city centre with the seizure of the party committee building and the massacre of demonstrators and bystanders. Early on in the strike, the workers had tried to notify other towns of their action — to this end, they stopped a passenger train on the Moscow-Rostov mainline — but the town was sealed off by the authorities with amazing speed.

This chapter analyzes, not the events of the early 1960s, but the changes that are occurring in the relations between labour and management in Soviet industry today. One can certainly question the appropriateness of beginning an analysis of the current restructuring of relations between workers and management with an account of events that took place 27 years ago under Khruschchev. On both the levels of discourse and practice, perestroika makes the Khrushchev era seem a timid affair. The present Soviet leadership has repeatedly declared its intention to carry through a deep, structural reform of the economy and has explicitly recognized that there can be no such reform without democratization of the state. And although what has been achieved until now falls far short of these declared aims, even if perestroika were to end today, it would still have been an incomparably more radical episode than the Khrushchev years.

In many ways, the official conception of perestroika appears aimed not only at improving economic performance but also at eliminating the very basis for Novocherkassk-type confrontations. "Probably the most serious social consequence of the period of stagnation in our country," write two Soviet economists,

> is the alienation of the bulk of the working masses from the management of production and the life of society, the split of society as a whole, of territorial communities, and work-collectives into managers and subordinates, rank and file and bosses, that has taken form and consolidated itself in the consciousness of all social groups. A direct consquence of this is the indifference, not only of the bureaucratic apparatus, but of many workers, toward concrete actions of

restructuring [perestroika] on their jobs, in their shops, enterprises, micro-districts, etc. Overcoming this division, the transformation of the worker into a real owner of the socialist property, is the goal both of the restructuring of the economic mechanism now occurring and of the growing democratization of management.[3]

Yet this passage typically directs its criticism at the "period of stagnation" i.e. the Brezhnev era. By contrast, favourable parallels are being drawn between perestroika and the Khruschev period. Indeed, Khrushchev, with official approval, has become something of a hero in the Soviet media. He had shortcomings, we are told, but he was moving in the generally correct direction, only to be cut short by the "forces of stagnation." The following examination of perestroika from the perspective of the shop floor (at least as it has manifested itself until now) does, in fact, give one a certain sense of *déjà vu*. And it leaves one wondering about the significance of the fact that, despite the current preoccupation of Soviet writers and journalists with the past, Siuda has so far been unsuccessful in his attempts to draw the Novocherkassk events into the realm of "glasnost'."

Worker-Management Relations Under the "Command Economy"

In the past, under the "command economy," workers enjoyed *de facto* job security.[4] In addition, although wages might vary from month to month, a worker's average wage was virtually guaranteed, as long as he or she observed basic discipline. Bonuses, premiums, participation coefficients and other supplementary payments — up to 50% of the takehome pay — that in theory depended on quality and intensity of work, were to a significant degree automatic. Instead of wages depending upon norms, as measures of labour, norms were often adapted to ensure a specific wage level, itself only loosely, if at all, related to productivity. Notices on Soviet factory gates commonly promised a takehome pay that already included bonuses and premiums.

This arrangement was necessary in order to attract and keep a large enough work force to meet plan targets in conditions of chronic labour shortage and the uneven supply to the enterprise of raw materials and semi-manufactured goods. The "command system" by creating and maintaining this labour shortage thus afforded the workers a certain bargaining power (they could "vote with their feet"), even in the absence of trade unions to defend their interests. At the same time, management had little countervailing incentive to economize on labour costs. The enterprise's wage fund came from the state budget and was calculated largely on the basis of past performance in such a way as to discourage too-significant rises in productivity (that would penalize the enterprise the next year) and to encourage managers to maintain the average wage and number of workers at relatively higher levels.[5]

An additional consequence of this situation was a pronounced levelling tendency in wages within enterprises and sectors. Although the spread in basic pay rates (tarifnye stavki) of different skill levels was quite broad, the effect of these differentials was undermined by the various supplementary payments, which, as noted, were to a significant degree automatic and which made up a large, and increasing, part of the takehome pay. This levelling tendency was further reinforced by the practice of assigning workers to the higher skill levels, regardless of actual qualification, as a means of attracting scarce labour.

The worker's wage thus bore a rather a loose relationship, not only to the intensity and quality of his or her individual labour, but also to the performance of the enterprise. Even if in principle a part of a worker's total annual wage and social benefits depended on enterprise performance — mainly, meeting and surpassing (though only slightly — to avoid an overly difficult plan the next year) gross output indicators — in practice the ministry would often intervene to lower the targets of failing enterprises. After all, it was also interested in the "success" of its enterprises.

The motivating role of the individual wage was further undermined by the relative importance of the social wage — free or subsidized goods and services — that, by definition bears no direct relationship to the individual labour furnished. The significant growth of the part of the social wage in incomes over the past few decades was a goal of the party programme adopted under Khrushchev, who saw this as a measure bringing Soviet society closer to communism.[6]

Under the "command system" relations between workers and enterprise management were fundamentally conflictual. Labour under this system, as under capitalism, remained alienated i.e. fundamentally coerced. And so workers saw their interest in witholding effort; management's task was to intensify it. But this antagonism was tempered by an element of shared interest and collusion. For, to a very large extent, management too was interested in concealing productive potential in order to avoid too-difficult plans imposed from above and to be able to deal with the irregular supply system. Neither side, for example, wanted "hard" norms. Workers — for reasons common to all alienated labour; management — because "soft" norms gave it the reserves needed to meet plan targets, especially by the inevitable "storming" at the end of the month and quarter, in conditions of chronic supply problems and frequent outside demands on its labour force (so-called "patronage tasks"). Management generally did its best, through legal and often illegal means, and in the face of contrary pressures from central authorities, to give the workers a relatively higher and stable wage. (It is now admitted, however, that because of price rises, "although the nominal wage in the national economy rose regularly over the past 18 years, from [an average of] 122 to over 200 rubles [a month], real incomes remained at the same level and in certain groups of the population even declined.")[7] It also looked the other way at certain infractions of discipline. In return, the workers helped management meet plan objectives by tolerating various violations of labour legislation and bad work conditions.[8]

While these characteristics of Soviet labour relations had existed in some degree since the 1930s, this system attained its fullest expression under Brezhnev. For this reason, some workers, only half-ironically refer to the last half of the Brezhnev era as their "golden age" — because it was relatively easy then to reach a working agreement with management. But it is important to emphasize that the extreme development of this system was the direct consequence of the régime's refusal to reform the economy, a refusal dictated by the corporate interests of its bureaucratic base as well as by a more general fear of the popular forces a structural reform of the economy might unleash. (The "Prague Spring" strongly reinforced these fears.) Brezhnev's régime was the bureaucratic régime par excellence. Brezhnev came to power declaring that he, unlike Khrushchev, would "respect cadres." Under his rule, the Politburo was eventually reduced to little more than the arbiter of particular bureaucratic interests.

It has been argued, especially by some members of the Soviet intelligentsia, that the workers were privileged under this system and corrupted by it. And yet, this system, in whose development the workers had had no say, was really directed against their fundamental interest in an efficient economy, responsive to popular needs. It did provide certain social guarantees, but they remained at a mediocre, inadequate level, and the price exacted for them was a heavy one: intensifying political repression, tremendous economic waste, widespread corruption, and the moral and cultural, and even physical degradation of society. The workers merely adapted as best they could, and the régime was forced to tolerate the situation in the enterprises as the cost of maintaining power. In theory, of course, the workers had an alternative: they could have sought collective, political solutions to their situation. But the failed wave of worker protest at the end of the Khruschev period (several years before the appearance of the "dissident movement") had shown that conditions were not then ripe for a successful popular mobilization. As for their being corrupted, as we shall see, dissatisfaction with the existing economic system is today no less strong among workers than in the rest of the population. If workers have so far shown no particular enthusiasm for the economic reform, it is not because they oppose change. It is rather that they have doubts about the nature of the change that is being offered them.

Reform Measures

The logic (if not necessarily, so far, the practice) of the "market reform" is to place enterprises under a "cost-accounting régime" (khozraschet), doing away for the most part with obligatory plan targets, and giving them broad autonomy to pursue profit within a regulated market context. The (central) state will continue to plan and regulate the economy, but through indirect methods, i.e. through control and manipulation of such economic (as opposed to administrative) levers as prices, credit, taxation and competitive state contracts.

This reform would end job security, since layoffs and bankruptcies become possible and, in fact, are already beginning to occur, though so far on a limited scale. It would also put an end to wage guarantees, since wages are to depend much more than before on the actual performance of the enterprise, as measured by profit, i.e what is left from sales after various payments have been made. The reform provides for two methods of calculating wages, one more "radical" than the other (the more radical one being officially preferred but so far rarely applied):

> a) Basic wages are paid as part of fixed costs according to state norms and so are guaranteed. But bonuses and

premiums are paid out of profits, after other financial obligations have been acquitted, and so depend upon enterprise performance.

b) No part of the wage is guaranteed. Wages are paid from what is left after meeting other financial obligations. In this case, the entire wage depends upon enterprise performance, as measured by profits.[9]

The wage reform also includes a review of skill classifications and norms, with a view to encouraging workers to raise their skills and to release hidden productive reserves. Accordingly, the part of the basic wage in takehome pay is to rise to 70-75%, and bonuses are to be made more difficult to achieve. To compensate this, basic wage rates are to rise on the average 20-25% (more for specialists and white-collar workers) over the course of the current five-year plan 1986-90. This rise, however, will not be financed by the state budget but must come from savings realized by the enterprise. That is why the specific timing of the reform's introduction is left up to the enterprise.[10]

An avowed goal of the reform is to increase wage differentiation in order to enhance the incentive role of wages. To the same end, there has been much discussion about the need to reduce the part of the social wage in incomes. This will be achieved through price reform, the reduction or elimination of subsidies, and the establishment of user fees for services that are presently free. "Levelling" stands officially condemned (as it has since Stalin's time, though perhaps now more insistently than ever) as economically inefficient as well as socially unjust, since, it is claimed, such egalitarianism contradicts the "socialist principle of distribution according to labour."[11]

The reform thus aims to tighten things up on the shopfloor. But another goal is to link the workers' well-being more closely to the performance of the enterprise, while the enterprise, on its part, enjoys significant autonomy in the pursuit of profit in a market context. The goal is to create a common motivation among managers and workers to discover and to release productive reserves, to increase individual and enterprise efficiency, and to produce quality goods that meet the needs of clients and consumers.

Those aspects of the reform aimed at democratizing enterprise management follow logically from this goal. In Gorbachev's words:

"The well-being of the worker will depend upon the abilities of the managers. The workers should, therefore, have real means of influencing the choice of director and controlling his activity."[12] This is a politically necessary corollary of enterprise autonomy. Otherwise, the Soviet enterprise director, freed from control from above in his or her disposition of the enterprise's resources and in setting prices, and newly armed with the means (the "stick" of dismissal and "carrot" of the reformed wage system) to extract an intensified labour effort, would resemble all too closely his or her capitalist counterpart. This would mean a unilateral abrogation of the old system of labour relations, which had allowed the régime to "buy" the workers' quiescence by affording them certain social guarantees and means of defence, at the same time as it fostered a collusive relationship with a paternalistic enterprise management. A "market reform" without enterprise democratization would be perceived by workers as a drastic and unjust undermining of their position vis-à-vis management, and it is not difficult to imagine them responding with massive unrest and/or the formation of independent economic (and almost by definition in the Soviet context) political organizations. Thus, for political and related ideological reasons, this is not a real option for the Soviet leaders.

Of course, the thinking behind enterprise democratization is not only political. It also has a more directly economic objective: together with the wage reform and cost-accounting, it is an attempt to overcome the workers' alienation, their indifference to the fate of the enterprise, and to foster a sense of responsibility toward this public property. Such an attitude has been woefully lacking (though not only among the workers, but also in management at all levels). According to the director of the research institute of the U.S.S.R. State Committee on Labour, "self-management today is designed to...awaken people, force them to feel themselves masters of production and of the country... Self-management is a way of uniting the interests of rank-and-file toilers, social groups and collectives with the interests of society."[13]

There are two main measures of enterprise democracy provided for by the "U.S.S.R. Law on the State Enterprise (Association)": the election of managerial personnel, and the empowering of the worker collective and its elected work-collective council to participate in management decisions and in the monitoring of their execution.

> Management of the enterprise is realized in conditions of broad openness (glasnost') through the participation of the entire collective and its social organizations in reaching highly important decisions and monitoring their fulfillment, the election of managers, and one-man management (edinachalie) in the administration of the enterprise. The pooling of the working people's efforts and the development of their initiative in achieving work results, the instilling of good work organization and discipline in personnel and the raising of their political consciousness are ensured on the basis of self-management.[14]

Before examining the present state of labour relations, it is worth pointing out the fuzziness and ambiguity of the law itself. The elected management "expresses the interests of the state and the work-collective", but the law does not explain what happens when the interests of the state and the work-collective come into conflict. Similarly, the director is elected by the collective but must be confirmed by the higher level agency, which can force a new election if it does not like the winner, although it must explain why. This veto power from above has been variously explained by possible "excesses" that can occur in the early stages of democracy and by the fact that the enterprise is state property, and the state must ensure its interests.

The law is equally unclear on the powers of the work collective and its council in relation to management. The appearance, without commentary, of the terms "democratic centralism" and "one-man management," notorious since the late 1920s for their authoritarian interpretation by the régime, is in itself worrying. The law also repeatedly uses the vague term "participation" to describe the role of the work collective and its council in the decision-making process. And it does not really clarify matters when the law finally states that "decisions of the work-collective council that are adopted within the bounds of its authority and in accordance with legislation are binding for management and the members of the collective." It is clear neither about the bounds of the council's authority nor about the other legislation that constrains its power. This absence of clarity cannot but raise doubts, since under Brezhnev work collectives also enjoyed broad powers on paper; yet it was the rare worker indeed who was even aware of their formal existence, let alone had ever seen them put into practice.[15]

In a similar vein, the call to revive trade-union democracy and to restore the unions' functions as defenders of the workers' interests appears as a strikingly incongruous element.[16] The provision for self-management and elected managers, whose aim is to overcome alienation and foster a real sense of ownership, would seem to obviate the need for trade unions. Even if conflict arose between labour and management, certainly the trade unions could be no more effective in resolving them than the work-collective councils, which after all, are elected by the same people but possess broader powers.

The Impact of Reform in the Factories

How have worker-management relations in industry changed so far under perestroika? First of all, it seems that the initial enthusiasm for the election of managerial personnel has waned. The authors of an article on the subject note that significantly fewer articles are being published on the subject, and their tone has become more sober, sometimes even pessimistic. "Such a shift in mood is the result of the fact that all those who especially wanted to have already tasted this 'dish'."[17] It seems that not all the workers (not to speak of managerial personnel!) were excited by the opportunity to hold elections and that those that were enthusiastic often found the "dish" less tasty than expected. Where workers did embrace elections as a means of changing things, of "putting affairs in order," they only too often had their hopes dashed.[18] This leads the authors of the above article to appeal "not to allow this important democratic principle to be 'buried'."

The new organs of "self-management," specifically the work-collective councils, have not fared much better. The head of the Department of Ideological Work of the party's Institute of Social Sciences concluded in mid-1988 that "the participation of the workers in management still remains a wish, a goal, rather than a reality." In a survey conducted by his school, only 14% of the respondents said they felt themselves the masters (khozyaeva) at work. (39% felt there was no owner, in the sense of someone concerned with, and responsible, for the fate of the enterprise.)[19] In another survey of 11,180 workers and white-collar employees of 120 large industrial enterprises from mid-1988, only 2.7% considered the councils to be "very active." 52.8% replied that they "have not yet fully shown themselves," and 18.3% said they were inactive. 11.1% replied that their enterprise had no council, and 15.3% were unable to give any opinion. V. Ivanov, the director of the Institute of Sociological Research interpreted this to mean that the attitude was one of "wait and see."[20] Another assessment made in the same period found that "the Law on the Enterprise is not functioning as it should. Collectives often refuse to take up the broad powers that have been given them. Democratization of management is clearing itself a path through outdated views and indifference only with great difficulty."[21]

As for the trade unions, by virtually all accounts, they have not responded to the calls for change: in conflicts between workers and management (not to speak of conflicts between workers' interest and those of the state at higher levels), they remain in solidarity with the latter.[22] A survey conducted by the research institute of the Central Trade-Union Council found that only one or two workers out of every hundred would turn to their trade unions in disputes involving wages. Meanwhile, although 80% of trade-union activists consider that the introduction of the wage reform in their enterprise is not in full accord with the law, the unions nevertheless remain silent.[23] In a letter to the trade-union paper *Trud*, a worker from Kharkov province wrote:

> It is no secret to anyone that trade unions don't always take the side of the workers. That may not be tragic if it's a minor issue and not one of principle. But when management takes revenge against a worker for criticism, and the trade union is either silent, or worse, supports the administration…I'll soon be 64 and I've often come up against such a situation.[24]

A trade-union activist from Novosibirsk asks:

> Why is it that our trade-union leaders, elected by the workers, again and again find themselves taking the side of the administration? …Earlier, I would not even have entertained the idea of going to management and demanding that it change this or that decision. But now we have democracy. Why are we not in a rush to use it?[25]

Of course, if self-management were becoming a reality, if the workers were acquiring a real voice in management and were adopting an attitude of solidarity with the administration in the common aim of improving the performance of the enterprise, the absence of trade-union combativity would not be an important issue. But not only is this not happening — the opposite is occurring. According to published reports from different Soviet sources, the number of conflicts between workers and management has risen sharply, this as a direct reaction to perestroika as experienced in the factories.[26] So far, at least, perestroika has failed to create in the workers a sense of ownership. Not only has it not reduced their alienation from enterprise management (let alone from the higher levels), but it appears to be intensifying their attitude of opposition, the sense of "us against them." It has done this by breaking down the old bases of collusion under the "command economy" without creating new bases for economically healthy worker-management co-operation.

This surely explains why the calls for the transformation of trade unions into militant organizations for the defence of the workers' interests have not yielded results: in circumstances of intensifying opposition and conflict between workers and management, neither the political leadership nor certainly enterprise management can really be interested in facilitating independent worker organization. Such organization could sabotage the reform (at least as presently conceived), and perhaps even threaten political stability. In private, and not so private, conversation, Soviet social scientists often advocate a firm hand, if not a "Cavaignac," to push through the reform. Or else they emphasize the need for a "responsible democracy" — as opposed to what the people, "unfortunately" want — a "democracy of desires."[27] At the June 1988 Party Conference, convened to discuss democratic reforms, the only speaker to even mention the trade unions was the chairman of the Central Trade-Union Council. And the theses published in preparation for the conference said nothing of the work-collective councils, which, after all, are officially intended as a form of democracy on the enterprise level.

Labour Unrest Under the Reform

An examination of the types of conflict occurring offers a more concrete picture of the situation in the factories. A major source of conflict is the arbitrary and illegal application of the wage reform. A group of electricians from the Simsk assembly factory in Chelyabinsk province complained to *Trud* about the manner in which management had recently introduced the reform. The director called a meeting of the workers, but "not to discuss ways of raising productivity, economizing on labour, etc.

but to get formal approval for the change that had already been decided without our participation." In fact, the director announced an across-the-board 20% reduction of bonuses and the demotion of all workers to lower skill grades.[28]

The wage reform is supposed to be carried out in close consultation with the workers. The review of skill classifications, according to government instructions, takes place in two stages. In the first, a commission of worker and management representatives is established. It looks at each case separately, considering the opinions of those who work with the individual — the other brigade members, the brigade leader, department head — and makes a preliminary evaluation. In stage two, the worker is invited before the commission and informed of her or his proposed classification in accordance with the new Unified Skill-Rate Handbook. If the proposal is a demotion, there must be an explanation, and the worker is provided with the opportunity to defend, through testing, his or her skill level. Only after that, on the basis of all the material, does the director make the final assignment.[29] The wage reform is also to be introduced gradually, as the enterprise assembles the conditions and means necessary, in particular those required for raising the basic wage rates, which are to constitute the major part of the total wage, the share of bonuses and other supplementary payments declining significantly.

But managers, in a hurry to show results, often resort to old trusted methods. The Vice-Director of the Department of Industrial Production and Wages of the Central Trade-Union Council has admitted that "in many cases the procedures of the reclassification are brutally violated. The first stage...is often totally omitted, and the affair...begins with an order that the worker is told to sign. And an order, as we know, is not open to discussion. [... This] is in total contradiction with the process of democratization of the entire life of our society."[30] The arbitrary, across-the-board reduction of workers' skill classifications is an easy way of conforming on paper to the wage reform: management indeed raises basic wage rates, but the worker is, in fact, left with the same basic wage as before, while facing new, harder norms and so lower bonuses, or none at all.

To make matters worse, this arbitrary and authoritarian approach is often accompanied by unconcealed discrimination against women. At a Chelyabinsk factory making construction materials, all men in the steel-fittings department were assigned to the fifth skill grade and all the women in the third. "This was openly explained by the fact that we are women and that men's skill classification should be two grades higher than women's." In other cases, women on maternity leave were illegally demoted in their absence.[31]

Despite all the talk about democratization, management, at least in the confines of the enterprise, still has the means to impose its will. (Even the official instructions appear to leave the last word with the director). At some factories, the workers were told to look for work elsewhere if they did not agree with the demotion.[32] At the Gidromontazh Assembly Factory in Tadzhikistan, the director gave the workers a choice: vote to reduce yourselves by one skill grade or else, as a result of the formal review of skill grades, you will be reduced two or three.[33] At another factory, "in the morning, as we came off the night shift, without forewarning, they organized a biased test for us. We were so tired, we couldn't make any sense of it." At the Biisk Garment Factory, "recently the management has begun to lower skill classifications for insufficient knowledge of the political situation. If a sewing-machine operator cannot answer how many delegates there were at the Nineteenth Party Conference, she can be demoted. Does this mean we should hire journalists who are experts in world politics to work at the machines?"[34]

In the workers' letters, the dominant sentiments are anger but especially deeply wounded human dignity. In the above-cited letter, the workers noted the "malicious joy" of the managerial personnel, as they administered the test. "Why such humiliation?" they asked. "They insulted us," wrote another group of workers, "removing our skill grades, without explaining or asking anything. Do we deserve such a lack of respect for our twenty years of honest labour?" And the workers see this as a test of perestroika: "Does the administration really think," concludes the letter, "that it can pass off this farce as restructuring?" "Is this what perestroika consists of?" "The whole factory is buzzing: 'So this is perestroika!'."[35]

In the absence of trade unions that defend them or even inform them of their rights, and given the prevalent authoritarian attitudes and practices of management, the workers' recourse is to the newspapers (which by law have to investigate complaints that are sent to them), to higher authorities (the joint commission of the State Committee on Labour and the Central Trade-Union Council charged with overseeing the reform is swamped with complaints) and/or the strike (increasingly frequent). The published reports of such conflicts usually indicate that the end has been successfully resolved, through a careful and differentiated review of skill classifications.

We do not know how often such appeals occur and how often they end satisfactorily for the workers. But we do know that many workers remain dissatisfied. For even in the course of a differentiated and careful review of skill classifications, a significant proportion of workers will find themselves demoted, since the reform is attempting to put an end to the common practice of assigning workers to higher skill grades than merited (a practice designed to attract scarce labour). Similarly, it is admitted that the introduction of a "cost-accounting régime," designed to restore the "socially just principle" of "payment according to labour," can, at least in the short run, lead to a decline in wages for "workers not possessing high skills and diligence."[36]

To the workers affected, these reforms really create injustice by making them pay for practices for which they bear no responsibility. As they constantly repeat in their letters, no one ever asked them their opinion about anything. Indeed, in the final analysis, these practices existed so that the régime would not have to ask the workers' their opinion about anything. More generally, these "past injustices" are a consequence of a planning and management system that was first established in the late 1920s in accordance with the interests of the bureaucracy. Much later, when it became clear that the system had become a major obstacle to further economic progress, the régime, guided by the interests of this same bureaucratic base, rejected structural reform. (It is, of course, an open question to what degree the system will be reformed even now.) The workers' sense of justice demands that if they are being asked to make sacrifices, the same should be asked of the real author of the "past injustices." Anyone familiar with the Soviet scene, knows the depth of popular anger at bureaucratic privilege and the workers' sense that they are being made to work for the upkeep of an unjustifiably bloated mass of parasitic "chinovniki." But despite the intermittent exposés in the media, there is little sign of this privilege being eliminated or even seriously diminished. True, there is to be a major reduction of staff in the various apparatuses, but at present it seems unlikely that the higher or even upper middle circles of the bureaucracy will suffer.

Typical of this type of conflict was the strike at Ryazsel'mash, an agricultural machinery factory in Ryzan' in the early fall of 1988. The coverage in *Sotsialisticheskaya industriya* reflects the official attitude (and that of most social scientists) to the issue of "past injustices." The conflict was between a brigade of about 50 electric welders and the new department head. According to the paper, things had been pretty lax there. Former department heads came and went, concerned primarily with meeting gross output targets (the main success indicator under the old system). They bothered little with such matters as economy of labour and materials. As for the workers, their attitude was "grasping" and "selfish," and they behaved according to the slogan: "After us — the deluge, as long as we get our wages." (We are not told why they should have cared about anything else, when the department heads and higher management themselves did not look past their bonuses and personal career interests, and when the workers had no say in how the enterprise was run nor virtually any material interest in the enterprise's real contribution to the economy.) Discipline was weak, continues the report, and wages did not correspond to the work done: norms were easy.

This situation had its origins several years back, when the department was being set up and it was hard to find workers. The easy norms were also a way of compensating workers for inevitable losses caused by difficulties in installing and mastering new technology. These circumstances no longer existed. Yet, because of the continued arhythmic character of production in the department, large sums have to be paid for overtime and other "incentive payments." "These are basically young workers," sadly noted a "labour veteran," "but look how they have been corrupted by easy money." Even stragglers here made more than experienced welders elsewhere. Such were the sad consequences of the "agreement" between workers and management. This, continues the report, became unacceptable under a cost-accounting régime.

The new department head set out to "introduce order with a firm hand." For failure to fulfill certain plan indicators in June and July, the welders were twice deprived of bonuses, even though they had overfulfilled output norms by a large percentage. "Having grown accustomed to 'indulgence'," the welders reacted "oversensitively" to these sanctions and warned the department head not to be so strict or he could expect a strong reaction. In all this, the trade union played no role — the workers acted through their own informal leaders. The department head had expected the support at least of the eight Communists among the workers. But, alas! "For them, too, charity apparently begins at home." As the department head stepped up his pressure, the workers retaliated with a slowdown strike, twice turning off the machinery to hold meetings. This is when the department head issued a "draconian" order that included many harsh punishments (we are not given the specifics), in response to which the workers put down their tools.

The reaction in the rest of the factory was mixed. "Some unconditionally condemned the brigade. Others, on the contrary, supported it. Yet another group simply could not believe such a thing could be taking place. A fourth group [the managerial personnel?] openly gloated: now they'll see what playing with democracy brings." The work-collective and the trade-union councils condemned the strike and threatened to disband the brigade if the strike was repeated. The two most active worker leaders were excluded from the trade union for one year. This means, among other things, a loss of important social benefits. Management was instructed to finally bring labour norms into line with the labour expenditures actually demanded by technology. The article concludes philosophically with the thought that the real losers are perestroika and democracy. "The brigade still feels that it was punished for trying to resist arbitrary rule. And the department head is certain that this is how order has to be introduced today. The victims are mistrust and a lack of faith."[37]

In the sixth sheet-rolling department of the giant Magnitogorsk Metallurgical Factory, an experiment, which subsequently became permanent, was introduced to fight levelling. Previous forms of "socialist competition" had had a mainly exhortatory, formal character, with little practical incidence on production. Under the experiment, the bonus is attributed not to each brigade, but to the department as a whole, on the basis of the final results. However, it is distributed in a very differentiated manner among the workers, according to the place their "coefficient of effectiveness of labour" (based on quality and quantity of output) takes in the competition. The difference between a winner and a loser can be 50-60 rubles. (The average monthly wage in the Soviet Union is 220 rubles).

According to *Trud,* under the new system, "no one holds back reserves, hides potential. Now it is not profitable..." Nevertheless, a large part of the workers have demanded an end to this form of competition. One problem is that in calculating results, conditions beyond the workers' control are not considered, such as the illness of a partner or failure of another department to supply the necessary parts on time. But the chairman of the trade-union committee feels that fundamentally the workers "fear the loss of the 'benefits' of levelling... Frankly, many of us have forgotten how to work intensely, thoughtfully, creatively. And it hurts now to have to pay for that with the ruble."[38] The report does not explain what the "benefits" of levelling are. But one can ask if it is fair to describe these workers as "corrupted" by the old system? Witholding of effort, while not a trait of human nature, is certainly inherent to alienated labour, which necessarily perceives any intensification of work as an intensification of exploitation, particularly when there is no control over the size and permanence of the reward. And so far under the reform, the immediate experience has often been an intensification of labour without a significant rise in wages. In conditions where "democratization" and "self-management" have yet to be translated into reality, "levelling" is still perceived by workers as an important means of defence against attempts at "storming". (How much income inequality they would choose even under completely democratic conditions is, of course, another question. Defence mechanisms aside, there are indications of strongly held egalitarian values in the Soviet population.)[39]

What political leaders, managers, economists and journalists portray as legitimate attempts to eradicate the injustices of the preceding era, workers tend to see as a unilateral abrogation by management of longstanding arrangements regulating their mutual relations. The new arrangements often amount to a deterioration of their immediate situation, and workers have little confidence that they might benefit from them at some later stage. In any case, it appears to them that they are being asked to bear all the sacrifices. Faced with this, workers, in their turn, are abandoning their tolerant attitude towards managerial shortcomings and the widespread failure to observe legal norms. They are encouraged in this by the political liberalization and the official policy (if not yet the practice) of democratization, which are creating a new sense of what is possible in a contest with management. As a result, conditions and practices which workers once grudgingly accepted are now also becoming objects of open conflict.

In March 1988, several dozen bus drivers at a Saratov transport enterprise struck when their wages for February, following the introduction of the wage reform and cost-accounting, turned out to be well below normal. When they complained, they were told to earn the difference. According to the newspaper report, these workers had grown accustomed to levelling and to management's toleration of slack discipline. Typically, the workers had not been consulted about the changes. "What can you expect," said one driver, "if they speak with us mainly from top down? No one gives a damn about our opinion, and management does whatever it likes. Meanwhile, the administrative apparatus is impossibly bloated." But the wage dispute was only the spark that ignited the strike. Management's unilateral action over wages allowed the release of years of pent-up dissatisfaction over the drawn-out construction of a new building, overcrowding, poor ventilation and lighting, failure to modernize the repair base, the shortage of spare parts and the poor quality of repairs. A party meeting placed the blame with management, the trade union and the party organization, who in the past reconciled themselves to indiscipline and poor work and now failed to prepare the workers for the shift to cost-accounting. It was decided to organize elections to management at all levels, to more carefully prepare the shift to new conditions and to work off the lost time outside of regular hours, the wages to be paid to the Children's Fund (a national charity).[40]

Overtime and its major cause — the arhythmic character of production, with long bouts of idle time followed by mad speed-ups — have always been an important source of worker dissatisfaction under the "command system", unable to assure regular supply of materials to the enterprises. Overtime in the Soviet Union is by no means always paid at higher rates, as the law prescribes (enterprises would greatly surpass their wage bills) and even when it is, it does not always make up for wages lost during periods of enforced idleness. More important, the irregular work hours wreak havoc with workers' lives. The overtime (regulated by law) is often illegal to boot. Nevertheless, overtime was usually begrudgingly accepted by workers under the old system of labour relations and only now is it becoming a major source of open conflict.

In December 1987, the workers of the Yaroslavl' Motor Factory struck for seven days. Management had compiled a work schedule calling for workdays of seven hours and 50 minutes and fifteen "black Saturdays" over the course of 1988. In past years, despite some grumbling, the workers had accepted similar schedules. This time it was different. They held 60 local meetings that yielded 60 resolutions, all calling for an eight-hour day and only eight Saturdays. (The ten minute difference in the workday over the course of a year equalled the seven extra Saturdays in the administration's schedule). Nevertheless, the work-collective council — chaired by the director himself! — ratified management's schedule, with only one opposing vote. So did the trade-union committee — without comment.

It was after this that the strike broke out. The next day the director met with the workers assembled in the yard. He explained why supply problems made fifteen "black Saturdays" necessary. From the crowd came shouts: "That's your concern!" He explained that the cafeteria would not be able manage. From the crowd: "That's your concern!" He explained that public transport could not cope and that the enterprise would have to pay 100,000 rubles in additional transportation costs. "That's your concern!" Workers who went to the platform told the director that he had had a whole year to prepare conditions for a normal work schedule but had done nothing. As for the transport question, the factory had busses that stood idle in the evenings. Even the intervention of the vice-minister did not sway the workers. "When are we supposed to rest?" asked one. "And what about our families?" "You say you are defending our interests?" interjected another worker. "You are thinking more about the motors... And we are there working day and night at the end of the month. That's illegal!" "But you get paid more for that," replied the director. To this a worker retorted: "We're idle at the beginning of the month and then [to make up for lost earnings] we get bonuses."

The meeting voted unanimously for the workers' "8-8" schedule. "A clean split has occurred," concluded the district party secretary. "The workers versus the general director, and there is no intermediate link." The trade union continued to side with management and applied pressure on the workers' informal leader, Makarov. But he explained: "It isn't just a question of rest. When we say an eight-hour day, we mean a real shift, with no idle time. Now, idle time makes up 9% of the shift. An 8-hour day would give management an incentive to intensify labour. As things stand now, it doesn't care, since the lost time can be made up on days when we aren't supposed to work."

The work-collective council decided to call a meeting of worker delegates. The hall was packed. Management explained that the plan targets could not be met with the "8-8" schedule. But according to one worker, fewer working Saturdays would leave more time for regular maintenance of the equipment which is old and is tended to only after it breaks down and stops production. But there was also the social aspect: "Many tie the demand for the eight-hour day to faith in perestroika." It was a question of new methods of work, discipline, renewed technology.

The meeting lasted five hours, and the vote was finally 359 vs. 296 for management's schedule. Applause was thin and it came mainly from the front rows (where management's people were seated). It is possible, noted the *Izvestiya* reporter, that management and the trade-union committee had applied pressure before the meeting. But more likely factory patriotism won out. After the vote, Makarov took the floor and proposed that in 1989 there would be a shift to the eight-hour day. Someone else called to put a total end to illegal Saturdays. Both resolutions passed unanimously.[41]

In a poll conducted by *Izvestiya* after the publication of this report, 69% of the worker respondents approved of the Yaroslavl' workers' refusal to work "black Saturdays", though half of these said they would have yielded in order to save the plan. All felt that the cause of the strike was dissatisfaction with the organization of labour — the irregular character of production, the poor quality of materials and of the goods produced as a result of this.[42]

This strike shows forcefully that workers hold management (at all levels) responsible for the poor state of the economy. This is quite a different understanding of the situation from that which one usually hears from social scientists, managers and journalists, who tend to lay a good share, if not all, of the blame on the workers' indolence, indiscipline and corruption. Some of this undoubtedly exists. But most workers sincerely wonder how they could work better in the given circumstances and they see the criticism directed at them as a way for managers to cover up for themselves. For example, a foreman at the diesel factory explained that "a regular pace of production determines everything else. But it does not exist. You work Saturday and Sunday. And then there is no work on Monday. In such circumstances it makes no sense to punish workers for lateness or absences, since idle time can last days."[43]

The strike at the Yaroslavl' factory illustrates how perestroika has not only not fostered beneficial work-management solidarity but has actually deepened the gulf between the two to an unprecedented degree. In the director's words: "The essence of perestroika is that there should not be "we" and "they", as is the case here now, but that the collective be united." The problem at the Yaroslavl' factory, and at most others, is that the organs of self-management, provided for by the Law on the State Enterprise, are not functioning as prescribed. At the diesel factory, neither the work-collective council nor the trade-union represented the workers. The council, chaired by the director himself, was clearly a tool of management, which thought it could continue to run things in the old authoritarian way. The workers had other ideas. However, they did not demand that genuine self-management be introduced, so that they could directly implement the changes they wanted. Rather they united behind an informal leader against management in defence of their interests, refusing responsibility for the administration of the factory.

This refusal is, in part, due to the workers' perception—generally a valid one — that management is not prepared to give them any real say in running things. They, therefore, see "self-management" as a trap to get them to take responsibility for failures of management and of the economic system as a whole. The leader of a brigade of mechanics, chairman of the work-collective council of the Kamaz Auto Factory, wrote to *Trud* in June that,

> although all managerial personnel in the factory are elected, so far this democratization is more external than deep. In its relations with the work-collective council, management, as before, adheres to the military code: an order from a higher rank is not open to discussion. For example, the administration orders the workers to appear on their days off, and neither the work-collective council nor the trade union even try to protest, even though we have passed the limit of [legally] allowed overtime.[44]

At the Perm' Motor-Repair Factory, the director was also chairman of the work-collective council, which had met only once in its nine months of existence. Workers here struck over delayed payment of wages. Asked why they would act thus against their own interests when the new cost-accounting régime means that the losses from the strike come out of their own pockets and when they now had their own organ of self-management, a turner replied simply that the "workers don't believe in that council."[45] As the letter from Kamaz indicates, elections have not given the workers real power. In the case of lower managerial personnel, at least, the elections are often "organized" by the director to make sure his or her candidates get through, and, in any case, the director retains the final say.[46]

Political leaders and the press often lament the workers' passivity in face of perestroika, attributing this to the corrupting effects of the old system. But the workers' apparent indifference to self-management is based much more on their disbelief in the possibility of making it a reality under the present régime. When they have decided to give it a try, the results have been disappointing. In 1987, at an electoral meeting of the trade-union council of the jewellery department of the Moscow Jewellery

Factory, in the spirit of perestroika, the workers let it be known that they "were sick of working in the old way," in conditions of disorganization and arhythmic production requiring massive overtime and "storming" that were turning them into nervous wrecks. So they elected a new trade-union committee with the mandate: "Put the place in order."

The committee began by holding elections for department head. The workers saw this measure as real. It "gave them confidence in their own forces, showed them that they can, all the same, influence matters in the department." But at a union meeting a year later, the gulf between workers and management was deeper than ever, as the workers complained about norms, wages, skill classifications. What happened? According to the author of the report, "the workers demanded changes and were ready to actively participate in them... But their insistence apparently irritated the managers. The latter still did not have answers to many of the production problems. Instead of calming the workers and explaining the situation, they used the old trusted methods of command: your business is to do what you are told." "You know," one of the workers explained,

> after the election of the department head, when we saw that we could run things in our department, our spirits rose and the desire to work better appeared. But then we understood: the administration had been playing at democracy with us. It turns out that we are the masters more in theory. They listen to our opinion when it coincides with the boss's, when its in their interest.

And so at the latest union election meeting, there was total indifference. "People had lost interest in what was occurring in the hall; they kept glancing at the exit, in a rush to get to the cafeteria."[47]

Management's reluctance to give up or to share power is not surprising, given the constraints and pressures placed upon it by the still largely unreformed "command" system. Prejudices and other considerations aside, to give the workers a real voice in these conditions is to make a manager's hard life even more complicated, to deprive him or her of the flexibility (a familiar theme to Western ears) needed to meet taut plan objectives in conditions of irregular material supply (still administered from the centre).

But management's resistance is not the only reason self-management is having trouble getting off the ground. For even where the work-collective councils are genuinely participating in enterprise decisions, the workers often remain indifferent and mistrustful. In an interview given to *Trud*, the chairman of the work-collective council of a Leningrad machine-construction factory, himself a turner, painted a picture of genuine council involvement in enterprise management, including negotiations with the ministry over various plan targets. Still he complained of indifference and lack of faith in democracy among the workers. They take their complaints to the party, to the soviets or to the press, rather than to the work-collective council, a workers' organ. This is because "they do not know what we can achieve. They do not believe that the work-collective council is a real force."[48]

The workers' continued mistrust of "self-management" even in those rare cases when management welcomes their genuine participation, has the same source as the managers' reluctance to give the workers a real say: the continued power of the ministries and other external bureaucratic forces that still largely determine the fate of the enterprise. In these circumstances, even if management is prepared to share power, the workers still perceive a trap to get them to accept responsibility for something they cannot effectively control. This emerges clearly from an article in *Komsomol'skaya pravda* by a young mechanic-assembler, a brigadier at the Kazan' Motor Factory. This is one worker who is definitely enthusiastic about self-management. But he finds himself constantly frustrated by the unreformed system:

> Perestroika is for all without exception! But, all the same, let's look the truth in the face. As long as the ministries, as is stated in the Law on the State Enterprise, bear full responsibility for the branch, the most militant work-collective council will inevitably find itself against a brick wall. You can't bear responsibility without at the same time taking rights away from the enterprises. And so too, our work-collective council does not "make the weather" in the enterprise. Not because it doesn't want to — because it can't... How can you ask me to feel myself the master, when practically nothing depends upon me?[49]

The article is appropriately entitled "We're Sick of Being Pawns."

At the Ural'mash Machine-Construction Factory, the work-collective council, along with management, was successful after heroic efforts in resisting an attempt by the ministry to impose new, impossibly high plan targets (in the new form of a "state contract"). At Ural'mash, with its liberal director, the work-collective council appears to be genuinely participating in management. But, notes its chairman, a brigadier, of late the council has been receiving letters from the councils of client and supplier enterprises, asking for special favours, such as extra deliveries or special parts not specified in the contracts. In other words, the councils are becoming a "democratic" variant of the old "pushers" sent out by management. Instead of coming with complaints and proposals about production, they are acting as the errand boys of management in an unreformed management system.[50]

A roundtable discussion on the work-collective councils in the coal-mining sector made clear that the major problem facing the councils is that the law itself is vague on the relative powers of the councils vis-à-vis the ministry and that, in practice, the ministry rules. "The work-collective council has no say in planning for the enterprise. It all comes from above."[51] "The ministries are violating right and left the rights of the enterprises," states the director of the State Labour Committee's research institute.[52] Indeed, a new form of conflict has emerged recently: work-collective council against ministry over losses to the enterprise caused by apparently illegal ministerial actions.[53] Besides the imposition of new "state contracts" in mid-stream, complaints include ministerial refusal to extract fines from its own enterprises for non-respect of contracts when the losses are incurred by another of its enterprises ("It's all in the same family"), and the attachment of indebted and failing enterprises to more "profitable" ones.[54] Such "levelling" practices by the ministries stand officially condemned, but they largely continue, despite reports of bankruptcies.[55]

One reaction to this situation, one that is reported most frequently by the press (that has been exhorted recently by Gorbachev to support the reform), is for the work-collective councils to demand real enterprise autonomy: only thus can self-management become real. But one suspects that this reaction comes mainly from enterprises that would be favourably situated in a market reform, because of the type of goods manufactured, geographical location, technological level of equipment, etc. (Actually, given the fact that resources are still centrally allocated, most directors are not eager to be freed from "state contracts."[56]) Thus, the secretary of the party bureau of a Tallin machine-construction factory describes how the work-collective council successfuly beat back efforts by the ministry to shift the factory to a newly created trust. "We were united and had rationality on our side. We were accused of worrying about our own profits. But we fought for the cost-accounting régime, for the flourishing of our enterprise that produces goods that are in demand — and thus for the interests of society."[57]

This is clearly the attitude of a part of the skilled workers, especially the younger, well-educated ones who are brimming with energy and initiative and have been straining to put these to productive use. The young brigade leader from the Kazan' Motor Factory cited earlier suggests the leasing of the machinery to the workers. But despite the official and media support for these views, they do not seem to have the support of most workers, who have serious doubts about the market as an agent of rationality and social justice. The Kazan' brigadier, after calling for enterprise autonomy and the leasing of machinery, continued:

> But there are people today who are energetically pushing public opinion to condemn the worker-"graspers" (khapugi), who feel no embarassment in talking about high wages. They shout: mercenary interests, petty philistine passions! Come on! Who is it then that moves our economy, that is the main support of production if not the "grasper", the one who breaks all norms, who is keen-witted and full of initiative, taking care of his means of production — his lathe and instruments. Of course, today's transitional situation does not please the lazy yes-man, who always keeps one eye on management: "At your service!" But it's a case of "either — or."[58]

Workers and Socialist Democracy

When there is no immediate prospect of democracy at the centre of power (and unfortunately, this is still the situation in the Soviet Union), this way of seeing the alternatives — either the market and the enterprise as guarantors of efficiency, or centralized bureaucratic management and continued waste — comes naturally to those who impatiently seek a creative outlet for their initiative. But ultimately this is a dead end. Self-management and the market in a non-democratic political context are in fundamental contradiction. For when workers' power is limited to the enterprise level, they use it to guarantee their jobs and salaries. This means there can be no real labour or capital markets. This is one of the lessons of the Yugoslav experience.[59]

Most Soviet workers are wary of the market as the ultimate arbiter or rationality and justice.[60] V. Vishnyakov, a law professor at the Trade-Union Institute, expressed these fears when he called recently for genuine democratization of trade unions and their real participation in state policy-making:

> The cost-accounting and self-financing régimes in the enterprises, the new labour legislation, have made more acute the problem of the social protection of the individual: *will not the humanism of socialist principles be sacrificed in practice on the alter of economic gain?*[61]

In the current Soviet political context, such concerns are usually condemned as reactionary advocacy of "levelling" and "social dependency." But they are real fears and they are greatly exacerbated by the absence of genuine democratic control over the reform, either at the central or the enterprise levels. And a "Cavaignac" at the helm, rather than facilitating structural reform, ultimately only makes its introduction more unlikely, because it deprives the reformers of the support of the working class, the only political base potentially strong enough to carry through the reform against the resistance from within the bureaucracy.

The concerns of Soviet workers do not mean structural reform of the economy and democracy are incompatible. All the evidence shows that Soviet workers want reform, they want to "put the economy in order." Nor do their concerns mean they would reject any application of the market mechanism in the economy. Rather, it is a question of whether the market will impose its criteria of efficiency and justice on society or whether society will subordinate the market mechanism to the type of development it collectively chooses. For the latter to be the case, the central state must retain key powers to plan and to regulate the economy. Despite past Soviet experience, this need not be a formula for continued economic waste and stagnation — if the state is democratic, i.e. freed from bureaucratic control. Only when national economic policy is decided in a democratic context can constraints placed upon enterprise autonomy cease to appear as external, to provoke resistence and the concealment of reserves.

The sincere proponents of self-management in the Soviet Union see it as a way to resolve the fundamental problem of the Soviet economy — the coherent linking of the interests of rank-and-file workers, managers, social strata and regions with each other and with the overall interests of society. The reform so far has patently failed to do this. It has deepened the divisions, and the level of conflict has risen sharply. The evidence analyzed here points to the undemocratic context in which the reform is being decided and promulgated as the underlying cause of this failure. The conclusion that presents itself from Soviet experience with reform to date (and from the experiences of other Soviet-type societies) is that for self-management to be effective, it must extend to all levels of economic decision making, including decisions about the character of the reform and the economic system it is designed to create.

What has been happening in Soviet factories can be seen as a qualitatively new, if still limited, stage of labour activism. So far the workers have organized only episodically around informal leaders and for essentially local ends. But before perestroika, strikes involving entire enterprises (and the bulk of Soviet workers are concentrated in huge factories) and lasting several days were rare events. The main factors that have contributed to this change are the political liberalization, the absence of genuine democracy (the main reform measures to date have all been dictated from above, albeit with public discussion of the details), and the introduction of a wage reform that is putting an end to the collusive ties with management and their corrupting influence on worker consciousness.

As — and if — the market reform progresses in its present fundamentally top-down manner and is experienced more concretely by the workers, one can see developing more permanent, large-scale, independent working class organizations. There are some signs of this happening already. In Yaroslavl', a "workers' group" composed of representatives of the major industrial enterprises has been formed as part of the city's "Popular Front." (This is an independent movement of citizens that arose at a mass meeting on June 8, 1988 to protest the "election" of the unpopular Yaroslavl' provincial party committee first secretary to the 19th Party Conference in Moscow.) The moving force behind the formation of this group was the workers' club of the Yaroslavl' Motor Factory, formed (against the opposition of management and the party committee) following the seven-day strike over the "black Saturdays."[62] A similar "workers' group" exists in the town of Andropov. Toward the end of 1988, in the Lithuanian city of Kaunas, 300 delegates from 70 enterprises founded the Kaunas Union of Workers. Its basic goals are defined as the "struggle for restructuring of the trade-union committees in the enterprises, for the corresponding restructuring of the content of the local factory newspapers, and for the protection of the rights of workers against managerial arbitrariness." Similar unions were being set up in Vilnius and Klaipeda.[63]

A price reform, without which there can be no market reform, might give a major push to such organization. Opposition to it is very widespread in the population, and the authorities are, accordingly, refusing to say anything precise about it, while they discuss the matter in secret. This could serve to unite workers on a larger scale in defence of their interests, since, unlike the wage reform, it would be a measure promulgated from the centre. Rather than mean an end to perestroika, such a development would set the scene for a genuinely revolutionary restructuring in the Soviet Union, one in which the initiative comes from below, the only one that has a realistic chance of succeeding.

Are contemporary Soviet workers really capable of independent political activity? Needless to say, many inside and outside the Soviet Union are sceptical about this and even doubt the workers' interest in socialist democracy. But the events of 28 years ago in Novocherkassk have something to tell on this score. Perhaps the most striking thing about them is the level of class consciousness displayed by the workers. This was a spontaneous movement of workers, with no participation of the intelligentsia. Despite provocations, it was a sober movement, without "excesses" on the workers' part — they occurred only on the side of a régime that showed how much it feared the workers when they took soviet power seriously. There was none of the "anarchism" supposedly inherent in the Russian "masses." These people identified themselves and their movement with the working class. They tried to establish contact with their comrades in other cities. They claimed the Soviet revolutionary tradition as their own.

And yet, Novocherkassk had no traditions of working class struggle. It was and remains a backwater provincial town that at the time of the revolution had no industrial workers. All of its large-scale industry dates from the 1930s and after. According to Siuda, the working class consciousness and traditions and even many aspects of the strike itself — so reminiscent of strikes in Tsarist Russia — came from the workers' schooling, from books and films and, of course, from their shared situation. Isaac Deutscher's discussion of this issue comes to mind:

> The fact that the rulers and leaders of the Soviet Union have never stopped evoking their revolutionary origins, has also had its logic and consequences. All of them, including Stalin, Khrushchev, and Khrushchev's successors, have had to cultivate in the minds of their people the sense of revolutionary continuity. They have had to reiterate the pledges of 1917, even while they themselves were breaking them; and they have had to restate, again and again, the Soviet Union's commitment to socialism. ...The educational system has constantly reawakened in the mass of the people an awareness of their revolutionary heritage.[64]

Novocherkassk was only partly about prices and wages. On a deeper level, it was about socialist democracy, something the workers had never experienced but which they had no difficulty in understanding. Siuda describes the atmosphere in this way:

> The time — excuse me because this might sound blasphemous in view of the tragedy that followed — but the time was a happy one, a time of spiritual emancipation, a full emancipation of the protest that had surely been accumulating in everyone's hearts. It was short-lived, but it was still freedom, independence. You must understand that we were always living with the slavish feeling: careful, what will the authorities [nachal'niki] think, say?... If you ask any worker for a chronological account of the events, they couldn't tell you. Because we felt so strongly our freedom that we lost our sense of time. I never again felt such total emancipation. Personally, I don't feel it now either. Because I see the reality and not what is being said or written in the papers.

A group of workers from the Urals, after reading Siuda's essay on the Novocherkassk events, wrote him the following letter dated June 17, 1988:

We have read your letter about the tragedy of June 1-3, 1962 in your town and we express our sympathy and solidarity. We want to send this information to some paper, to Komsomol'skaya pravda, for example.

The workers, on the whole, believe the account of the facts in your article, but for the good of the cause, we would like to receive personally from you a confirmation with a brief account of the course of events. This will be a document of sorts against the local bureaucrats, opponents of the revolutionary renewal, in whose hands, unfortunately, the real political power rests. This is a treacherous class of exploiters of the toilers, that uses as a cover that which is most sacred to the working class — Marxism — and passes itself off as the true representatives of the party of the working class, of Soviet power, of the people, and against them one must fight skillfully, with their own arms. Of course, after this deception of the workers, unprecedented in the history of humanity, it will take a certain amount of time for the course of democracy and glasnost' to yield fruit: the dictatorship of the working class, its full power though its own institutions — the soviets, in their Leninist understanding.

We are sending a letter to Gorbachev, N.S., signed by a group of workers of the metallurgical factory. In this connnection, we would like to know your critical comments on this letter and your advice on the methods of struggle against the enemies of the working class — the bureaucratic bourgeoisie, or, as Lenin called them, the sovbours.

We await your answer as soon as possible. It is needed for our struggle for the cause of the working class.

January 1989

NOTES

1. The following is from an interview I conducted with Siuda in the summer of 1988 as well as from his unpublished essay that has been circulating in the "informal" movement.
2. See. V. Belotserkovskii, "Les soulevements ouvriers des années soixante," L'-Alternative, no. 3, March 1980, pp. 28-31.
3. V.I. Gerchikov and B.G Proshkin, "Vybornost' rukovoditelei: pervyi opyt, pervye problemy," *EKO*, no. 5, 1988. p. 90.
4. See my article "Economic Reform and Democracy," in *Socialist Register* 1988.
5. "Norma truda v novykh usloviyakh khozyaistvovaniya," *Sotsialisticheskii trud*, no. 5, 1988, p. 38; V.I. Shcherbakov, "Kardinal'naya perestroika oplaty truda," *EKO*, no. 1, 1987, p. 38; G. Konstantinov, "Perestroika zarplaty — chto yei meshaet", *Agitator*, no. 13, 1988, p. 17.
6. W. Brus, "Utopianism and Realism in the Evolution of the Soviet Economic System," *Soviet Studies*, vol. XL, no. 3, July, 1988, p. 440.
7. S. Minaeva, Director of the Central Trade-Union Council's Department for Social Development, in *Trud*, Jan. 12, 1989.
8. See, for example, V. Dement'ev and Yu. Sukhotin, "Sobstvennost' v sisteme proizvodstvennykh otnoshenii sotsializma," *Kommunist*, no. 18, 1987, p. 71; "Economic Reform and Democracy..." pp. 139-42.
9. *Sotsialisticheskii trud*, no. 2, 1987, pp. 57-96, and no. 3, 1987, pp. 54-66.
10. V.I. Shcherbakov, "Kardinal'naya perestroika oplaty truda," *EKO*, no. 1, 1987, p. 37-52.
11. See D. Mandel, "La perestroika et la classe ouvrière," *L'homme et la société*, winter 1988-9. There has been no serious debate about what this principle should mean in practice. It goes without saying that it is open to diverse and contradictory interpretations. For a discussion of this, see A. Zimine, *Le stalinisme et son "socialisme réel"*, Paris: La brèche, 1983.
12. *Pravda*, Jan. 28, 1987.
13. Interview with E.G. Antosenkov, *Nedelya*, no. 49 (1497), 1988, pp. 6-7.
14. *Pravda*, July 1, 1987.
15. On this, Antosenkov stated: "If we are to be honest and do not close our eyes to reality, in the past there was talk about the participation of toilers in management but not their real participation," *Nedelya*, no. 49(1497), 1988, p. 7
16. See, for example, the speech of Shalaev, chairman of the All-Union Council of Trade Unions, at the Trade-Union Congress, *Pravda*, Feb. 25, 1987. This has also become a constant, though not unambiguous, theme of the central trade-union paper *Trud*.
17. Gerchikov and Proshkin, "Vybornost' rukovodyashchikh rabotnikov predpriyatii, uchrezhdenii, organizatsii, *Sovetskoe gosudarstvo i pravo*, no. 1, 1988. p. 56.
18. See, for example, A. Kozlov, "Nachinal tsekhkom s zhelaniem," *Trud*, Sept. 29, 1988.
19. Zh. Toshchenko, "Soznanie, nastroenie, deistvie," *Agitator*, no. 12, 1988, p. 11.
20. "Stimuly i tormoza," *Sotsialisticheskaya industriya*, June 19, 1988.
21. G. Konstantinov, "Perestroika zarplaty...", p. 18. Discussions at a conference on the work-collective councils organized by the Leningrad "Perestroika" club at the end of June 1988 similarly made clear that their impact so far has been small.
22. V. Vishnyakov, "Prosit' ili trebovat'?", *Trud*, Oct. 6, 1988.

23. E. Terent'ev, "Sotsial'naya sfera i profsoyuzy," *Trud,* July 8, 1988.
24. *Trud,* July 8, 1988.
25. Ibid., June 1, 1988. An exceptional case of a trade union actively defending the collective interests of workers and even leading them in a strike is that of Khabarovsk Regional Committee of the Union of Workers of Local Industry and Communal Services. In a striking letter published in *Trud,* the chairman of the regional comittee admitted that this was an extreme measure but he recalled Lenin's justification of strikes as a legitimate means of defence against "bureaucratic deformations" in the Soviet state and he warned that such means would continue to be used. G. Tkachenko, "Dlya raskachki vremeni net," *Trud,* Oct. 12, 1988. This case, written up in the central trade-union paper is, indeed, significant and therefore deserves mention. If at the same time, I have relegated it to a footnote, it is because it is an isolated case. It is also worth noting that it involves a distant region and a politically marginal category of workers scattered in a myriad of very small enterprises.
26. See, for example, I. Leshchevskii, "Idti vmeste," *Sotsialisticheskaya industriya,* June 26, 1988; E. Terent'ev, *Trud,* July 8, 1988; V. Kazachenko, "Rodoslovnaya zhaloby," *Trud,* Sept. 3, 1988; G. Konstantinov, "Perestroika zarplaty…", pp; 15-18.
27. See, for example, A. Ulyukaev, "Perestroika — kto 'za', kto 'protiv,'" *Nedelya,* no. 18, 198, pp. 11-12.
28. *Trud,* July 8, 1988.
29. A. Levina, "Operatsiya 'stupeni masterstva'," *Rabotnistsa,* no. 10, 1988, p. 17.
30. Ibid.
31. Ibid., and Konstantinov, "Perestroika zarplaty…", p. 15.
32. *Trud,* July 8, 1988, and Levina, "Operatsiya…" p. 17.
33. Konstantinov, "Perestroika zarplaty…", p. 16.
34. Levina, "Operatsiya…", p. 17; O. Zhadan, "Dekol'te na samsvale", *Trud,* Jan. 17, 1989.
35. Levina, p. 16-18, and Konstantinov, p. 16.
36. A. Mineev, "Evolyutsiya obshchestvennogo soznaniya," *Moskovskie novosti,* Jan. 15, 1989, p.8.
37. V. Lifanov, "Zhestskii pressing," *Sotsialisticheskaya trud,* Oct. 4, 1988.
38. A. Rostarchyk, "Protiv uravnilovki," *Trud,* Nov. 24, 1988.
39. See Mandel, "La perestroika…" V. Chervyakov of the Institute of Sociological Research states that research shows a widespread "psychology of levelling", but he blames this on the effects of what he maintains was the past state policy and philosophy of levelling. "Formula spravedlivosti," *Trud,* Jan. 18, 1989.
40. A. Vorotnikov, "Konflikt nazrel," *Pravda,* April 13, 1988.
41. "Sem' dnei," *Izvestiya,* Dec. 25, 1987.
42. "Sem' dnei," *Izvestiya,* Jan. 6, 1988.
43. "Sem' dnei," *Izvestiya,* Dec. 25, 1987.
44. *Trud,* June 15, 1988.
45. V. Konstantinov, "Profkom v prostoe," *Trud,* September 4, 1988.
46. See, for example, the letter from Izhstal' in ibid., July 8, 1988.
47. A. Kozlov, "Nachinal tsekhom s zhelaniem," *Trud,* Sept. 29, 1988.
48. *Trud,* July 7, 1988.
49. C. Bulatov, "Nadoelo byt' peshkamy," *Komsomol'skaya pravda,* Oct. 5, 1988.

50. *Sovetskaya Rossiya,* June 26, 1988. See also "Uchitsya upravlyat' samim!," *Nedelya,* no. 49, Dec. 5-11, 1988, p. 7.
51. *Trud,* June 17, 1988.
52. "Uchitsya upravlyat' samim!," p. 7.
53. V. Kazchenko, "Rodoslovnaya zhaloby," *Trud,* Sept. 3, 1988.
54. Ibid., 16 June, 1988.
55. See, e.g., "Bankroty," ibid, Sept. 16, 1988.
56. P. Bunich, "Goszakaz ili prikaz?" *Ogonek,* no. 44, Oct. 1988, pp. 14-16.
57. Ibid., July 16, 1988.
58. C. Bulatov, "Nadoelo byt' peshkamy…"
59. See, C. Samary, "De la yougoslavie a l'URSS", *L'homme et la société,* winter 1988-9.
60. See Mandel, "La perestroika…"
61. V. Vishnyakov, "Prosit' ili trebovat'?", *Trud,* Oct. 6, 1988.
62. A. Mineev, *Moskovskie novosti,* Jan. 15, 1989, p. 8
63. N. Belyaeva, "Natsional'nyi ili nardonyi," *Moskovskie novosti,* p. 10, Dec. 25, 1988.
64. I. Deutscher, *The Unifinished Revolution,* London: Oxford University Press, 1967, p. 36.

Chapter 2

Perestroika and Women Workers

Nearly half of the workers in Soviet industry, and a quarter of those in construction and transport, are women. Although many of the basic problems facing Soviet women workers are common to all Soviet women, this chapter will limit itself to a brief discussion of some aspects of the situation of women workers as workers and to the impact that perestroika has had and is likely to have on it.

As in Soviet society generally, so too in the situation of women workers, perestroika has so far brought few positive material changes, changes that can be felt on the level of social practice. Indeed, to judge by letters to the press and opinion polls, a very large part of women workers feel things have grown worse. While this perception has a basis in reality, it is also fostered by "glasnost'," the policy of political liberalization that has allowed a much freer (but not totally uncontrolled) flow of information about society. This in turn has created a heightened awareness of social problems. This liberalization (not to be confused with democracy, in which the people collectively decide the key social questions that affect their lives) represents major progress because of its potential impact on popular consciousness. In particular, it has allowed public discussion — often very passionate — in the mass media of issues relating to women workers that were previously discussed, if at all, only in limited-circulation scholarly publications. (Whatever "women's problem" was previously admitted publicly was portrayed as a demographic one, a view still widely held, unfortunately, even in progressive "informal" circles.)

One of these issues is dangerous, unhealthy and onerous work conditions. Although male workers also suffer from these, there is some basis to argue that they are relatively more women's lot — despite the existence of legislation specifically protecting women. Official statistics put at 4.8. million the number of women working in conditions that violate legal norms of work safety.[1] Depending upon the basis of calculation, this could be as many as one third of the female industrial work force. Moreover, men are more routinely compensated materially for bad work conditions. For example, the wages of underground miners, a profession from which women are excluded by law, are among the highest in the Soviet Union, while those of workers in "light" industry, with its overwhelmingly female labour force, are among the lowest. Yet in 1988, conditions in 1800 enterprises of the latter sector were officially recognized as unsatisfactory.[2]

Over the past two years, a series of exposés have shown conditions in the textile industry frequently to be horrendous. This is the largest sector of female industrial employment. The equipment and structures of these mills tend to be ancient, the noise, heat and dust levels extremely high, the level of mechanization of lifting operations primitive. This is one journalist's description of Moscow's Frunze mill:

> A white haze hovered above the shop. Dust swirled in the air and settled on my hair, crept into my eyes and mouth. My ears ached from the incredible din, the monotonous knocking — you cannot hear even the sound of your own voice — of dozens of huge looms pulling thread. One of them suddenly began to rumble: a thread coming out of its bowels broke. Immediately a girl in a worn smock ran out from somewhere. Harmonious, almost mechanical movements — and the thread once again grew taut, giving food to the insatiable loom... "Rugacheva Nadya," she introduced herself in the corridor... "Yes, it's hard. My hands go numb and get all black — it's unbleached thread. Eight hours of running. When you come back to the dormitory, your feet are aching. All you want to do is collapse on your bed. Every day the same thing. And the noise — outside after work you keep on shouting from habit. We'll probably be deaf when we get old."[3]

Morbidity among textile workers is high compared to women in white collar jobs of the same age.[4] It is not surprising that turnover and recruitment of young workers are serious problems in this industry. Of course, it is not only in the textile industry that women work in such conditions. For example, in some enterprises of the tractor and agricultural machinery industry, which has a large female work force, the concentration of manganese dioxide is 25 times the allowed norm, and the noise and vibration levels extremely high. The rate of occupational illness here is four times the national average.[5] Workers in jobs officially designated as harmful do receive special benefits: wage supplements "for harmfulness", longer holidays and early pensions. But these practices are also the object of criticism, since they are based upon the state and management's consideration that it is cheaper and simpler to pay wage supplements than to protect the workers' health by improving conditions. Trade-union spokespeople admit that relatively little is spent on health and safety. At the same time, the policy of "harmfulness benefits" creates among workers a material interest in staying in such conditions and not pressing collectively to eliminate them.

Labour legislation strictly limits the weight women workers can lift. Yet women are frequently employed in unmechanized jobs that require heavy lifting that violates legal norms. Thus, in the Tadzhik Republic, 42% of women workers are employed in unmechanized manual jobs. Nationally, women in woodworking, paper, glass, food and light industry make up 30-50% of the work force doing heavy physical labour.[6] In brick factories, women workers regularly move over 30 tonnes of silicate mass in a single shift, while the legal norm is seven. In construction, the most common job for women is painter, requiring women to carry 30 kilogramme pails from floor to floor. As for "light" industry, women commonly complain that this is a misnomer.[7]

An important contributing factor to industrial accidents among women is the failure of machine designers to take into account woman's physiology: levers that cannot be reached, that are too hard to pull. This is especially true in the textile industry. It was found that about one half of industrial accidents occurring in light industry result from faultily designed machines, and that 80% of the accidents occur on automatic machines designed specifically for "women's branches".[8] In the tractor and agricultural machinery industry, accidents resulting in death are double the national average.[9]

One of the most serious sources of dissatisfaction among women workers is night work, a practice that has come in for harsh criticism. Although forbidden by law, except as a temporary measure dictated by special needs of the industry, almost all textile mills have been on three shifts at least since the war. But even in industries where night work is necessary, such as petrochemicals and baking, more women work at night than men. 3.8 million women — more than men! — are engaged on any given date in night work. Although special benefits are paid — wage supplements and early pensions — Soviet studies show the body cannot get used to night work, which is generally unproductive and results in high morbidity rates and turnover among workers.[10] A related issue is the large amount of overtime and worked holidays made necessary by the arhythmic nature of production. Although this problem is general, it is felt more acutely by women who bear the bulk of family responsibilities.

Women's double shift has been a public issue since the 1960s, though it still continues to be discussed largely as a demographic issue: the rate of women's participation in the labour force is felt to be a major cause of the low birth rate. Among the principle solutions discussed are extended paid leave for women with children under three years, flexible work schedules, part-time work, home work. Limited space precludes any discussion of these proposals here. Suffice it to say that they all take for granted that the family and home are mainly a woman's responsibility.

There are, however, some dissident voices that condemn Soviet culture's "consumerist attitude" towards women, and the fact that women are most frequently portrayed with a child.[11] *Rabotnitsa* last year published an article on paternal leave in Bulgaria that argued that "we need to shift the emphasis and speak less of motherhood and more of parenthood."[12] But these views are still rarely found in the mass press. It is not surprising, therefore, that job segregation, one of whose main sources is the double shift, has not become a major topic in the media.

While the problems of women workers are discussed more openly, practice itself has changed little. The new Law on the State Enterprise gives elected work-collective councils broad powers to deal on their own with social issues, but so far ministries continue to control most of the funds that could be used for these purposes. Yet if enterprise autonomy and competition do become realities, as the reform prescribes, the result will be increased socio-economic differentiation. And it is by no means clear that most women workers, who are principally in low-skilled jobs, stand to benefit. Certainly one could conclude from the experience of Western market systems so far that sexual equality is unattainable in a society whose essence is socio-economic inequality. Any improvements in industrial health and safety conditions and in the relative situation of women workers that have been achieved in these systems has not been the result of market forces but of collective pressure on the part of workers. Indeed, when asked how the reform will help women, most Soviet radical marketeers point to increased consumption as the main benefit and do not mention work. This was the response of the noted woman sociologist, T. Zaslavskaya, in an interview on

International Woman's Day last year. And her example of the consumption benefits to women was the telling: a broader variety of shades. After all, she said, not all women want to be blonds.[13] But a woman from Kemerovo wrote: "They have finally begun to speak about us women in full voice. And the papers are full of reports: here they opened a fashion salon; there a dietologist offers consultations about how women can be slim. All that's fine. But if you are going to think really seriously about women, then you have to start from work conditions."[14]

Women workers' experience under perestroika has so far often been discouraging. There are many reports that pressures to reduce personnel exerted by the new "cost-accounting regime" are leading first of all to the unjust dismissal of women with small children, as well as older workers, these being the least productive. (The law permits women to be absent from work to care for sick children.) As one women complained to *Rabotnitsa:* "Perestroika is not only personnel reductions and dismissals, but also compassion and sensitivity towards people."[15] The right of women with small children to work part time without management's agreement is generally not respected by management. Many women have not even heard of this right.[16] And not only is women's night work not being reduced, but state and trade-union authorities appear to have shelved the issue, now that the government, as part of the reform, is encouraging enterprises to move to three shifts in order to make more efficient use of productive capacity.[17]

The present reform does not address itself to job segregation, vertical or horizontal. Many abuses have been occurring in the course of the review of skill classifications that is part of the wage reform. Management arbitrarily demotes entire groups of workers: for example, all men are placed in the fifth grade and women in the third. When the women complain, they are told openly that they are women, and men's skill grade should be two higher than women's. Similarly, the legal right of women with small children to study to raise their skill grade during work hours is simply ignored by management.[18]

If the economic reform offers nothing for women as workers, what of the officially proclaimed "self-management" and "democratization", that are said to be integral parts of perestroika? Unfortunately, with some rare exceptions, these have yet to materialize. Nor have the trade unions reformed themselves: numerous reports decry their continuing solidarity with management and passivity when it comes to enforcing legal norms and improving conditions. As for the revival of the women's councils, judging from the trade-union press, they have had little impact in the factories. It is telling that their voice, like that of the trade unions, has not been heard on the issue of night work, now that official policy calls for its extension.[19]

If women workers have not yet benefited as workers in any material sense from perestroika, the political liberalization is without doubt an important gain (though lacking any guarantees), since it opens the way for women to a more critical understanding of their situation and to the consciousness of the necessity to seek collective solutions that correspond to their interests, rather than passively placing their hopes in the present political leadership. (On International Women's Day 1988, during Gorbachev's visit to a Moscow ball-bearing plant, half of whose 20,000 workers are women, none of the issues raised related specifically to women.[20]) The current reform, designed and promulgated from above in an authoritarian manner, based upon deepening socio-economic differentiation and increasing dependence upon market criteria of rationality to guide social development, offers little that is attractive to the vast majority of women workers. The same is true for the working class as a whole, whose shared interests indeed call for a fundamental restructuring of the economy, but one that places democracy at the centre of the economic system, with social solidarity, based upon democratic decision-making and a real concern for social justice, gradually becoming the fundamental motivating factors of economic actors.[21]

June 1989

NOTES

1. "Zhenshchina v zerkale statistiki," *Agitator*, no. 3 1988, p. 33.
2. *Trud,* Mar. 3, 1988, plenum of the Central Committee of the Trade Union of Light and Textile Industries.
3. I. Chernyak, "Kto v rabochie poidet?" *Sobesednik*, no. 29, July, 1988, p. 13.
4. N.V. Dogle, "Usloviya zhizni i zdorov'e tekstil'shchits," Moscow, 1977, pp. 77-93.
5. "G. Bilyalitdinova, "Ne zhenskaya nosha," *Pravda,* June 6, 1988.
6. Ibid.; "Zhneshchina v zerkale statistiki".

7. "Tysyachi tyazheliykh kirpichei," *Nedelya*, no. 6, 1989, p. 14; "Osvobozhdennyi trud na khozrschete," *Sobesdnik*, no 23, p. 6.
8. "Tysyacha tyazhelykh kirpichei." p. 14
9. Bilyalitdtinova, "Ne zhenskaya nosha."
10. A. Levina, "Tysyacha i odna noch'," *Rabotnitsa*, no. 4, 1988, p. 12.
11. S. Kaidash, "K voprosu o zhenskom voprose," *Moskovskie novosti*, Aug. 8, 1988, p. 13.
12. D. Akivis, "Materinstvo i 'otchestvo'," *Rabotnitsa*, no. 6, 1988, p. 21.
13. *Izvestiya*, Mar. 8, 1988.
14. Bilyalitidinova.
15. *Rabotnitsa*, no. 10, 1988, p. 1. See, for example, *Trud*, May 14, 1989, p. 2, report of the working group on employment of the All-Russian Trade-Union Council and State Committee on Labour.
16. "O svoikh l'gotakh," *Rabotnitsa*, no. 1, 1988, p. 20.
17. A. Levina, "Tysyacha i odna noch'."
18. "Operatsiya 'stupeni masterstva'," *Rabotnitsa*, no. 10, 1988, p. 17.
19. Levina, "Tysyacha..."
20. *Pravda*, Mar. 8, 1988.
21. I have argued this at greater length in "Perestroika and the Working Class," *Against the Current*, May-June 1989, pp. 22-31.

Chapter 3

THE REBIRTH OF THE SOVIET LABOUR MOVEMENT: THE COALMINERS' STRIKE OF JULY 1989

Between July 10 and 24 1989, over 400,000 miners took part in a strike that embraced the four major coal basins of the Soviet Union. This marked the emergence for the first time in over 60 years of a labour movement in that country. As the first large-scale, independent labour action of perestroika, the strike merits careful analysis for what it can reveal about the nature of the Soviet (especially Russian and Ukrainian) working class and its aspirations. In the unanimous judgment of Soviet officials and media, the strike was an expression of support from below for the government reforms. But this claim appears at odds with Gorbachev's own admission before the Supreme Soviet:

> This was the most difficult trial for us in the entire four years of perestroika. We had Chernobyl. We had other difficult trials. Nevertheless, I would single out present events as the most serious, the most difficult.[1]

Background to the Strike

"Perestroika has shaken people up, especially the youth," commented A. Evsyukov, chairman of the Kemerovo strike committee in the Kuzbass in Siberia. "Over the past few years, the development of people's political consciousness has moved ahead especially quickly."[2] Two important changes have occurred in the workers' relations with the political and economic bureaucracies. On the one hand, having tested the waters in small-scale strikes, workers have gradually shed their fear of repression. The barrage of criticism which the central authorities and the press have been directing at the economic administration has also had the effect of encouraging worker protest.

On the other hand, the effect of the wage reform, "cost accounting" (khozraschet)[3], and other innovations in enterprise management has been to undermine the traditionally collusive relations between workers and the administration, but without so far replacing them with economically healthy co-operation. This has undermined the traditionally paternalistic relations between managment and workers and freed the latter to protest collectively against miserable work and living conditions and managerial arbitrariness, that they once grudgingly tolerated in return for management's "favours." Something of the miners' changing outlook was reflected in the words of Yu. Boldyrev, a member of the Donetsk strike committee:

> In the coal industry an especially disrespectful attitude of managers to subordinates has flourished. Rudeness and the trampling of human dignity are widespread. Just yesterday people considered this the normal "business" style in the branch. But today with the process of democratization, this way of managing is totally inadmissible... and that is why we frequently express our lack of confidence in the managers.[4]

The miners' strike was fundamentally a protest against bureaucratic mismanagement of the economy and the system's inherent tendency to treat the the population not as the goal of production, but as a residual factor whose needs could be ignored so long as social peace was not threatened. This was particularly blatant in the coal industry after the 1958 decision to shift the energy balance from coal to oil and gas. This meant a decline in priority for investment in coal, which in turn translated into a low level of social spending in the coal regions, since most of the investment in housing and social infrastructure depends upon the ministry.

The chairman of the mine strike committee in Mezhdurechensk in the Kuzbass described social conditions in the following terms: numerous families living in dormitories, overcrowded buses, a shortage of day-care spaces, schools that work in three shifts — the lights stay on past midnight — lines at the polyclinic "as long as lines for imported shoes," only two cafeterias accessible to the general public, one cinema, no sports or youth centre. "In a city of 107,000 that extracts 31 million tonnes of coal annually, we thus live without rights."[5]

Coalminers' wages and pensions have traditionally been among the highest in industry, but their work conditions are among the most onerous and dangerous — life expectancy among miners is under 50 years. However, the coal enterprises, like those in other extracting industries, have been less able to exploit the provisions of the economic reform to obtain additional income: they make essentially one product and so cannot change the profile of their production to concentrate on higher priced goods; they cannot jack up prices by claiming improvements in their product; nor could they, before the strike, exchange above-plan production for consumer goods or construction materials, since their entire output was covered by state contracts and they had no direct access to consumers. Wages in coalmining have risen at only half the national rate during the current five-year plan (1986-90). The industry has lost 34,000 workers over the past three years.[6]

According to Boldyrev, "work conditions of the Donbass miners are not only not improving, they are getting worse... The occupational prestige of the miner has fallen to zero; the value of his labour has been cheapened. Wages in many mines have become lower than those on the surface, and their miserly increase is eaten up almost at once by sharp jumps in the price of goods and services."[7] "We began to feel the tension mount in the mines after January 1, 1989," reported V. Medevedev, secretary of the central committee of the Union of workers of the Coal Industry, "when the industry shifted to new conditions of economic management. The basic reason was that the mines were not ready to work in conditions of cost accounting and self-financing and all our shortcomings became visible to everyone. In this connection, strikes occurred in several regions."[8]

Industrial pollution is another important source of dissatisfaction. In large part because of it, life expectancy in Novokuznestsk and Kemerovo is ten years below the national average.[9] The ecological situation is worst of all in the Kuzbass with its open-pit mines. "The region is drowning in industrial waste," said Evsyukov. "Its water resources and scarce arable land are drawing their last breaths. The thinning taiga is being reduced to nothing under the shovels of the giant excavators and the iron heels of new industrial monsters."[10]

The miners' official workday was six-hours, but they were often at the mines for more than ten hours because of time spent in travel to and from the coalface and in changing. This time was not paid.[11] The miners were also not being paid the supplement for evening and night work provided for in a 1987 decree.[12] In addition, the system's inability to assure a regular supply of materials for production causes periods of idleness and loss of wages that are especially painfully felt now with the new cost-accounting régime. Finally, the effect of any wage increase that the reform may have made possible has been neutralized by inflation and the deteriorating supply of consumer goods in the state sector.

The miners' shifting schedule of holidays, which eliminated Sunday as a common day off some ten years ago (this was done with the trade union's blessing — the workers were not consulted) was another focus of discontent. This arrangement typifies the ministry's lack of consideration for the workers' interests. This measure, which allowed an increase of output with minimal capital investment, was entirely at the miners' expense, since they rarely had days off which they could spend together with their families.

Another key factor in the outbreak of the strike was the arbitrary power and corruption of the local authorities. These were not new problems, but they have become intolerable under perestroika. Many of the workers demands could have been met by the local authorities and even, in principle, by the workers' self-management councils. But there had been no real democratization and the local authorities continued to consider only the wishes of their bureaucratic superiors worthy of their attention. On the other hand, bureaucratic privilege remained intact. "Saunas, summer vacation trips, the chance to rest in the summer — that's only for the bosses," complained one miner. Another miner from Makeevka in the Donbass described how his section director sold his car each year and purchased a new one, while workers waited nine or ten years for a car. Many miners had long since lost hope of receiving an apartment, but the director owned a house and was "having built" an apartment for his son. While managers benefit from subsidized and free trips to sanatoria and spas, workers are lucky to obtain one in fifteen years. In Makeevka, the party authorities had recently constructed a luxurious "house of political education" in the centre of a city that has no youth centre, rehabilitation or chronic care facilities for miners. A Soviet journalist reported hearing such complaints, "full of anger and bitterness, innumerable times at meetings and in ordinary conversations. It had been building up for a long time and demanded expression."[13]

At the middle and central levels of power, the workers saw looming above them a grossly inflated, uncontrolled and wasteful bureaucracy, which they viewed, like the local management, as little better than an army of parasites. Since the price system meant that many coal enterprises worked at a loss, they depended upon the good will of this apparatus for capital and social investment. But they received so little that it seemed that the wealth they produced disappeared into thin air, that is, when it did not fall into the pockets of the bureaucrats. When told that the strike was costing the country millions of rubles, miners angrily pointed to the huge stores of coal that were catching fire on the railway sidings because there were no cars.

The Strike Movement

The depth of the miners' dissatisfaction was no secret to the authorities. In January the trade-union paper *Trud* published a letter from three decorated workers of Mezhdurechensk who complained bitterly of "total neglect in the resolution of social problems" and of the ministry's "anti-perestroika attitude" of "take where the taking is easy." But the ministry responded to all criticism with empty promises. This time it did not answer at all.

The miners' strike came on the crest of an unprecedented strike wave in the Soviet era: two million worker-days lost in the first half of 1989, an average of 15,000 workers on strike each day (although a significant part of these strikes involved national issues, themselves, of course, not devoid of social aspects).[14] The coal industry itself experienced twelve strikes in the first half of 1989 over many of the same issues as in July. But they yielded only partial concessions and promises of more to come.

The miners of the Shevyakov mine in Mezhdurechensk finally forced the issue. At the start of July, they presented a list of demands to the central committee of the coalworkers' union, the city party committee and the director of mines and gave them until July 10 to satisfy the demands or face a strike. Negotiations with management on July 4 led nowhere. The strike began with the night shift of July 10-11. By midday the four other mines of the local trust as well as other enterprises in the town had joined. 12,000 miners in their work clothes marched down the main street and sat on the asphalt in the city square next to the building of the party committee. They elected a city strike committee which presented a list of 41 economic and ecological demands.[15]

That day, *Trud* published an interview with the chairman of the All-Union Central Council of Trade Unions (AUCCTU), Shelaev, who explained the coal workers' union's "ultimatum" to the minister. It included the following demands: the right of mine collectives to determine their own work and rest régimes; a common day off on Sundays; a 40% supplement for night shifts; payment for time spent in travelling to and from the coalface; priority to social needs in centralized capital investment. But not only did this "ultimatum" not cover all the workers' demands, it gave the ministry a year to act and then only threatened symbolic protest.

On July 12, the Minister arrived from Moscow. The meeting lasted all night and into the next day, while on the central square 5,000-20,000 workers held a continuous meeting. At three p.m. on the July 13, the strike committee announced that 36 of the 42 demands had been met and recommended a return to work. The miners rejected this. That day the city strike committee sent an open letter to the Soviet government demanding improvement in the food supply to Siberia and the Far East, an end to official privileges and an immediate opening of a public discussion of a new draft constitution to be adopted by November 7, 1990. The letter also demanded that the leaders of the party and government themselves come to the Kuzbass. And in order to expedite their arrival, it called for a general coalminers' strike in the Kuzbass. Mezhdurechensk itself returned to work on July 14.[16]

Everywhere the picture was the same. The miners occupied the central squares in permanent meeting. Worker detachments maintained order. (In Donetsk, veterans of the Afghan war played an important role in this. Among the miners' demands were increased pensions for the veterans.[17]) In Kemerovo, crime declined by 52% during the strike. The strike committees stopped the sale of alcohol, sealed liquor stores and set up drug inspection points on the main roads. In Donetsk two miners were dismissed for appearing drunk on the central square.[18] With a few exceptions, the miners assured operations necessary to maintain the mines and continued to ship coal to metallurgical enterprises whose furnaces would otherwise have been ruined. Arguing that they were putting forth demands for the entire community, the miners asked workers in other essential branches not to strike. People began turning to the committees for help in matters such as pension allocations, obtaining telephones, construction and housing repairs, food supply and labour disputes (outside the coal industry) where they had been unable to obtain recourse through the official channels.[19]

On July 15 in the hall of the Palace of Culture of Novokuznetsk, overflowing with miners, the Minister and oblast' first secretary repeated the volatile bargaining marathon of Mezhdurechensk. But this time they were dealing not with five mines and 12,000 workers but 158 mines and 177,000 workers. And the bargaining was much tougher. The miners were demanding the presence of Gorbachev and Prime Minister Ryzhkov as the only guarantee they would not be deceived again.[20]

These two were not about to come, but on July 16 Gorbachev informed the miners by telegram that a top level delegation, including Politburo member and Central Committee secretary Slyun'kov was on its way, and in view of this the miners should return to work. But the workers wanted concrete results. On July 18, the regional strike committee, stating that the talks were going well and the basic demands were being met, recommended a return to work starting with the night shift. Many heeded this call, but the next day 64,015 workers (91 mines) were still out. It was only on July 21 that all workers in the Kuzbass returned.[21]

The strike in the Donbass began on the evening of the July 15 in Makeevka. Despite goverment assurances that the Kuzbass agreement covered the entire industry, the Donbass miners insisted that top government officials talk directly to them. Indeed, the strike movement in the Donbass spread out of Makeevka only on the 18th, — it was as if the agreement and return to work in the Kuzbass spurred the others to action, fearing they would otherwise be passed by. A regional strike committee was formed in Donetsk. In all, 110 mines struck in the Donbass with up to 90,000 miners out on a single day. Besides the large number of economic demands, the Donbass miners also put forth political demands. On July 20 the strike spread to the other mining centres of the Ukraine.

The government commission arrived in Donetsk on July 20, and the protocol was signed on the July 22. That day, Gorbachev and Ryzhkov called the miners to return. By the morning of July 24, 73 mines in Donetsk oblast' had ended their strike, but 50 were still out, insisting on legislative guarantees. A delegation of members of the Donetsk strike committee and People's Deputies from the Donbass flew out to Moscow and met in the Kremlin with Ryzhkov on July 24. A concrete programme of action for the whole industry was outlined. Ryzhkov again called all miners to end the strike. On July 25 it was decided to return to work. A majority of those still out returned, but in Donetsk they held out for two more days. The strike in the Ukraine and southern Russia did not completely end until July 27.[22]

In the Pechora basin in the far north, the strike began on the July 19 and was called off on July 24 only after People's Deputy V. Luzhnikov formally apprised the Supreme Soviet of the miners' demands. Even so, most miners did not return until the next day when they received a photocopy of the signed accord.[23] The strike in the Karaganda basin in Kazakhstan, the country's third largest coalfield, began on the night of July 19-20. Explaining the strike, a representative of the strike committee stated that the mass media were not revealing all the demands of the Kuzbass miners. Work resumed with the night shift of July 22-3.[24]

With the end of the strike, the strike committees did not disband but transformed themselves into workers' committees, whose main task was to monitor the execution of the agreements.

The Demands

The full lists of the miners' demands were *never* published in the central press, and their more political demands which did not figure in the signed accords were given only fleeting mention. The demands can roughly be divided into four categories: wages and benefits, work conditions and work régime, ecology and political power. In the Donbass, the major demands in the first two categories, according to a list given to Western reporters by the Ukrainian Central Information Services, included a wage supplement for evening and night shifts, full pay for travel to and from the coalface, Sundays off, recognition of a series of diseases as work-related, retirement after twenty years of continuous underground work, additional pension benefits, three years maternity leave at average wage, full pay for idle time that is management's fault, no loss of wages for changing jobs, prohibition of punitive job transfers, and the destination of earnings from all-union subbotniki (voluntary worked holidays without pay) to be decided by workers' assemblies.

Other economic demands that went beyond the limits of the enterprise were resolution of problems of water, gas and electricity supply, a review of soap quotas, an apartment for all miners within ten years, supply of food in accordance with medical norms. Then there were the more "political" economic demands: reduction of managerial personnel, payment of wages during the strike from union funds, regional self-financing (khozraschet), prohibition of the establishment of new co-operatives and the disbanding of existing medical and food co-operatives. (Hostility to the co-operatives, many of which employ hired labour, is directed particularly against those whose high prices and incomes are not justified by additional labour inputs; to the ordinary Soviet citizen this is still "speculation," even if now formally legal. They are also seen as contributing to the shortages of cheap materials and goods in state stores, since these are often the co-operatives source of supplies. Opposition to medical co-operatives stems from fears of the creation of a two-class health system and the view of free health care as a right.) The Vorkuta miners also demanded that 25% of the foreign currency earned from the export of their coal be left at the disposition of the labour-collective councils and that the government's decision linking wage rises to productivity growth be rescinded. The Kuzbass miners demanded that the ministry pay more into local government budgets.

It is worth noting here that the demand for enterprise autonomy did not appear among the original 20 demands of the Mezhdurechensk miners nor on the Donbass or Vorkuta lists. It also did not figure in the demands presented by the central committee of the miner workers' union to the ministry that were published on June 11. On the list of 25 demands presented by the Kuzbass miners, enterprise autonomy was only eighteenth.[25] At some point, however, enterprise autonomy came to be presented officially — and possibly seen by a part of the miners themselves — as the central demand.

Besides the general demand to repair ecological damage, some of the specific local environmental demands were the construction of a purification plant in Mezhdurechensk and a halt to contruction of the Krapivinskii hydro-electric project on the Tom' River and to atomic testing in Semipalatinsk in Kazakhstan.[26]

Other demands attacked bureaucratic power and privilege directly. Like the demand to ban co-operatives, which flies in the face of the economic reform's basic orientation, these were treated more gingerly by official spokespeople and the press — in fact, they received little mention at all. The callous attitude of local officials was a major theme of meetings, where these officials were often met with remarks such as "Here comes the town mafia."[27] Everywhere the miners demanded "the removal of any privileges enjoyed by officials of the administrative and party apparatuses." Some workers in Prokop'evsk took it upon themselves to inspect the apartments of local officials. There were also widespread demands "to reduce the numerous apparat personnel," including that of the coal ministry, by 40%, to replace enterprise and trust directors, work-collective councils, as well as local soviet, party and trade-union officials, and to hold new elections immediately, particularly to the local soviets."[28]

The miners wanted to replace them with their own leaders from the strike committees. In Chervonograd in the Western Ukraine, where the Ukrainian national movement was stronger, the workers also demanded the resignation of the first secretary of the Ukrainian Communist Party, Shcherbitsky, as well as the city party first secretary, the police chief, the head of the KGB and the creation of an independent trade union to be named "Solidarity."[29]

There were also demands for changes at the central level. The Vorkuta miners called for the removal of the coal minister and of the chairman of the Union of Workers of the Coal Industry, "as leaders of the branch who have shown themselves incapable of developing effective, balanced, economic and social policies." They also demanded the repeal of article six of the Soviet constitution which allots the Communist Party the "leading role" in the state (in fact, it is a euphemism for the bureaucratic monopoly of power) and election of the Congress of Peoples' Deputies by universal suffrage, in effect, calls to end bureaucratic power. The demand for direct elections of the chairperson of the Supreme Soviet implicitly called Gorbachev's own legitimacy into question. In the Kuzbass, the workers demanded a national discussion of a new constitution, which should be adopted on November 7, 1990 (the anniversary of the October Revolution).[30]

In light of these demands, statements such as that of a Makeevka strike committee leader that "our demands are not political but socio-economic," seem surprising.[31] The level of politicization did vary from one region to the other, it being the highest in Vorkuta. (The demand to rescind article 6 of the constitution was proposed by the chairman of the Voshagorskaya mine strike committee, himself a party member for over ten years.)[32] The Donbass miners, the least politicized, did not want to put forth political demands "on principle," possibly for fear that their socio-economic demands would be pushed into the background or because they did not want to provoke the authorities.[33] In fact, insofar as many of the "socio-economic" demands were directed at the central authorities and challenged their policies and their power to make economic decisions without the consent of the workers, the strike from the start was everywhere highly politicized. And this even if one chooses to ignore the demands to abolish bureaucratic privilege and the repeated expressions, in words and actions, of non-confidence in the political authorities at all levels. But the popular Soviet view of what is political is often a curious one. Thus, the chief of the police in Mezhdurechensk could calmly report "no anti-state or anti-party manifestations."[34]

The Government's Response

Gorbachev's narrow social basis strictly limited his options. Repression would have totally discredited his economic reform in the workers' eyes and played directly into the hands of the anti-perestroika elements in the apparatus. On the other hand, the depth of the miners' scepticism towards the government and of their frustration ruled out buying them off in the usual way with concessions and vague promises. Yet a serious response to the miners' demands raised the spectre of a chain reaction of strikes across the country.

Gorbachev did not want this strike. But once it was there, he was determined to make the best of a bad thing to strengthen his weak social base in the working class and further undermine his enemies in the bureaucracy. The formula was simple but ingenious: he declared the strike a popular movement in support of the economic reform. At the same time, a concerted attempt was made to direct the workers' anger at local officials and especially at the ministry, who were accused of holding back the reform. Hence the repeated affirmation that the "central" and "essential" demand was enterprise autonomy, even though there is no indication that this was prominent in workers' minds at the start of the strike. Indeed, there is ample evidence that not all workers were enthusiastic about this demand.

The emphasis on enterprise autonomy made it possible to blame the ministry and local authorities for the miners' situation. Typical was the statement of the chairman of the Donetsk regional trade-union council:

> In the breakneck development of the industrial might of the Donbass, the social sphere was neglected. This is the consequence of the dictatorial and arbitrary power of the ministries and central agencies, with the connivance of the local organs.[35]

In reality, of course, the neglect of the social sphere is the consequence of the bureaucratic system itself, of the bureaucracy's arbitrary power over the Soviet people. This could not have occurred in a genuinely democratic system, regardless of the degree of central planning and regulation. If blame were to be honestly apportioned, certainly the topmost leaders, the party politburo and secretariat deserve the greatest part. They are supposed to set basic policy for the ministries to carry out.

This same tactic allowed Gorbachev to exploit the strike to further weaken bureaucratic opposition to perestroika. On the background of the growing strike movement, he reassured the party secretaries that the party (i.e. its apparatus) was destined to remain the ruling party, though it would have to change its methods of domination. At the same time, by calling for a renewal of cadres from top to bottom, he sent warning to fall into line or to risk losing one's posts. He also called for special local party meetings with government and trade-union officials to consider workers' demands, including the ouster of unresponsive officials.[36] A move to forestall a national strike wave, it was also an attempt to use the workers to get rid of local officials nurturing anti-perestroika sentiments or lacking in initiative.

While the idea of enterprise autonomy was being promoted with the full force of the ideological apparatus, to which the liberal intelligentsia willingly lent its services, other demands that challenged bureaucratic privilege or went against the spirit of the economic reform, in particular the closure of co-operatives, were hardly mentioned. Gorbachev did refer to it in one speech, only to dismiss it as "an easy way, but is it the best?"[37] The miners had many complaints about "glasnost'": "The media did not transmit our thought and our pain to the whole Soviet people," complained a Pavolgrad miner. As already noted, the central media never fully reported the workers' demands, especially the more political ones and those that went against the current of the government's economic reform, but they constantly emphasized the losses the strike was causing to an economy that was already in serious condition.[38]

The official position was that the demands were justified but the strike was not a good way to obtain their satisfaction, and the government tried to mobilize public opinion to pressure the miners to return. The local authorities adopted the same position, verbally supporting the demands while opposing the choice of means. In practice, however, with few exceptions, they lost control of the political situation, though some did play a not unambiguous role as consultants.[39] The trade-union organizations were also supportive of the movement, organizing free meals, transport, even legal advice. But in extremely few cases did they lead the strike.

While adopting a tolerant attitude to the miners' strike, the government took measures to dissuade other workers from following suit. One of these, as mentioned, was Gorbachev's instruction to local party committees to hold meetings with workers' representatives. The government also entered into direct negotiations with representatives of the railroad workers who were threatening to strike August 1. At the same time, it let the railroad workers know they could not expect the same indulgence as the miners. A worker from Chernigov oblast' wrote that he and his colleagues had been forced to sign commitments not to strike. This was after a meeting at which a government telegram about raising discipline and stopping strikes was read out. "Only prohibitions and demands that we sign. This sort of attitude towards us on the part of the leadership in no way fosters mutual understanding and the desire to work better. It only intensifies the existing confrontation."[40]

Once the protocols were signed, the benevolent attitude of the authorities began to change. For example, in the Donbass, most miners went back to work without awaiting the return of their delegation that was in Moscow negotiating modalities for the concrete application of the accord. But in Donetsk oblast' they wanted guarantees. It was at this point that management stopped strike pay and declared that henceforth strikers would be counted as absentees. It also set up guards to keep members of the strike committees out of the enterprises. The government, on its part, refused legal status to the workers' committees (the renamed strike committees), which meant that they had no formal powers and their members received no wages from their enterprise and they risked losing their underground seniority. Finally, although the signed protocols specifically gave the workers the right to resume the strike if the accords were not carried out, when the Vorkuta miners tried to do this in November, their strike was declared illegal (The Soviet had passed in the meanwhile a new law on labour conflicts), exposing the strikers to very stiff penalties.[41]

The Accord

The settlement was in two parts: the signed economic accord and the political accord. The latter was not published as such in the press, but consisted of different measures that responded partially to the demands of a more political nature.

The economic protocols in the different regions were similar in their basic elements but also responded to specific local demands. The Kuzbass protocol published in *Trud* had seventeen points (though Gorbachev referred to an accord with 35 points.)[42] Article number one grants full economic and juridical autonomy to the mines, in accord with the Law on State Enterprises. Enterprises can adopt different forms of property — state, co-operative, leasing, joint stock and others. Article two gives enterprises the right to sell production beyond that covered by state contracts at contractual prices at home and abroad. The extent of state orders is to be reviewed accordingly.

Article three calls for a rise in the price of coal in accordance with the real costs of its extraction, including the full cost of recultivation, and considering changing natural conditions. Enterprises are also given the right to apply certain correctives to performance indicators. Article four allows enterprises independently to set output norms and wage rates, the basin-wide norms being only recommendations.

These four articles were the government's answer to the demands concering wages and social investment. An increase in these is thus made dependent, to a degree at least, on increased productivity and effort on the miners' part. Under the old system, increased productivity tended to lead to a decline in wage rates and an increase in output norms and plan quotas, thus penalizing more efficient enterprises.

Other articles met the wage demands for night and evening work, payment for travel time to and from the coalface, Sundays off, pensions and retirement (a central demand), maternal leave, vacations, professional diseases, and the shedding of excess managerial staff.

The elements of the political accord included increased supply of scarce consumer goods to the regions and a rise in the regional wage supplement for the Siberian workers. There was provision for new elections of trade union committees and work-collective councils. Directors who did not enjoy the workers' confidence were removed after the strike. In the Donbass medical, food and trade were prohibited. Many co-operatives were also closed in the other regions.[43]

Gorbachev responded to the demands to remove local officials and hold new elections by proposing that the Supreme Soviet reverse an earlier decision to postpone local soviet elections from the fall of 1989 to the spring of 1990. This had been a concession to local bureaucrats who feared they would be turned out or discredited if not given more time to prepare. (In the end, the elections were held in the spring.) In the meanwhile, local party plenums with representatives of workers would take up the question of renewing cadres. No decisions were made regarding the further democratization of the USSR Congress of People's Deputies and the Supreme Soviet or discussion of a new draft constitution.[44]

Worker Consciousness

The miners' strike challenged the widespread view among the Soviet intelligentsia of the workers as a brutish, alcoholic, déclassé mass, a potentially fascistic social basis for bureaucratic reaction. According to this view, workers are not capable of governing; the parliament and government should be staffed by "competent" people, members of the "educated classes."[45] Although the movement arose and spread spontaneously — the strike committees were formed only after the strikes began — the miners displayed remarkable discipline and organization.

The strike also revealed a high level of political consciousness among the workers. They are certainly no bait for rightwing nationalist ideologies. A survey that asked Kuzbass miners in whom they placed their confidence, found no supporters of "Pamyat'" or the "Fatherland" (Russian chauvinistic organizations).[46] Although the miners are a mixed ethnic group, national divisions played no visible role in their movement. Miners typically explain that the dangerous nature of their work does not permit such luxuries, and besides, underground, everyone looks the same. The Ukrainian national movement, "Rukh," has had difficulty finding a social base in the Donbass (whose Ukrainian population is often Russian-speaking). Nor do the miners support the "Democratic Union," a liberal party that calls more or less openly for the establishment of a capitalist democracy.[47]

At the same time, the strike was a massive expression of non-confidence in bureaucratic power. If the the strike began as a movement for economic demands, the miners understood at once that the more basic issue was that of guarantees and that the only real guarantee was power, i.e. democracy. Indeed, one cannot help but be struck by the depth of the mistrust toward bureaucratic power at all levels, including the highest. The miners brushed aside the local authorities and were not satisfied to negotiate with the minister. They ignored Gorbachev and Ryzhkov's appeals to return to work before the conclusion of negotiations. And once the agreement had been reached, many still insisted that it receive legislative guarantees — the Supreme Soviet is at least a quasi-democratic body. Gorbachev had to make an embarassing admission before the Supreme Soviet:

> In Donetsk the miners want the Supreme Soviet to be formally apprised of the documents worked out jointly with the commission. Among the people there has arisen a, so to speak [!], lack of trust... It is the same in the other coal regions too.[48]

The fact that Gorbachev had to recruit Yeltsin, who appealed, not in the name of the Supreme Soviet, but of the parliamentary "radicals" for the workers to return, shows that shortage of confidence in the authorities is the most serious shortage of all in the Soviet Union. The strike would have been brief and limited to the Kuzbass had the miners in the other regions believed the repeated assurances at the highest level that the Kuzbass accord covered the whole industry.[49]

Even when they decided to return to work, most miners were not convinced they had won anything real. An independent journalist who was in the Donbass wrote that the leitmotif was:

> "They will inevitably trick us." And the miners cited examples from their experience of the last twenty years. Hence their call for control, including control over the middle-level bureaucracy, that will inevitably resist the agreement. In this they showed considerable political maturity, even though they did not put forth political demands.[50]

Hence the miners decision in all regions not to disband the strike committees and their warning that the strike had merely been suspended, not terminated. "We are returning to work," declared the chairman of the Pavlograd strike committee. "But we will wait one month. If it turns out that we have been deceived once again, then we will continue the struggle to a victorious conclusion."[51]

As it turned out, the miners' suspicions were justified. When the Vorkuta miners went out on strike again in November 1989, the government admitted that many points of the accord were not being carried out. The Prime Minister himself confessed that the government signed the accord without fully considering its capacity to live up to it. But the government was reneging even on parts of the accord that required no new allocation of resources, such as the right to resume the strike if the agreement was not carried out.[52]

Soviet journalists reported that they did not feel the presence of the party committees, ordinarily the real power in the towns, during the strike and that these were the object of many bitter words on the part of the workers. *Pravda* also criticized the various local authorities who seemed to have faded into the scenery.[53] The void was filled by the strike committees. "A peculiar situation arose," commented *Trud*.

> The strike committees, in essence, became the authority in the towns. They were occupied with questions of trade, transport, maintaining order. From morning to night people who for a long time had been unable to get help or support from any other organization came to the committees. And their members looked into each problem, asked specialists, and helped where they could with medical treatment, repairs, job placement... We saw how the working class closes ranks and organizes itself, how it boldly defends the interests of all toilers, demands resolution ot the most important problems facing the country. We saw how the strike revealed extraordinary, independent, capable and bold people, ready to serve the common cause. We saw this and we wondered: why were they not noticed before, why are indifferent, faceless people put at the head of public organizations, people who are prepared to agree with any opinion of higher-ups? Maybe that was easier, more convenient?[54]

A Movement In Support of the Government Economic Reform?

Among the social-science intelligentsia and journalists, who overwhelmingly support the "radical market reform" (many favour the restoration of capitalism but the word is still unacceptable), the view is widespread that the mass of workers are hostile to the government's market reform. Hence the almost audible sigh of relief from journalists, commentators and official spokespeople, who repeatedly emphasized that the demand for enterprise autonomy made the strike a pro-perestroika action.

But since it does not appear to have been a central issue for the workers before the strike, one can surmise that it initially appeared as a solution offered to the miners by the government to the problem of financing their social and economic demands. They were told in effect: if you work harder and more efficiently, we will henceforth let you use the extra fruits of your labour to meet your needs. The workers accepted the offer. But does this mean that they have been won over to Gorbachev's market reform? Only the future can definitively answer this. But there are some grounds for scepticism.

In the end, the strike was about power. The workers, in essence, were asking for control over production and over their surplus product. In accordance with the logic of the reform, and the interests promoting it, the goverment tried to channel these aspirations away from the idea of collective planning and regulation on the national level and exclusively toward decentralized group control on the enterprise level. This directs workers away from the struggle for collective control over the conditions within which the autonomous enterprises are to function.

One strike leader did call on television for a national congress of coal miners without senior industrial officials, which could serve as a forum for discussing collective solutions to the industry's problems. But this proposal was apparently not taken up.[55] (Despite calls for an early national meeting of miners, the Congress of the Union of Workers of the Coal Industry met only at the end of March 1990, and less than a fifth of the delegates were miners. This prompted a walkout of miners and representatives of the workers committees, who described the meeting as a "congress of apparatchiki and employers"[56]) And yet, enterprise autonomy, as described by the Soviet media, makes the least sense in a resource extracting industry, where profits will depend heavily on natural conditions. The Donbass coalfields are deeper and have been mined out to a significant degree, and so costs there are higher than in the Kuzbass, where the coal lies near the surface. What little is known about worker consciousness indicates that their sense of justice would make them consider as unjust competition among autonomous mines in conditions where prices are set by the market. Even in Poland, where Solidarity's leaders are strongly pro-market, only four percent of industrial workers, according to a survey conducted in the summer of 1989, said they agreed that wages should be tied to enterprise profitability as determined by the market.[57]

In the Donbass, at least, there was considerable scepticism about enterprise autonomy. According to an opinion survey of Donbass miners conducted during the strike, only 16% of the miners favoured "cost-accounting" (khozraschet), i.e. enterprise financial autonomy, as a means of getting the industry out of its crisis, though one third did consider leasing the enterprises to the worker collectives as desirable option.[58] Many miners felt that enterprise autonomy would benefit the more productive mines but penalize those that have been neglected or largely mined out. And there are many of these in the Donbass. Furthermore, any application of purely market criteria to the Donbass coalfield would lead to the closure of a large number of mines, the displacement of tens of thousands of miners' families, the death of entire communities. Only a few years ago, the British miners fought bitterly against the application of just these criteria to their mines. When asked about this, Yu. Boldyrev, member of the Donetsk city strike committee, replied:

> There are no 100% just demands. We need to support the reform. That is the position of the strike committee. Yes, there are some voices saying that in conditions of full cost-accounting some mines will close. But that is a social question... We don't want to be a brake on the reform.[59]

While Boldyrev's views represent the thinking of a certain stratum of worker activists, not all miners are as confident that "social questions" can be so easily separated from questions of the economic reform. According to A. Dubovik, a member of the Donbass regional council of strike committees, "rumours are constantly circulating to the effect that the Donbass will be closed in five years. There is no way that we will allow that."[60] The point is that if a restructuring of the Donbass economy is called for, this restructuring will not occur in a manner corresponding to the workers' interests if enterprises are left to make decisions in isolation and to fend for themselves within a free market context. Indeed, it is precisely this kind of problem —

one that faces the Soviet economy as a whole — that calls for democratic, collective solutions on national and regional levels.

To the extent that workers find the concept of enterprise autonomy attractive — and there is no doubt that many do — it is because they see it offering conditions for self-management, for more efficient organization of production and for earning more for social investment. But this is not the same market reform, with its weakening of social guarantees and deepening socio-economic inequality, that most liberal intellectuals and Gorbachev's team have in mind. Indeed, their reform, in its moderate or more "radical" versions, which is being touted as "democratization of the economy," is more correctly seen as a substitute for democracy, if the latter is understood as popular control over the economy. M. Anokhin, a member of the bureau of the Porkop'evsk city workers' committee in the Kuzbass, described what he saw as the likely scenario:

> The workers demand full autonomy. They will try it, gain experience and maybe suffer through the difficulties it will bring. Then they will decide themselves: You know, comrades, it is bad for us when we are isolated. We should unite.[61]

In any case, it is not at all clear that the July agreement itself corresponds to the official conception of the market reform, since it does not create a unified price for coal (something the workers reject[62]), but rather calls for a rise in coal prices in accord with the real costs of extraction and recultivation. Moreover, enterprises are given some latitude in adjusting performance indicators. This would seem to mean that prices for coal will be based on local costs and not on competitive market criteria. If so, is this not more of the "levelling" that is being so vigorously condemned?

A major effort is underway to channel widespread feelings of exploitation — one works hard yet sees no improvement in one's life — along centrifugal, regional and corporatist lines. According to the strike committee chairman of Kemerovo, "The residents of the Kuzbass have understood one thing: a colonial policy has been applied until now to the basin: take out as much as possible, invest as little as possible."[63] But this is exactly what separatists in the national republics are arguing — Moscow is exploiting us! There is probably not a single region in the Soviet Union whose inhabitants do not feel this way. Yet, an economist recently wrote that

"Muscovites not only do not live better, but in many ways they live worse than the inhabitants of other cities."[64] The problem is obviously not one of the unjust redistribution of income and wealth among regions, but the anti-popular, wasteful nature of bureaucratic management, not to mention that part of the national income that is consumed by bureaucratic privilege. But it does not necesarily follow from this that regional and enterprise autonomy are the magic solutions they are made out to be.

At a roundtable discussion several months before the strike, a researcher at the Institute of the National Economy of the Council of Ministers explained the growing strike wave as a movement provoked by the government's reform:

> With the shift to full self-financing, the financial well-being of the collective shapes up in different ways. And it often depends not so much on the collective itself as on outside economic conditions and on the branch to which the enterprise belongs. The market mechanism is oriented toward money stimuli. Whoever can raise prices on his products lives in clover...
>
> Workers see that their earnings do not grow in the same proportion as in branches with more favourable conditions. We observe these same processes in the coal and in the ferrous metal industries. In some mines the workers stop work...until their demands are met. Thus are decided questions relative to the improvement of food and living conditions...
>
> The rise in prices of food and supply shortcomings are also contributing to the strike movement. The co-operatives cannot fill up all the holes. In fact, they ravage the state purse rather than improve the life of the population. There is a pumping of funds from one vessel to the other, from state to co-operative trade. Another cause is the unequal development of regions. Regions with highly developed heavy industry and weak agriculture find themselves in more difficult conditions. Sometimes in conditions of self-financing a region is not capable of feeding itself. Before,

> specialization was demanded, i.e. basically one-sided development. Priority was given to production of the means of production. Agriculture lagged behind seriously. Workers feel that they work harder and get less.
>
> The prognosis for the future is not good. The negative tendencies favouring strikes, and mainly — the strengthening of market elements in the economy — remain. Therefore, strikes will continue and the situation of the working class will continue to decline.[65]

This analysis was not challenged by the other participants, who support the "radical reform". The only real argument they could muster was that the old system was no less unjust. True enough, but is the only alternative another form of injustice? The above analysis was recently confirmed by a group of prominent (and undoubtedly pro-market reform) social scientists in *Pravda:*

> The threat of insufficient social protection of people has made its appearance under the new conditions of economic management in cases of massive layoffs, in the carrying out of structural changes, the liquidation of enterprises. This has been the basis of an upsurge of social discontent, of an intensification of social, but weakening of work, activity among the people. This situation is also pregnant with a slowdown in the tempo of change."[66]

Perspectives

The underlying issue of the strike — power — has not been resolved. If the fundamental problems that provoked the strike are to find resolution in the workers' interests, and not at their expense, they cannot be entrusted to market forces. Nor can they be left to the bureaucracy. This is why, objectively, the miners' strike poses question of workers' power — at all levels. The miners must be able to decide themselves the framework within which enterprise self-management will function. Among other things, this means deciding what centralized functions the ministry should retain and how to democratize it so that it is responsible to the workers of the enterprises that belong to it and to the population as a whole. These same issues confront the entire working class: to democratize national planning and to create a real framework for self-management *at all levels;* not to eliminate planning and to leave whatever central regulation remains in bureaucratic hands.

From the time that commodity production first became predominant in Western Europe, the popular classes have fought against the "free" market and for public economic regulation to ensure social security and justice. There is strong reason to believe that an independent working class movement in the Soviet Union will do the same. The key word is obviously "independent". Although the workers' committees contain within themselves the beginnings of an independent workers' organization, in the face of the tremendous ideological pressure exerted by liberal quasi-monopoly of the mass media, it is not clear whether the workers will succeed in mobilizing around their own alternative programme, as opposed to purely defensive actions against the social consequences of the "radical reform". The only "socialist" opposition that finds its way into the mass press is the "defenders of socialism" (who claim it already exists, however imperfectly), linked to the conservative wing of the apparatus and enjoying very little worker sympathy. The programme of self-managed socialism of the democratic socialist opposition, which sees the plan-market controversy as secondary and largely a distraction from the central issue of democratic control at *all* levels of economic decision-making, corresponds best to the workers' concerns. But this political current, which began to organize seriously only after the strike, has not succeeded in establishing broad contact with the labour movement.

The coming elections to the local and republican soviets will be an important political milestone. After the experience of this strike and in the presence of militant workers' committees, it will be much harder in the mining towns — and in other industrial centres — to get away with the undemocratic election procedure used to choose the Congress of People's Deputies and Supreme Soviet. This presents the possibility that geniune soviet power (i.e. independent of the party bureaucracy) will be re-established in the localities. It is anyone's guess how long it would be before these soviets take on the regional and higher party bureaucracies. The people's deputies of the Kuzbass recently recently met in Prokop'evsk and resolved: "Considering the demands of the strike committee, examine the question of elections to local soviets already in October." But the oblast' party committee, however, would not hear of this.[67]

The miners' strike has opened a new act in perestroika: the working class has made its appearance on the political stage.

August 1988

Postscript

In the nine months since the miners' strike, the coal industry has witnessed a continous series of local strikes aimed principally at forcing the implementation of the July accords and the resignation of discredited officials. The mining regions are seething. Although many points of the accords have been implemented and significant personnel changes have occurred in local political and economic authorities as well as in the trade-union and self-management committees, the miners have so far not seen substantive improvement in their material situation. Nor is there any sign of this happening in the proximate future.[68] And economic grievances were, after all, the starting point of the movement.

Over time, political divisions have appeared and weakened the worker committees; their level of activity seems to have somewhat declined since the fall. But these tendencies could easily be reversed in the event of a renewed labour upsurge, which virtually all observers view as inevitable. A crucial element of the present situation is the failure of the July strike to resolve the underlying economic problems in the coal industry, as the overall situation in the country continues to decline. This, in turn, is related to the fact that the general framework of the economy and of the political system have not significantly changed. As a result, increases in earnings have been eaten up by inflation. Similarly, although many enterprises did not obtain real autonomy, those that did found that the economic mechanisms that would allow them to make use of it are lacking.

This is not to say that illusions were widespread among the miners concerning the strike's ability to resolve their problems. Evidence presented above points rather in the oppposite direction. Already on October 10, 1989, the Vorkuta miners, in an "Appeal to the Toilers of the Soviet Union" stated that "The experience of economic strikes shows that without a decisive scrapping of the totalitarian-bureaucratic system, it makes no sense to put forth economic demands."[69] In mid-November a conference of worker collectives of the Kuzbass established the "Union of Toilers of the Kuzbass" and declared that the nature of change would continue to be painfully slow and and partial unless the revolution from above was supplemented with a revolution from below. Declaring itself for socialism, the Union called for genuine, consistent democratization of the state and adopted an economic programme that combines free market relations, free enterprise zones, regional and enterprise autonomy, on the one hand, with self-management and planning, on the other, while explicitly rejecting capitalist private property and unemployment.[70]

This eclectic attempt to combine elements of the liberals' (and now also the government's) "radical" reform with basic worker interests reflects the workers' failure so far to find their own alternative to the discredited bureaucratic "command economy." This is the central issue facing the labour movement at present.

It now appears that the second, and perhaps decisive, act of the new labour movement, following the miners' strike, has been postponed at least until the fall of 1990. Referring to the government's decision in April to delay introduction of its "radical" reform (the draft laws were to be presented to parliament that month and take effect July 1), a senior Soviet editor explained: "They approached the edge, looked over and were horrified by what they saw."[71] In the incomparably more tense social and political atmosphere nine months after the strike, it is not hard to imagine the nature of the abyss that the Soviet leadership peered into. The next wave of labour protest will not be limited to the mining regions but will embrace all major sectors of the working class, including the large urban centres that have heretofore not seen mass co-ordinated actions. After announcing the postponement of the reforms, Gorbachev and his colleagues dispersed to the major industrial centres to assure the workers that there would be no "shock therapy," that they would be consulted and their interests protected. Judging from the press — which, incidentally, has quite accurately reported on economic developments in Eastern Europe — the workers are particularly worried by the prospects of price rises and a decline in living standards, bankruptcies and unemployment, as well as the questions of control and ownership (rumours of mass privatization are rife).[72]

The July strike demonstrated the workers' capacity for independent organization, as well as their potential to shape the course of societal development. But the strike and its aftermath have also shown that the realization of this potential, and the fate of socialism in the Soviet Union, depend upon the workers' ability to mobilize around their own programme as an alternative to those of the liberal and conservative intelligentsia-apparatus alliances, which are competing furiously for the workers' support.

May 1990

NOTES

1. *Trud* (Moscow), July 25, 1989.
2. *Sobesdnik*, no. 31, July 1989, p. 10.
3. Under "khozraschet", enterprises enjoy varying degrees of autonomy in disposing of their incomes, after making certain fixed payments to the state budget. On the other hand, depending on the model of "khozraschet", bonuses and/or wages and other benefits are no longer guaranteed, as they generally were under the old system.
4. *Trud*, August 2, 1989.
5. *Trud*, Sept. 27, 1989.
6. *Trud*, Aug. 11, 1989.
7. *Trud*, Aug. 2, 1989.
8. Unpublished stenographic report of conference "Economic Consciousness and Economic Behaviour in Conditions of Restructuring," Zvenigorod, Nov. 20-5, 1989.
9. *Moskovskie novosti*, no. 30, 1989, p.3.
10. *Sobesednik*, no. 31 1989, p. 10.
11. *Trud*, July 21, 1989.
12. *Trud*, July 11, 1989.
13. *Argumenty i fakty*, no. 30, 1989, p. 7.
14. *Trud*, July 29, 1989.
15. *Sotsialisticheskaya industriya* , Aug. 3.
16. *Trud*, July 14, 1991.
17. I. Konstantinov, "Zabatovska v Donbasse," *Rubikon* (Leningrad) no. 10, 1989, p. 34.
18. Yu. Apenchenko, "Kuzbass. Zharkoe leto," *Znamya* (Moscow), no. 10, 1989, p. 171-3. 1989; *Trud*, July 4 and 12, 1989.
19. *Moskovskie novosti*, no. 30, 1989, p. 14. *Trud*, 15 July, 1989;
20. *Argumenty i fakty*, no. 30, 1989, p. 4; *Sotsialisticheskaya industriya*, Aug. 3, 1989.
21. *Trud*, July 19, 1989; *Moskovskie novosti*, no. 30, 1989, p. 3.; *Argumenty i fakty*, no. 30, 1989.
22. *Argumenty i fakty*, no. 30, p. 7; *Vesti iz SSSR (Munich)*, no. 13/14 , 1989, p. 21; *Trud*, July 25, Aug. 2, 1989.
23. *Vesti iz SSSR*, no. 13/14, 1989, p. 21; *Trud*, July 22, 1989.
24. Ibid.; *Trud*, July 23, 1989.

25. Apenchenko, "Kuzbass," pp. 165-66; *Zapolyar'e* (Vorkuta), July 22, 1989; unpublished list of Kuzbass demands; *Manchester Guardian Weekly*, July 30, 1989, p. 7.
26. *New York Times*, July 14, 1989, p. A-3; *Libération* (Paris), July 15-6, 1989, p. 18; *Sotsialisticheskaya industriya*, Aug. 3, 1989; *Trud*, July 22 and Aug. 5, 1989.
27. *Sotsialisticheskya indystriya*, July 15, 1989; *Liberation*, July 22-3, p.7.
28. *Globe and Mail* (Toronto), July 26, 1989; *Trud*, 16,25 and 26 July, 1989; *Sotsialisticheskaya industriya*, Aug. 3, 1989; *Argumenty i fakty*, no. 30, 1989, p. 8.
29. *Manchester Guardian Weekly*, July 30, 1989, p. 7; *Vesti iz SSSR*, no. 13/14, 1989, p. 21.
30. Ibid; *Trud*, July 17, 1989; *Zapolyar'e*, July 22, 1989.
31. *Moskovsie novosti*, no. 31, 1989 p. 8.
32. Personal communication
33. I. Konstantivnov , "Zabastovka…", p. 33.
34. *Trud*, July 13, 1989.
35. *Trud*, Aug. 2, 1989.
36. *Trud*, 21 July 1989.
37. *Sobesednik*, no. 31, 1989, p. 2.
38. *Trud*, Sept. 28, 1989.
39. Konstantinov, "Zabastovka…", p.34.
40. *Argumenty i fakty*, no. 32, 1989, p. 1.
41. K. Mikhailov, "Zapolyarnyi ofsaid," *Sobesednik*, no. 49, 1989, pp.13; Stenographic report, Zvenigorod; Konstnatinov, "Zabatovska…", p. 35.
42. *Trud*, July 23 and 25, 1989; *Vesti iz SSSR*, no. 12/13, 1989, p. 22.
43. *Argumenty i fakty*, no. 30, p. 4; *Trud*, July 30 and Aug. 2 1989; *Vesti iz SSSR*, no. 13/14, 1989, p. 22; Stenographic report, Zvenigorod; V. Andriyanov, "Gornyi udar," *Dialog*, no. 1, 1990, pp. 62-5.
44. *Le monde*, July 26, 1989.
45. See "Rabochie vne politiki?" *Agitator*, no. 16, 1989, pp 4-5
46. K. Mikhailov, "Zapolyarnyi," p. 12; *Soviet News and Views*, no. 17-18, 1989, p.6.
47. Interview with Yu. Boldyrev, *Rubikon*, no. 10, 1989, p. 37.
48. *Trud*, July 25, 1989.
49. *Trud*, Aug. 8, 1989.
50. Konstantinov, "Zabastovska…", p. 33.
51. *Trud*, July 21, 1989.
52. Mikhailov, "Zapolyaryi…", p. 13.
53. *Argumenty i fakty*, no. 30, 1989, p. 4, *Pravda*, July 25, 1989.
54. *Trud*, Aug. 3, 1989. See also *Moskovskie novosti*, no. 31, 1989, p. 8.
55. *Gazette* (Montréal), July 21, 1989;
56. *Izvestiya*, Apr. 1, 1990.
57. *Zycie gospodarcze* (Warsaw), Aug. 1989.
58. *Izvestiya*, Aug. 11, 1989.
59. Interview with Boldyrev, *Rubikon*, no. 10, 1989, p. 32.
60. *Sotsialisticheskaya industriya*, Sept. 9, 1989.
61. Ibid.
62. Zvenigorod stenographic report.
63. *Sobesednik*, no. 31, p. 10.
64. V. Kuvarin, "Dorogaya moya stolitsa…", *Nedelya*, no. 34, 1989, p. 12.

65. "Zabastovski v SSSR: novaya sotsial'naya real'nost'," *Sotsiologicheskie issledovanioya,* (Moscow) no. 1, 1989, p. 32.
66. *Pravda,* July 16, 1989.
67. *Sotsialisticheskaya industriya,* Aug. 3, 1989.
68. V. Federov and H Zhankin, "Kuda poidet Kyzbass," *Nedelya,* no. 17, 1990, pp. 6-7.
69. K. Mikhailov, "Zapolyarnyi ..." *Gazette* April 24, 1990, p. A-14.
70. Photocopied document.
71. *Gazette,* April 21, 1990, p. A-14.
72. For Gorbachev's visit to the Ural workers see *Rabochaya tribuna,* April 26 and 28, 1990; and for Ryhkov's visit to Leningrad, *Pravitel'stevennyi vestnik ,* no. 18, 1990, p. 3.

Chapter 4

SOVIET TRADE UNIONS AT THE CROSSROADS

The real functioning of the Soviet trade unions has changed little under Gorbachev, despite the increased openness of the trade-union press and its appeals to the unions to democratize themselves. Workers still see the unions as mainly administrators of social programmes. But when it comes to defending workers' interests, they are mere appendages of enterprise management and of the state. The recent coal strike was itself a massive vote of non-confidence in the unions. The miners completely bypassed them, electing their own strike committees and everywhere demanding new democratic elections of the union committees.

There are various reasons for this state of affairs. The tradition of union subservience is almost 60 years old. In the 1920s Soviet trade-unions enjoyed a good measure of autonomy. Strikes were legal and did indeed occur. Lenin justified trade-union autonomy in a workers' state, since this state suffered from a "bureaucratic deformation" and the workers needed to be able to defend themselves. But in the late 1920s, Stalin finally elevated this deformation to a virtue and crushed the unions. Henceforth their role was that of "transmission belts" of state policy.

But this tradition by itself explains little. It was certainly never accepted willingly by the workers. It rested, in the final analysis, upon the threat of repression. The 1962 massacre that put an abrupt end to the Novocherkassk general strike — this during the high point of Khrushchev's "destalinization" — was an object lesson that independent workers' collective actions, let alone organizations, would not be tolerated. On the enterprise level too, management possessed an array of arbitrary powers to discourage thoughts of union independence. These included, among other things, loss of bonuses and wages (great arbitrariness ruled in calculation of wages), loss of one's place in the queue for housing, transfer to less desirable jobs, demotion in skill grade and dismissal. While there was some recourse in the courts or at higher levels of power, success was very uncertain and required sacrifices that most workers were not prepared to make.

But repression was only one element of this system — albeit the fundamental one. The workers' grudging toleration of this system, especially during the Brezhnev period, depended also upon the paternalistic nature of worker-management and worker-state relations. Some have called this a social contract, though the workers were given no choice about whether they wanted to enter it. On the enterprise level, in return for toleration of management's legal violations and miserable work conditions, workers could count on job security, a more or less guaranteed — and until the late 1970s rising — income, often higher than what was legally due them, and a generally tolerant attitude of management in the area of labour discipline.

Perestroika has fundamentally changed this situation. On the one hand, under the régime's liberalization, workers have gradually lost their fear of repression. On the other hand, the economic changes that Gorbachev has introduced have undermined enterprise paternalism. Job security is slowly becoming a thing of the past. The same is true of the guaranteed wage. And in any case, inflation and growing shortages of consumer goods over the past eighteen months have caused a serious decline in real incomes. Management's new interest in economizing on labour costs has also made it generally less tolerant in its relations with workers.

In theory, the economic reform provides for self-management in the enterprises through democratically elected labour collective councils. But, like the unions, these too have been largely the playthings of management. (The miners called for new elections of these councils too.) In reality, the régime does not want independent labour organizations. On one level it understands that that is really the least it can offer the workers who are faced with an economic reform that threatens certain of their fundamental interests without being able to offer the increased consumption in the near — and probably intermediate — future. But at the same time, it is reluctant to encourage such organization because it could sabotage or veto the market reform and the whole restructuring of bureaucratic power, of which the economic reform is a central part. As for enterprise managers, in their great majority they see enterprise democracy and independent trade unions at best as unnecessary complications in their work and at worst as threats to their positions.

As a result, the workers have begun to organize and act independently of the trade unions and labour collective councils. The coal strike, the high point (so far) of a strike wave unprecedented in the Soviet era, has finally forced the issue. In the coal regions, the strike committees have become workers' committees which stand ready to replace the trade unions if this round of elections fails to make them into fighting labour organizations. Analogous organizations have begun to appear in other sectors, such as oil and railroads.

The crisis of the official trade unions was the central point of discussion at the sixth plenary session of the All-Union Central Council of Trade-Unions (AUCCTU) on September 5-8, 1989.[1] "The question is," declared a foreman from the oilfields of Turkmenia, "are the trade unions to be or not to be." "Alternatives...already exist in embryonic form," noted the chairman of the Byelorussian TUC. The background of this crisis is the workers' declining material situation. In the evaluation of the chairman of the Moscow TUC, "The economic reform, cost-accounting, leasing relations, co-operations, despite expectations, have resulted in a series of negative phenomenon and have aggravated the socio-economic situation in the country...This situation is not only not improving but is constantly declining." A sign of the seriousness of the crisis was the presence of Central Committee secretary and Politburo member Chebrikov — few could recall the last time a Politburo member had attended such a meeting, such has been the low standing of the trade unions in the Soviet system. Also invited for the first time were representatives of enterprise union committees and of the coal regions' workers' committees.

The report by Shelaev, Chairman of the AUCCTU, began with the official line that the coal strike had been an expression of "decisive support for perestroika," even though it took a "dramatic, acute and unusual form for our society." But the rest of the report, and the ensuing discussion, painted a devastating picture of the workers' situation under perestroika:

> There is no doubt that cost-accounting and self-financing, market and leasing relations, cooperatives, the creation of enterprises with participation of foreign capital significantly broaden the economic independence of enterprises and facilitate the growth of production efficiency. But at the same time, these same forms of management in many cases, especially in the transitional stage, are accompanied by a whole series of negative phenomena that hit directly at the interests of workers and [white-collar] employees.

In many work collectives deformations have occurred in the payment of labour, group egoism of certain categories of toilers is developing; the desire to obtain the maximum income pushes into the background concern for the health and leisure of people, for job safety. In these same aims, the production of cheap sorts of goods declines, including those for children and older people. To our great chagrin, we more and more often meet with situations where collectives forget about the needs of their veterans and families with many children, where they squeeze out women with small children and often sick workers. It often turns out that access to cost-accounting collectives is closed to young people who have not yet been able to obtain a sufficiently high level of skill.

The wage reform has given rise to a whole series of abuses. Though these in themselves are not new to Soviet workers, they have become much more widespread, and the workers are reacting more and more aggressively. These include unjustified raising of output norms and reduction of workers' skill grades, outright cheating in calculation of wages, frequent delays in payment of wages. Workers are also less and less willing to work "black Saturdays" and holidays and overtime to compensate for the failings of the economic system and poor enterprise management.

Bad work conditions, especially in the area of job health and safety are another major source of dissatisfaction, which perestroika has done nothing to remove. According to Shelaev, professional morbidity in machine construction, the light and lumber industries, and in metallurgy are 3-8 times above the national average. In these branches "10 to 26% of the workers are working in conditions that simply degrade human dignity."

At the same time, living standards are declining. Speakers attributed this to several related government policies. First is the uncontrolled rise in prices. The search for "profits" under the new economic conditions has led enterprises in the consumer sector to concentrate on high priced goods and to cut back on production of cheaper ones. At the same time, price rises are justified by minimal changes in product characteristics that are presented as improvements in quality. There is also the sale at "contractual," i.e unregulated prices of goods produced beyond what is specified in state orders. A party plenum in March, against AUCCTU opposition, decided to allow "contractual" prices for potatoes, fruits and vegetables, including conserves. Officially this is to begin on January 1, 1990 but not all suppliers are waiting. (In July, the trade-union paper *Trud* noted the slogan "Down with contractual prices!" on the posters of the striking miners.[2]) The workers are "dissatisfied with the uncontrolled rise of prices," complained a brigadier from the Novolipetsk Metallurgical Factory. "One gets the impression that no one in the country is in charge of them." Pensions were recently raised to 70 rubles a month, i.e. the minimum wage level. But, "if prices continue to rise at these rates, even a person with a 120-ruble pension will soon find himself below the poverty line."

The co-operatives, bitterly attacked by virtually every speaker, were also blamed for inflation. They were accused of buying goods cheaply in state shops, contributing to the shortages, and then reselling them at triple and quadruple the price after having added little or no labour of their own. These goods are accessible only to people with high incomes from the "shadow economy."

This gradual freeing of prices — with no official introduction of the "price reform" that popular opinion has so unanimously rejected — causes all the more anger as wages in the producer goods sector have effectively been frozen at 3%. According to the new Law on Taxation of Wage Funds of State Enterprises, when payments from the wage fund rise more than 3%, for each ruble increase, one ruble is paid in taxes. If the rise is 5-7%, two rubles are paid in taxes for each additional ruble; if over 7% — three rubles. This means that any rise above 3% is neutralized by taxes and any rise over 5% actually leads to a net loss of income.[3] One speaker noted: "Inflation today is at 7% and the growth of wages is in practice limited to 3% — we are deliberately laying the basis for decline in living standards." After January 1, 1990 when contractual prices are officially introduced for vegetables and fruit, prices can be expected to rise by several times. This wage freeze, it should be noted, was enacted by the Supreme Soviet, an indication of how far it really is from popular interests.

Another growing concern of workers mentioned by many speakers is the loss of job security and the growth of unemployment. Under pressure from reform measures to economize on labour, managers are becoming reluctant to keep or hire less productive workers. This hits first of all women with small children, older workers and pensioners, and youth. If unemployment has long been a problem in areas of Central Asia, it is now making its appearance in industrial towns of European Soviet Union.[4] A locomotive engineer at the plenum complained that staff reductions on the railroads were reaching the point where they posed a danger to passenger and personnel because of the inability to maintain the equipment properly.

"The measures for improving the economic mechanism that are being prepared and discussed by the Supreme Soviet of the USSR and the union republics should not create the preconditions for the appearance of unemployment," argued the chairman of the Moscow TUC. But has not Gorbachev promised there would be none under his reform? "Today on the national level," complained the chairman of a trade-union committee from Kuybyshev, "there is no programme for dealing with redundant workers, for retraining them. And by the way, there are no programmes on the branch and regional levels... We need a programme to create new work places, a system of retraining, social guarantees. How can we be silent in such a situation?" This is almost two years after the joint party-state-union resolution calling to set up such a programme and guarantees.

The co-operatives came in for the most criticism at the plenum, and this only reflects the mood in the population. The closure of trade, food, and medical co-operatives was a demand of the striking miners in the Donbass and Karaganda basins. And many have already been shut there by the workers' committees. In a town in Turkmenistan, when local authorities ignored the inhabitants' demands to shut the co-operatives, 29 were sacked in a single night. The shooting of two co-operators by an army officer in the town of Chita was met with widespread satisfaction by the population.[5]

But the central government's policy has been one of hands-off — the encouragement of the private sector is an integral part of the economic reform. It has left regulation to local governments, with the implicit understanding that they should act only when social tensions leave no choice. "We have to pose the question to the government," declared the chairman of the Chemical and Petrochemical Workers' Union: "When will it finally introduce order in the economy and the country in the matter of defending the toilers from robbers, crooks, speculators, racketeers and co-operative prices?"

The speakers were not opposed to co-operatives as such. Only to those they considered covers for speculation and unearned income. The worker from Liptesk explained:

> We tied our hopes for an improvement in trade and services
> for the population [...] to the development of the co-opera-

tive movement. But this did not occur. Many co-operatives seek income not from good work but by exploiting parasitically the shortcomings of [state] trade. When you get off the train, already at the station you meet all the "delights" of the co-operative movement. Here you have to pay three times more for everything — from a glass of water to, you will pardon me, the toilet. Everything is in the hands of the cooperators. The so-called commercial-purchasing cooperatives undermine the stability of the markets, cause price rises and give rise to speculation.

We workers are "for" co-operatives, but the kind that use local secondary raw materials, that produce and process their own agricultural products, that make goods that people need, but not those that are involved in buying and reselling... In the first half of this year the co-operatives in Lipetsk received 11 million rubles from the banks, but they returned only two million. Meanwhile workers cannot always receive their wages or loans to construct housing, garden cottages, since the banks haven't the money.

The Lipetsk Soviet has decided to close down these co-operatives. But "someone must bear responsibility for the distortions, and maybe this should be at a level even higher than the region."

"Medical co-operatives are springing up like mushrooms," complained a worker from Voroshilovgrad. "Yet we claim that medical care is free in our country. Hospitals lack the simplest medicines. But for three times the price in a co-operative — by all means... 'Who is looking after all this?' ask the workers in alarm?"

Many speakers complained of the growing practice of state enterprises leasing out cafés, shops and entire sections of factories to co-operatives on very profitable conditions. The high wages in these co-operatives cause an outflow of skilled workers at the expense of the basic production and pit workers against each other. The press has also reported a growing number of cases of corruption involving state enterprise managers and co-operatives.

The consensus at the plenum was that the trade unions, if they are to survive in these circumstances, have to give priority to defending the workers' rights and interests on both the state and enterprise levels. This was reflected in the resolution on "The Current Moment and the Tasks of the Trade Unions" which calls for a "radical restructuring of the activity of the trade unions, a shift in their focus toward the function of defence" and for the abandoning of activities related to the organization of production that rightfully belong to management. Among other measures proposed, union organizations were instructed to defend the workers' "right to strike in accordance with the law as a form of struggle in defence of their interests when all other means have mean exhausted." At the same time, the resolution called for passage of a "dependable and effective" law on the resolution of collective labour conflicts. It should be noted that the recently published draft law on resolving collective labour conflicts would in practice forbid strikes in entire sectors where they create "a threat to the life and health of people." As one worker wrote, this could be interpreted so broadly as to include almost any sector.[6] However, this law and the role of strikes generally were scarcely touched, according to the published report of the plenum.

The unions are to use collective agreements and the broadened enterprise autonomy to improve the workers' conditions. They are to fight for full employment and to press the Supreme Soviet to adopt a plan of struggle against unemployment, including job creation, a national job placement, a retraining and data collection system, strengthened guarantees and increased payments for workers made redundant, conditions favouring the hiring of youth, pensioners and the handicapped, and "strengthened guarantees against dismissal at the initative of the administration." (Does the latter mean that only workers can decide to dismiss workers?) Local union committees are given more autonomy, and rank-and-file union members are to have the possibility of directly electing delegates to higher level union committees. Finally, the resolution came out in support of broad republican economic autonomy and real sovereignty in dealing with socio-political and national cultural questions, while calling on unions to promote internationalist values and to distance themselves from those who would undermine the Soviet Union's integrity.

On the issue of living standards, the resolution demands a price freeze for basic goods and maximum prices for potatoes, fruits and vegetables. It calls on the government to strictly control the prices of state and cooperative services, to fully compensate lost real income due to inflation and to eliminate within the next months shortages of such basic goods as milk products for chldren, soap, toothpaste and school notebooks.

As for the co-operatives, the unions will support only those that sell goods and services at state prices, not those out for illicit gain through deals with state commercial and industrial enterprises. The resolution calls on the government to conduct a new registration of all co-operatives, shutting those involved in resale of state and imported goods at speculative prices as well as those formed within state enterprises that sell goods above state prices. At the same time the state should strengthen its financial control of the co-operatives and make sure that they attract mainly people not already employed in the state sector — pensioners, invalids, housewives, students. Finally it calls to limit strictly the use of contract labour in co-operatives, as this is merely a form of hired labour (which is not covered by labour laws or collective contracts).

Is this a turning point for Soviet trade unions? There is certainly a new tone and content in these resolutions. But since these come four years into perestroika when mounting pressure from the workers threatens to sweep the official unions away, one must doubt the sincerity of this change of heart both in the upper levels of the union bureaucracy and in the leadership of the party-state bureaucracy that controls them. It would be an illusion to think that this "turn to the workers" is in its intention (its consequences are unforeseeable — this, and much else, depends on the extent to which the workers mobilize) more than a coming to terms with the inevitable in the hope that it will allow the régime to retain some control over the workers while it carries through a reform that conflicts fundamentally with their interests and aspirations. The plenum resolutions demand that the government do many things that in practice go against the basic orientations of its reform. Yet no one directly called this reform into question.

On the face of it, this is surprising since it was implicit throughout the discussion that the economic reform and the government carrying it out are alien to the workers' interests. After all, the phenomena that were being condemned were not really aberrations but direct consequences of reform measures, and they would certainly be much more serious if the market reform were being implemented in a consistent manner. The anti-worker thrust of the reform was also implicitly recognized in the call by some speakers for union veto power over government measures affecting the situation of workers. But are not the workers the vast majority of the population? And is not this supposed to be a popular, if not quite democratic, government? Others proposed putting workers — even a majority of workers! — in the Politburo. It is very possible that this and similar proposals are manoeuvres by conservative, anti-perestroika bureaucrats desperately trying to build a popular base. Their lack of a positive programme makes it doubtful that they will succeed. But whether sincere or not, their criticisms of the reform reflect real and growing concerns among workers.

"What sort of society are we to have?" asked the chairman of the Central Committee of the Union of Automobile Transport and Highway Workers.

> We have to do everything to safeguard [!] the socialist system, the most just and democratic. We must take into account the lessons of Poland, where the leaders of "Solidarity" at first said: we are for socialism, but when they took power they said that Poland would be the first to restore capitalism... The leaders of certain currents are trying to lead us astray, when they hide behind a perestroika shield — incidentally, this is very much in style now — although the ears of capitalism and nationalism are sticking out from behind that shield.

More sincere, but in the same vein, was the declaration of a woman chemical worker from Grodno: "The many thousands of workers in our collective are trying to understand why it is that in conditions of democracy and glasnost' the priority of the working person is proclaimed while in practice there is total indifference to him, especially on the part of the higher economic authorities."[8] This statement reflects the position of most Soviet workers today. They are dissatisfied with the results to date of the economic reform, but they are told by the liberalized propaganda apparatus that this is because evil bureaucrats are not letting it go forward fast enough. They oppose many of the concrete measures that are an integral part of the reform, such as price reform, unemployment, increased income inequality based upon market criteria, marketization of basic services, etc., but they are told that this is the only way to "civilize" Russia and to raise living standards to levels in the West. They are told that the market reform is the only alternative to the totally discredited bureaucratic "planned economy," that it is the "democratic" alternative to the "command-administrative" system (a term which denotes everything from Stalin's terror to state planning and regulation (by *any* state — authoritarian or democratic) that uses direct administrative means).

It is certainly not the "restructured" trade-union apparatus that will lead the workers in a struggle for a workers' alternative, though under pressure from below, it might become a loyal opposition that takes up partial workers' demands. The emergence of a workers' alternative awaits the formation of a genuinely independent workers' movement. The miners' strike provided a strong push in this direction. But such an alternative also requires an ideologically independent movement, something that will be much harder to achieve without organic contacts with the Marxist minority of the intelligentsia.

The "objective" conditions would seem to be ripening. The miners' strike created the political conditions for an independent workers' organization. As the plenum showed, the impact of the reform has made the workers increasingly critical. In the midst of that strike Gorbachev complained that

> Of late the growth of significant social strata under the influence of radical leftist positions has become evident. Populist ideas, leftist speculation on demands for social justice in the spirit of universal equalizing are circulating broadly.[7]

What is missing and will be much harder to create, is the "subjective" element, a leadership with a coherent, credible socialist programme.

September 1989

NOTES

1. Reports of this plenum appeared in *Trud,* Sept. 6-9, 1989.
2. *Trud,* July 16, 1989.
3. Ibid., Sept. 6, 1989.

4. See N. Menitskaya, "Ne khochu byt' bezrabotnoi", *Rabotnitsa*, no. 7 1989, pp. 1-12. According to Menitskaya:"Cost accounting dictates harsh rules, introduces new production relations in the collective. Labour productivity is rising not only on the basis of technological improvements but also by increasing work loads. There is no escape from this physical and psychological strain, since it is a matter of common sense: if you work poorly, someone else will take your place. And you will find yourself out on the street with your three months allowance. But if you push yourself so as not to be fired, will you have any energy left for your family? And your factory has neither a nursery nor a youth camp."
5. "Trud, Sept. 7, 1989; *Komsomol'skaya pravda*, July 29, 1989.
6. *Komsomol'skaya pravda*, Aug 31, 1989.
7. *Trud*, July 19, 1989.

Chapter 5

"A Market Without Thorns": The Ideological Struggle for the Soviet Working Class

Introduction

The miners' strike of July 1989 marked the emergence of the working class as an active political force, whose attitude toward the reform of the economic system will be a decisive factor in determining the shape of Soviet society for years to come. The appearance of a workers' movement, for the first time in over sixty years, has given rise to an intense ideological struggle for its allegience among liberals of different shades, partisans of a reformed bureaucratic system, and socialists. So far, this has been a rather one-sided struggle favouring the liberals, who enjoy privileged access to the means of mass communication. Indeed, one can almost talk of a liberal monopoly in this area, whose task is nothing less than to break the workers' attachment to socialist values and to the socialist idea as a system qualitatively different from — and superior — to capitalism.

This chapter will offer an analysis of this ideological struggle and of the position of the industrial workers within it, in an attempt to assess the prospects for the development of a socialist alternative in the Soviet Union. The discussion of worker consciousness will focus mainly on Russia and, to a lesser degree, on the Ukraine, omitting those regions where national questions overshadow social issues. Throughout, the sometimes impressionistic nature of the data on worker consciousness should be borne in mind: not only are Soviet workers an extremely diverse group, but reliable, systematic data on their attitudes and behaviour remain scarce even in this sixth year of perestroika. Moreover, in a turbulent period of historic changes, attitudes evolve quickly.

Political Attitudes

The politicization of the working class has proceeded rapidly since 1985 and especially over the months since the elections to the First USSR

Congress of People's Deputies in the spring of 1989. When the Vorkuta miners renewed their strike at the end of October 1989, they issued a Declaration to the Toilers of the Soviet Union: "The practice of economic strikes shows that without a decisive scrapping of the bureaucratic-totalitarian system, it makes no sense to put forth economic demands." There followed a series of political demands: confirmation of the status of the workers' committees (the transformed strike committees) as permanent bodies for the social defence of the toilers; the right of toilers to unite in independent trade-union organizations; inclusion in the agenda of the Supreme Soviet of the following questions: abolition of article six of the constitution (guaranteeing the party's "leading role," subsequently abolished), the right of all citizens "to unite in political associations, parties and groups on a platform of non-violent actions; the right of every citizen to freely express his views."[1]

Although the politicization of the workers has probably gone farthest among the miners, who are also the best organized, no group has been left untouched. This is certainly one of the most important achievements of Gorbachev's perestroika. Workers who even three years ago showed scarcely any interest in politics, now regularly follow developments in the media, discuss them with their comrades. As for the orientation of this political consciousness, it is marked by strongly anti-bureaucratic, democratic sentiments, which were demonstrated in the elections to the Congress of People's Deputies and a year later in the elections to local and republican soviets. In the areas of large industrial concentration, the candidates of the apparatus and of the chauvinistic movements were roundly beaten.

The miners' strike, during which the workers repeatedly expressed their lack of confidence in the régime at all levels and demanded, implicitly and often explicitly, an end to bureaucratic privilege and power, was probably the most powerful single expression of these democratic attitudes. As a member of the Vorkuta strike committee put it:

> We are used to talking about workers' power, but where is it? There is no popular power. We have to strike just to force someone to talk to us. That is also why we are fighting for official status for our workers' committees. We are returning to the sources, to Lenin's writings, "Better Less, but Better," and "How to Organize the Worker-Peasant Inspectorate."

The worker-peasant inspection had the status of a people's commissariat, with the right of oversight even of the Politburo. No document ever took these rights away. Beria and Stalin merely buried them.[2]

"Pamayt'" (Memory) and similar nationalist organizations have failed so far to find a social base in the industrial working class of the Russia, even though the deepening economic crisis, on the background of the government's own reform measures (which encourage regional and localist sentiments of all kinds), as well as of the rise of the separatist movements in the periphery, would seem to offer fertile ground for this. In Moscow, with its socially heterogenous and unstable working class, the nationalists won only four of 65 seats in the March 1989 soviet elections. "The so-called patriots showed that their real backing among the people is very limited," concluded the head of Moscow's anti-fascist centre.[3] A survey conducted in the Kuzbass that asked miners in whom they placed their confidence found no supporters of "Pamyat'" or "Fatherland."[4] According to Yurii Boldyrev, a member of the Donetsk strike committee, the Ukrainian movement "Rukh" will not be able to build a serious social base in this area of the Ukraine, largely Russian-speaking, until it makes clear that it is a democratic, rather than a nationalist, movement.[5]

The political section of the programme of the Union of Toilers of the Kuzbass, adopted at the Fourth Conference of Workers' Collectives of Kemerovo Oblast' in Novokuznetsk on November 18, 1989, is a good example of this democratic outlook. It is a harsh condemnation of bureaucratic rule and a call for genuine soviet power, with a multi-party system, public institutions that are accessible to the people, a free and accessible press, direct elections and referenda on major questions.[6]

But if the workers' democratic aspirations are straightforward and coherent, flowing directly from their experience of oppression in the factories and in the larger society, their views regarding the social content of this democracy, specifically the economic reform, present a more complex, often contradictory and confusing picture. They can fully be understood only within the context of the growing sense of urgency, fostered by the deepening economic crisis, and of the ideological framework that the government and liberal intelligentsia, through their control of the reform process and the mass media, are attempting to impose on society. This intense ideological pressure — indeed, the term "oppression" is perhaps more fitting — has effectively excluded from the public debate any genuine alternative to their vision of a "market economy" — i.e. an economy in which the market is the *dominant* co-ordinating mechanism imposing its logic on society, rather than vice versa — to replace the discredited "command-administrative system."

The Liberal Message

The "leading intellectuals" today in the Soviet Union, i.e. those who control or enjoy privileged access to the mass media, as well as most of those who have managed to get elected or appointed to political office or advisory positions, are liberals. Although their stated views vary from "neo-liberalism" to "Swedish-style socialism" (tending increasingly toward the former), the essence of their message is to identify the market with economic freedom and political democracy, and state planning and regulation with dictatorship. In their speeches and writings, one encounters passages lifted almost literally from Western prophets of the "free-market" economy, such as Hayek and Friedman. Even the ubiquitous term "command-administrative" economy implicitly identifies, by means of its hyphen, an authoritarian political régime with administrative methods of regulation and management. The implicit message is that *any* directive planning and management (and for the most "radical" liberals — any planning or regulation whatsoever) are necessarily undemocratic and oppressive. Hence the calls for the "destatization" of the economy, issued without regard to the nature of the state, whether democratic or bureaucratic.

Boris Yeltsin's criticism of the government's economic programme at the Second the Congress of People's Deputies in December 1989 illustrates how the liberals united around the Interregional Group of deputies formulate their positions for the public. The government programme called for a period of consolidation before moving to the market. Yeltsin criticized this as a compromise between the interests of society and those of the apparatus. He began, not by attacking the economic reform, but rather the timidity of the government's democratic reforms. He noted that if Honoeker had been asked during his last days in power how long it would take to introduce democracy, he would have answered — years. But the people did it in weeks. He asked why the apparatus cannot decide to give up its privileges instead of waiting for them to be expropriated. Then, almost imperceptibly, he moved to the economic reform, calling the government's proposal an unviable mixture of market and bureaucratic elements. He demanded the dismantling of the "command-administrative" economy, its "de-ideologization," the creation of a system based upon "collective and other forms of property," including state, co-operative and private, all of which should have equal status.

The ideological core of his message was contained in the following phrase: "The deformation of the form of economic relations gave rise to its twin in the political sphere," i.e. the root of totalitarianism lay in the command economy.[7] Of course, the historical truth is rather different: the bureaucratic usurpation of power, which certainly built upon conditions that arose during the civil war, blossomed to full maturity under the New Economic Policy of the 1920s (which liberals now hold up as a model), a period when Russia had a market system of sorts. It was only when this system had fallen into crisis that Stalin transformed it along "command" lines, in a manner that corresponded fully with the interests of his political base, the apparatus. (The point is, of course, that Soviet experience cannot be cited as "proof" that central planning leads to dictatorship, just as the experience there and elsewhere with the market does not "prove" the market is a basis for democracy.) The liberals' message is twofold: the market means economic freedom, because economic actors are autonomous, free to use their property as they like, free of direct state regulation and intervention; at the same time, the market is the only social basis for political democracy.

The Soviet liberals have gone out of their way to portray themselves as the most consistent democrats. It was the Interregional Group that unsuccessfully called a political strike on the eve of the congress to force the inclusion in its agenda of a debate on article six of the constitution. There is more than a small dose of posturing in this. In private, many of these same people admit that the their market reform requires an authoritarian régime to impose it against popular opposition. After the miners' strike, some prominent liberals even stated this in print.[8] When the Supreme Soviet created a strong new presidency and made Gorbachev "dictator officially" (in the approving words of *Ogonek's* liberal editor, Vitalii Korotych), Nikolai Shmelev, perhaps the "radical" economist best known to the West, only expressed fear that Gorbachev would not be "bold enough to use his powers to drastically increase the role of private enterprise in the economy."[9] In the wake of the popular protest against the government's accelerated reform proposal of May 1990, economist N.Engver, member of the Interregional Group, wistfully cited his American colleague Vasily Leontief in this connection: "It's a pity that glasnost came to you before the radical reform connected with the transition to the market." Obviously a supporter of "Western-style democracy," Engver argued that elected representatives should not feel bound by pre-election promises.[10] Academician O. Bogomolov, another member of the Interregional Group, called the government's idea of a referendum on price reform "absurd," since the population would obviously oppose it.[11] Yet, all liberals admit that freeing prices is a crucial part of their reform.

In reality, the liberals' programme needs the support of the reform wing of the apparatus, although this does not prevent them from attacking its timidity. By the same token, the apparatus reformers need the liberals if they hope to emerge as winners, individually or collectively, from the reform process they have unleashed. Nevertheless, the liberals' successes in the spring 1989 soviet elections (the mayors of Moscow and Leningrad and the President of the Russian Republic are prominent liberals — who, incidentally, have not had much trouble winning the support of their respective apparatuses) attests to their success in identifying themselves in the public's mind with the democratic and anti-bureaucratic struggle. But this success is so far only partial: as we shall see, they cannot yet carry the population behind them in realizing their economic programme. Yelstin, an astute demagogue, might criticize the government's timidity, but he does so in the name of a market reform in which no one will suffer.[12]

Another key element of the liberal message is that the market guarantees "social justice," i.e. material reward corresponding to one's "real" contribution to the economy. The "command-administrative system," on the other hand, with its "levelling" ideology (another liberal historical myth[13]) rewards the indolent at the expense of conscientious workers and encourages "social parasitism." Sociologist A. Batygin informs the readers of *Izvestiya's* weekly that in a market economy, the wealth of the rich is the result of their labour and savings; the poor are simply losers. Social equality is the ideology of the poor, and that explains why the Soviet Union is poor. "The dictatorship of the proletariat won, the resistance of the bourgeoisie was crushed, property was socialized, money lost its value, exploitation of man by man is absent. Only one thing is missing: the benefits don't flow. Society is rich only when it has a lot of rich people. Nothing needs to be done. Just don't bother those who want to get rich and who know how to do it."[14] A few weeks later, sociologist Bestuzhev-Lada, who hates bureaucratic privilege, tells readers that the egalitarianism of the Soviet population is nothing but "black envy," the ideology of lumpen, déclassé elements that make up so much of the society, a consequence of rapid industrialization and social upheaval. The ideology of the "mass marginal" is "levelling, destructive, malevolent envy and aggressive obedience." These people oppose the market and would bury perestroika "in slobber, if not blood."[15]

A third pillar of liberal propaganda is the "natural" character of market relations as the only "normal" basis of economic organization, the one that corresponds to human nature. Academician E. Shatalin, economic advisor to Gorbachev, complains: "People often talk about a 'planned-market economy', a 'socialist market'. We've had enough ideology and ideologization of certain processes. We need to direct our efforts so that a modern, normal market appears." People's Deputy N. Travkin just returned from a junket to Sweden, where he "was overcome by impotent anger. Did the people who taught us that 'capitalism is exploitation' ever visit that country? Of course, they did. That means they consciously frightened us with a normal economy." He discovered goods in Swedish stores that Soviets had never even heard of.[16]

Increasingly, the qualitative difference between socialism and capitalism is denied: there are only different mixes of regulation and market. Sociologist Bestuzhev-Lada: "It's time to stop playing ping-pong with balls marked 'capitalism' and 'socialism'... It is time to move not from capitalism to socialism, but from a realized utopia, from an abnormal society, one literally gone mad, to a normal, a real one."[17] Along with this, goes the idea, repeated ad nauseum in virtually every newspaper article dealing with economic issues, that "there is no other way" but the market economy — as conceived by the liberals or the government. "Let us ponder how, when and what to do, to what to assign priority and where to begin," said Mikhail Gorbachev to the workers of Sverdlovsk in the spring of 1990. "These are questions of life, work and practice. But as concerns the fundamental choice, the basic direction of our policy, no one has yet proposed anything else that is serious or substantial."[18] He only failed to mention that this unique, serious "fundamental choice" has itself constantly shifted over the past five years and that it is Gorbachev himself who is the arbiter of what is "serious and substantial." *There has never been public discussion of fundamental, strategic alternatives.*

The absence of a serious alternative is implicit in the very way the media — and even top state officials[19] — portray the Soviet political spectrum: the liberals constitute the "left," while the conservative bureaucrats and other partisans of bureaucratic management are the "right". Since this leaves no room for socialsts, by implication there is no socialist alternative, or, even worse, it is identified with the "right," with the discredited "command-administrative" economy and bureaucratic domination. One can, however, make a strong argument that the liberals and the conservative bureaucrats are, in fact, only variants of the right: in different ways, their programmes represent anti-democratic and anti-popular choices for Soviet society.

The Evolution of the Government's Economic Orientation

The government's economic thinking has come a long way since the summer of 1985 when Gorbachev told a Central Committee meeting in no uncertain terms that there would be no market reform. As the months go by, the Gorbachev faction moves increasingly closer to his "radical" critics, even as the latters' vision of a "normal economy" for the Soviet Union grows more explicitly capitalistic. Indeed, some of the most "radical" liberals are not intellectuals but freshly-converted bureaucrats. The platform of the new Prime Minister of the Russian Republic, a life-long functionary in the aviation industry, is "market, private property, destatization, openness to foreign capital." "Either Gosplan or market, one or the other...," he has declared. "In the end, it comes down to the fact that, if socialism is really going to be built anywhere, it will be in Sweden or Japan, but not here."[20]

In December 1989, the government unveiled a five-year, two-stage "Programme for Economic Recovery and Deepening of the Economic Reform" whose utlimate goal was a "regulated market economy." 1990-1992 would be used to stabilize the economy, especially the consumer market, reduce the budget deficit and put in place necessary legal and regulatory mechanisms for the second stage, 1993-5, during which the shift to the "regulated market" would occur. Prime Minister Ryzhkov told the Second Congress of People's Deputies, that approved his programme, that the "left"'s call for an immediate shift to market relations in 1990 or 1991 was "completely irresponsible." Such a policy would inevitably provoke "galloping inflation, a decline in the role of economic incentives, a drop in production, massive unemployment, and mounting social tensions."[21] Hardly three months had passed, when Gorbachev, just elected to the new presidency of the USSR, declared that he would use his powers to accelerate the transition to "a fool-blooded domestic market."[22] Interfax, the press agency of Moscow Radio, reported that a government team was at work in a house outside Moscow on a series of laws to be presented to the Supreme Soviet in April. These laws were being prepared behind closed doors, "to avoid premature confrontation with society." Few specifics were given, but Interfax did reveal that the Polish reform was being closely studied as the "most appropriate for the Soviet Union" and that the government envisioned setting up soup kitchens to feed the victims of the transition period.[23] *Pravda's* economic editor commented that the time had passed when it was possible to stabilize the economy without "harsh unpopular measures" and that "serious social collisions are inevitable."[24] Rumours of an impending Polish-style "shock therapy" began to circulate widely as social tensions mounted.

Gorbachev explained his shift by saying that it was urgent to put an end to a situation in which new and old economic forms coexisted antagonistically. For the first time in decades, national income was reported to have declined in absolute terms in the first quarter (though this was at least partly due to problems of reconversion of the military industry and strikes in the Caucasus), while salaries and the budget deficit continued to grow. The central government was fast losing control over the economy, as enterprises, in their pursuit of profits, cut back on production and raised prices, disregarding formal restrictions. "In anger, we often say that nothing has changed in the last four years," remarked one economist. "But our economy is different. It is capable of beating back directive attacks from the centre, of subordinating any laws to group egoism."[25]

The erosion of the centre's power in favour of the ministries and trusts is a long-standing process dating back over three decades. But Gorbachev's reforms have greatly accelerated it, encouraging centrifugal and localist tendencies. Although the government continues to denounce "group egoism", this is the quite rational behaviour of monopolistic producers freed from central control. Under the "cost-accounting" (khozraschet) reform that preceded Gorbachev's conversion to a "full-blooded market," the government and the media constantly exhorted enterprises to fight for their autonomy, to increase and hold onto their "cost-accounting income." Producers' "group egoism" is all the more inevitable when the economic centre is perceived as alien and oppressive (and correctly so) and when there is no perspective of its democratization. In such conditions, and in view of workers' strongly anti-bureaucratic sentiments, any limitations on producers' autonomy emanating from this centre will be seen as unjust and to be resisted.

This is not to argue that democratization of the central economic authorities, that is self-management at the local and regional levels functioning in the framework of self-management at the national level, would automatically resolve the contradictions between centralized planning and regulation and enterprise autonomy and harmonize the interests of economic actors at the various levels, especially when the starting point is today's Soviet reality. These are indeed problems whose complexity should be openly recognized by socialists. But at least, it provides a social basis that makes possible the quest for solutions. As we shall see, this is the kind of reform proposed by Soviet socialists, even while they insist upon the ultimately dominant position of the central level of decision-making (of "the people's common [obshchenarodnaya] property") in any socialist economy. The Gorbachev régime seems to have ruled out this option. It is bent on canalizing the workers' desire for control of the economy into corporatist channels, while discouraging them from seeking collective solutions on a societal level. Its treatment of the miners' movement is an example of this policy. During the July 1989 strike, the government, aided by a strong media campaign, made great efforts to channel the miners' social and economic demands toward enterprise autonomy, a demand that even one year later has brought them nothing concrete. Few mines have actually obtained economic autonomy and those that have have found that the conditions do not exist to make use of it. At the same time, under various pretexts, the government and the trade union apparatus managed to postpone for a full year a national conference of miners. The demand for such a congress to enable the miners to discuss collectively the problems of their industry and the economic reform had been voiced in various regions during the strike.[26]

The government's gradual abandonment of producers' self-management, originally a central part of its reform, is another manifestation of its reform orientation. Self-management, which, in any case, has remained largely on paper, was severely restricted in a number of ministries by a decree in the fall of 1989, and at the Second Congress of People's Deputies,

Ryzhkov called for an end to election of management in state enterprises; it would be allowed only in leased and co-operative enterprises. Increasingly the government's emphasis has shifted from self-management, viewed more and more sceptically by the press and the liberals, to "making workers real owners" through leasing, buyouts, joint-stock companies. Economists point out that self-management would be an obstacle to the efficient transfer of capital and labour between enterprises and so undermine attempts to build a "full-blooded" market.[26]

Of course, enterprise self-management in Yugoslavia has been very problematic. But rather than this having proved the utopian nature of enterprise self-management as such, as Soviet liberals are quick to conclude, socialists have argued that the Yugoslav experience demonstrates the inconsistency of workers' power at the enterprise level with a larger structure of economic power dominated by the bureaucracy and/or the market.[27] In any case, the government's original orientation, that sought to combine self-management with "national" property of the enterprises, at least left the door open for seeking solutions through the extension of self-management to the regional and national levels. Privatization, even if it initially takes collective forms, would rule this out.

The accelerated reform package was late in coming, as Gorbachev and other political leaders, sensing the mounting tension and fearing a "social explosion" suddenly left on visits to industrial centres to "consult with the workers." "We have heard your cries of alarm," Gorbachev told the workers of the Urals, promising there would be no shock therapy and that social programmes would protect them from the effects of price rises and layoffs, even as he emphasized that there is no alternative to his market reform.[28]

The new reform programme that Prime Minister Ryzhkov finally proposed to the Supreme Soviet at the end of May 1990 was still much less than what the liberals had in mind, though he made clear that the government shared their strategic orientation. In his presentation, he acknowledged several times the logic of the liberals' positions. If he rejected them, it was because they were politically unacceptable.[29]

Worker Attitudes towards Economic Reform

"We must choose once and for all what we vitally need," stated an editorial at this time in the weekly paper of the Council of Ministers: "a free market or a command 'bazaar'? And here we can also expect many difficulties. For our consciousness, as M.S. Gorbachev recently noted..., is 'absolutely non-market'."[30] The negative popular reaction to the new reform package focused primarily on the proposed price rises for bread and other food items and manufactured consumer goods. People were not impressed by Ryzhkov's promise of compensation (30% of the additional cost of goods would not be returned as compensation, but, according to Ryzhkov, this would be revenue exclusively from the sale of luxury goods) and indexation of wages. (The liberals also attacked the price rise, but remained silent about the fact that if the government freed prices, as their own programme demanded, (something the government did not immediately envisage, except to a limited degree) they would surely rise much higher.) Commmenting on popular attitudes, economist O. Latsis complained: "The market system means free prices. But we, including those who say they are by all means for the market, only know to shout in unison: Don't touch prices! It is as if we've invented a rose without thorns. But a market is a rose with thorns."[31]

This is the conclusion that most often emerges from published materials and conversations with worker activists (who have had the greatest exposure to liberal ideas) and increasingly also with ordinary workers (though they tend to be more dubious): A market? By all means, if it is the only way to get the economy out of this deepening crisis and to fill the shelves. But without the social consequences that are an inevitable part of the "full-blooded markets" that exist under capitalism: unemployment, stark inequalities of wealth and income, poverty, exploitation, "unearned income" and the loss of societal control over social development. But with self-management and economic democracy. These atittudes prompted liberal historian I. Klyamkin to muse about the necessity of an authoritarian régime to carry through the market reform. The workers indeed want to modernize economic management, he admitted, but they also want social justice. For Klyamkin and his fellow liberals, these two things are incompatible.[32]

The economic programme of the Union of Toilers of the Kuzbass, which shows the undeniable influence of liberal propaganda, illustrates this well. It describes the main task as the "transfer of the right to dispose of wealth to those who produce it," calling for full autonomy of production units, which can be real only in the context of market relations, "an invaluable experience of human civilization." All forms of property, including national, state, republican, municipal, co-operative, individual-labour, joint-stock, mixed, private, etc., should be treated equally, and worker collectives should be free to choose the form of property and management they want, including leasing and purchase of the enterprise from the state. The document also calls for regional autonomy and the establishment of equal exchange between Kuzbass enterprises and their partners. In the Kuzbass itself, a free enterprise zone should be established to help resolve the social problems and raise living standards.

At the same time, many elements of the programme contradict, or at least strongly qualify, this market orientation. For one thing, it explicitly calls combining the market with planning, "one of the great inventions of the twentieth century." Social property must remain the predominant form in the main branches of industry and construction. "The Union of Toilers of the Donbass does not consider possible the use of private property based upon exploitation of man by man." It specifically rules out unemployment. "We are decisively opposed to those who call for pulling our economy out of its crisis by articificially studying capitalist private property." The programme also calls for electiveness and revocability of managerial personnel at all levels, with the right of the collectives to contest all decisions. The Union firmly declared itself socialist and ready to "welcome any new party that defends the principles of socialism and toilers' interests." (Unlike Eastern Europe, socialism, is not — yet? — a bad word among Soviet workers.)[33]

The workers' opposition to price rises (which is not to say they do not support higher prices for their *own* production), and all the more so to free prices, is not, as government spokespeople and liberals contend, necessarily an irrational unwillingness to make small immediate sacrifices for larger long-term benefits. At the most basic level, it is a healthy reaction to the undemocratic nature of the reform process and a means of asserting some control over it. After the Supreme Soviet decided to put off any decision on the reform package, economist and Vice Prime-Minister Abalkin complained to an interviewer that "you cannot keep a leader on a short leash and still expect success from him."[34] But the workers' historical experience tells them that reforms not subject to democratic control inevitably fail and it is the workers who bear the costs. Price reforms in the past have caused living standards to decline, despite promises of compensation, without stimulating production and efficiency. After the price rise, production costs themselves quickly rose, eventually restoring the old price proportions and annulling any stimlulating effects of the original price rise. As for a sudden freeing of prices, the "shock therapy" admired by many liberals, that could lead to a sharp rise and possibly galloping inflation, without any guarantee of increased production, given the existing monopoly conditions.

The following are excerpts from telegrams from worker collectives that poured into the Russian trade-union centre in response to the government's May 1990 reform proposals: "We demand a referendum and the publication of alternative reform conceptions." "People do not know what a regulated market economy is. There is little information. The toilers of our enterprise demand a national discussion of this question." "The immediate publication of alternative, less painful alternatives for the transition to the regulated market is necessary." "We must put an end, once and for all, to secrecy and incomplete information in discussing questions that are vital to people."[35]

N. Petrakov, a personal advisor to Gorbachev, has complained that, unlike the Poles, Soviets prefer empty shelves to high prices, i.e. they will accept queues but not free prices. In a national survey conducted at the end of 1988, 40% of the respondents supported rationing; by the beginning of 1989, this figure had risen to 58%. *Kommersant*, the organ of the co-operators' movement (an advocate of private enterprise), concluded that, while one cannot necessarily count all the supporters of rationing among the opponents of a market economy, neverthless, "fifty million more people moved farther from understanding what is necessary to improve the economic situation. Opposition to the economic reform is growing, and in this case, time is not working in its favour."[36]

One can argue whether or not the supporters of rationing know what will — or rather, what will not — improve the economy. But support for rationing stems to a large degree from an attachment to social justice. High prices might keep the shelves stocked, but many necessary goods would be inaccessible to average and lower income citizens, as is the case today in Poland and Hungary. At the same time, rationing potentially allows for democratic control over shipping, storage and distribution. This is no small matter in an economy, in which, according to Soviet specialists, the present level of agricultural production could meet the population's present demand for food, if spoilage, losses and illegal diversion of that production could be stopped or even reduced. Moreover, the technical and organizational measures needed to achieve this are relatively inexpensive and would not require a long time to be put in place. This leads socialist economist Yu. Sukhotin to ask if "someone" perhaps is not interested in taking these measures.[37] A citizen of Yakutsk explained his attitude to rationing in this way: "Of course rationing is a disgraceful way to regulate social life... But it is already a disgrace when in such a rich country in peacetime we have empty shelves. I think that it is basically the corrupted part of society that does not want rationing."[38]

The introduction of large-scale private enterprise also has major obstacles to overcome in popular consciousness. In an article at the end of 1989 on the results of a national survey of attitudes toward private property, it was reported that, while three quarters of the respondents favoured private ownership of small workshops, restaurants, shops, etc., only one quarter supported private property of large enterprises, and 57% strongly opposed it. As for hired labour (i.e. in private or co-operative enterprises), one half considered this permissible. But even of these, three fifths felt it should be strictly limited. The author of the article, a sociologist at the All-Union Centre for the Study of Public Opinion, concluded:

> Private property in the form most widespread in countries with a market economy [the word "capitalist" is still eschewed in the Soviet Union] has only 25-30% support. The majority, though not opposed to private property, want to keep it on a strictly limited scale, in strictly limited forms and spheres of activity. [... And so] the process of establishing private property will have to be accompanied by (and perhaps follow) the development of collective forms, based upon leasing, the purchase of enterprises by worker collectives, creation of joint stock companies, joint enterprises, etc.

Although this is not the large-scale private property that is the reform's ultimate goal, at least in the author's opinion, he concedes that the population should be allowed to get used to the idea by first passing through group forms of property, since "more radical transformations are pregnant with social explosion. Mass consciousness might simply not be able to withstand such an overloading."[39]

The opposition to capitalist enterprise is related to the workers' concept of "unearned income." N. Belous, a welder and a member of the Interregional Group, explained that he, for one, does not fear private property. But the law should strictly regulate incomes drawn from it and it should completely outlaw "unearned income."[40] The Russian term is literally "non-labour income," and for the average worker — and probably for Belous too — income arising from the purchase of others' labour or from cleverly exploiting market conjunctures is unearned. Hence the deep and widespread popular hostility to trading co-operatives that make profits by buying cheap and selling dear and to producers' co-operatives whose high prices are not justified by the small amount of labour added to materials bought at low state prices. Hence the Kuzbass document's explicit rejection of exploitation.

Even the widespread support for enterprise autonomy should not automatically be interpreted as support for the government's or liberals' reform concept. Workers see this as creating conditions for self-management, for more efficient organization of production, for earning more for social investment and for freeing themselves from an oppressive bloated bureaucracy, which they rightly regard as the main source of inefficiency and injustice. But the vision of most workers is a far cry from autonomous enterprises competing in a free market environment, with the inevitable mass bankruptcies, layoffs, unemployment and economic insecurity that this would entail. (Estimates as high as 40 million unemployed, in an active population of 125 million, are cited by journalists and economists as the immediate consequence of "shock therapy." Some liberals add that unemployment payments cannot be much higher than the subsistence minimum, or else "many will prefer to receive it rather than work, and social parasitism will develop."[41])

The "Right"

Whether their experience will lead workers to seek collective, socialist solutions depends ultimately on the ability of the socialist political forces to challenge successfully the current orientation of the reform by presenting a credible social and political alternative.

At present, however, the only "socialist" critics of government policy to which the broad public has any significant exposure through the mass media are the "right," i.e. conservative elements in the party (e.g. the Russian CP, founded in June 1990, has a strongly conservative orientation[46]), "workers'" organizations like the United Front of Toilers, and the official trade-union apparatus. All of these have some links with the conservative wing of the party-state apparatus, which itself dreams of a return to a modernized, revamped version of the "command" system. Despite periodic sorties against Gorbachev, and their undoubted strength in the apparatus, and to a much lesser extent in the mass party, the "right" appears quite isolated in society as a whole. It does not offer a coherent alternative. In fact, for the most part, it claims to accept the government's "regulated market," taking exception only to selected aspects and demanding social guarantees for the population.

The UFT (United Front of Toilers) was founded in Leningrad in June 1989 and soon appeared in other cities as well as on the national level. It received political and material support from the trade-union apparatus, and was widely seen as a "populist" manoeuvre by the apparatus preparing for the coming soviet elections. It loudly proclaimed its socialist credentials and included among its programmatic demands lower prices, a reduced work day, longer vacations, an end of night shifts, equal economic conditions for workers in the state sector and co-operatives, power to democratically elected soviets, referenda as the key form of consultation with the people, popular control over the creation of all joint enterprises and over the use of natural resources, conservation and restoration of cultural and historical landmarks. This last demand gives a hint of the organization's "patriotic" bent: it has taken up the defence of Russian minorities in the national republics as well as the integrity of the Union, and is known to have some links with Pamyat'. The UFT has also made an issue of the small percentage of worker deputies in the renewed elective assemblies. Other demands are currency reform and strict regulation of the co-operatives, both directed against the growing *nouveau riche* stratum.[42]

Although the UFT had the reformers and liberals scared for a time, as it organized demonstrations along with the trade union apparatus in support of currency reform and against the co-operatives, Gorbachev seems to have tamed it considerably over the last months. In particular, he appointed the UFT's national co-chairman, V. Yarin, to his advisory Presidential Council. Yarin, a metallurgist (dubbed by some a "nomenklatura worker"), who never tires of repeating that after thirty years in the factory, all the property he has accumulated is what you see on him, accepted his appointment in order to help "restore the prestige of the authorities." He claimed his appointment was a response to demands to include "people of toil in the highest state formations" and a guarantee against the ambitions "of certain forces striving for power in order to use it for aims foreign to socialism."[43] Yarin has endorsed Gorbachev's basic reform orientation. "Of course, we can criticize, add some concrete things, but it is time to get to work, turn the government's programmes into reality."[44]

After the miners' strike, the trade-union apparatus also took a populist turn, realizing that its very existence was at stake. Its position has been one of critical support for the government's reform, with the accent on support. But while it endorses the overall reform conception and is helping to sell it to the workers as the only alternative, it has been sometimes taking sides with workers in economic conflicts and insisting on measures to protect workers against the social and economic consequences of the reform. In the winter of 1989/90, the trade-union leadership lent its support to workers who were already forming strike committees, protesting against a wholesale price rise on fuel, energy and transport that would have severely cut enterprise earnings in energy-intensive industries like metallurgy. The government was forced to retreat and compensate the enterprises.[45] Although initially the chairman of the All-Union Central Council of Trade Unions (AUCCTU) appeared to endorse the accelerated reform package of May 1990, in the face of popular reaction, the trade-unions' representatives in the Supreme Soviet opposed the price rise and called for other ways to shift to the market that would not "so suddenly hit the pockets of millions of people."[46]

Despite the obvious ambiguity of the trade-union apparatus's attitude to the government's reform, it has adopted, at least in principle, some progressive positions that go beyond mere damage limitation. The AUCCTU's legislative proposal on employment reaffirms the constitutional guarantee of the right to a job as well as the government's responsibility to ensure full and productive employment. People losing their jobs would be entitled to their past average wage while seeking new employment, with special guarantees for women, young people, invalids. (However, the draft also calls for unemployment payments to be made for a maximum only of twelve months at not less than the official minimum wage but not more than the average republican wage, and those seeking work for the first time would be entitled to only 75% of the legal minimum wage.)[47]

More fundamental is the trade-unions' demand to democratize the reform process. While the government has grown cool to its own initial proposal of a referendum, this idea is being pushed by the union leaders for all basic issues of the reform. Explaining the unions' rejection of the proposed price rise, the chairman of the Russian trade-union centre stated: "We do not reject the market, because the people do not reject it, as far as we can tell at present. But people want to clarify things and understand. And they also have to have confidence in the authorities, the conviction that such major, vitally important decisions will not be taken behind the back of the people, without its agreement. ...We have to say that such an imposed and incomprehensible price rise, whose very possibility has stirred up the whole country,...will not happen."[48]

As important as these positions are in principle, their practical significance depends upon the unions' willingness to defend them. And while the official unions are fighting to retain worker support, one should not be too optimistic about their taking on the government in any decisive struggle. Besides, without an alternative to the "full-blooded market" which constantly reproduces the very social and economic ills the unions oppose, even a more militant stand would achieve little more than to sabotage reform without stopping the economic decline. This would be not unlike the Polish situation of 1982-9, which paved the way for the present attempt to "leap into capitalism."

The Socialists

The socialists have begun to organize only in the past several months and they have no mass-circulation publications. The academics among them publish in specialized journals or monographs. From time to time, the "right" press will publish an article or an interview reflecting their positions.

The principal, more-or-less organized, socialist groups are the "New Socialists," which arose out of the left wing of the Moscow Popular Front and will hold its founding congress in June 1990, and the "Marxist Platform in the CPSU," which held its first national conference in mid-April. There are also small Marxist-oriented groups in the Urals and other provincial industrial centres that are seeking to forge boarder links with the workers.[49] Despite the rudimentary organization among the left, a rough consensus has emerged over the past year or so in relation to economic reform. The following is an attempt to summarize briefly some of the main ideas.[50]

The socialists, the vast majority of whom are Marxists, do not oppose the use of market relations under socialism (though there are differences about their ultimate fate at a more developed stage of socialist society, which is quite far off). Socialism can accomodate and requires both types of economic co-ordination: market relations and administrative methods, and the Soviet Union at its present stage of development clearly suffers from an hypertrophy of the latter. The ongoing debate between "left" and "right" over market versus administrative co-ordination is to a large extent a diversion from the central question: power relations in the economy.

The bureaucratic usurpation of power, the disenfranchisement of the real owners of the economy, the people, and not administrative planning and nationalized property, are at the base of the economic crisis that led to perestroika. By the same token, power is a basic criterion for judging whether market relations are compatible with socialism. If they function in a way that gives one social group power to determine the social and work conditions of others, these cannot be called socialist. Of course, this does not mean that even capitalist relations have no place in the concrete historical conditions of the Soviet Union today, just as Lenin saw a place for them under NEP. But these proposed new forms of property should be recognized for what they are and not be camouflaged as socialist. Their introduction requires a conscious, democratic decision. At the same time, people working as hired labour should not lose their right as joint owners of the national economy to take equal part in the decisions affecting it and to share in its benefits.

While not denying an important role in economic progress to the development of collective forms of property, the transfer of certain activities to co-operatives, regions, etc., the socialists oppose the liberals', and increasingly the government's, orientation toward wholesale denationalization, with their accent on producer collectives as the "real subjects of the national property." The nationalization of the "commanding heights" of the economy is an essential element of socialism, as a system in which economic development is subordinated to democratically determined social goals. It is essential if market relations are to be put at the service of socialist development, rather than the market subordinating society to its own logic. A capitalist market has no goals except profit. The talk of "equality of all types of property" is less than sincere: in any system, one type must dominate. Despite liberal claims, the difference between socialism and capitalism is qualitative, not a quantitative difference between more or less market, more or less state regulation. From a liberal viewpoint, there are undoubtedly economic costs to socialism, a trade-off between social justice and efficiency. But there is no small element of tautology in defining efficiency through the market.

Market relations should, therefore, be expanded in a controlled, gradual manner, through a genuinely democratic process which allows the population collectively to decide the kind of society it desires and to set parameters and limits to the market relations accordingly. The market in the hands of a liberalized bureaucracy can turn out to be a more potent and flexible means of oppression that the old administrative system. And the reform process so far, and all the more so the liberals' call for a "cavalry assault" on the administrative system and its wholesale replacement with the market, bear all the marks of the bureaucratic voluntarism they are supposed to eliminate. This is an adventuristic, forced imposition of a new order that would completely ignore the existing socio-economic structures and interests in the society. The failure so far of the reforms to yield the expected results — indeed, they have generally exacerbated the crisis — is not due to their timidity but to their hurried nature and the reformers' failure to analyze deeply the causes of the crisis and the nature of the system they want to transform.

If the beneficial introduction of market relations requires a gradual, well-thought out process, it is clear that market relations cannot serve as emergency measures to correct the present economic crisis. Of course, it is not a question of restoring the old system or eliminating all the innnovations. But the wholesale liquidation of the administratative mechanism and structures of management is equally absurd. The relative liberalization that has occurred so far has merely continued the *de facto* expansion of the autonomy of the ministries and associations that began in the 1960s. The centre is losing what little power it had retained under Brezhnev. At the same time, the shadow economy is being legalized and is expanding in a growing symbiotic relationship with the state monopolies. All this to the detriment of the ordinary citizens, who as consumers remain as powerless as before. The results of the introduction of market relations in these conditions are growing inflation, shortages, declining production and living standards, deepening socio-economic differentiation.

The fundamental cause of the majority of the ailments of administrative management is *social* — the weakening or elimination of the power of the owners, in this case — the Soviet people. In those conditions, any form of economic stimulation to more effective work is foredoomed. Waste, negligence, and low quality work are directly related to the impunity of managers, their freedom from responsibility for the real results, the secrecy with which administrative appointments and dismissals are made. Waste and shortages elevated into general norms of economic life make managers' jobs easier — less is expected, and their positions are more secure; they also facilitate earnings in the shadow economy. Not much has been done under perestroika to change this: the freedom of the bureaucratic apparatus from society's control has scarcely diminished. The tauted reduction of managerial personnel is more apparent than real. And, as before, this social force is called upon to be the main instrument of the reform; it pushes workers to move "voluntarily" into the seemingly new structures.

Obvious ways of reducing shortages and improving living conditions that are immediately available are ignored, such as reduction of the incredible waste in the storage and delivery to the consumer of agricultural production or the introduction of available improved technology in industry that is held up by the administration. Instead of open public inquiries into the most glaring sore spots of the economy that would lead to clear, practical decisions concerning those responsible, including their dismissal and, if warranted, legal prosecution, the apparatus continues to dominate all forms of public control. Such an elementary "introduction of order" — a demand voiced frequently from below but unheeded by the reformers — i.e. the reestablishment of managerial responsibility toward the owners of the economy, should be the starting point of any reform, regardless of the final correlation that is arrived at between centralism and enterprise autonomy, direct and indirect methods of management and regulation.

The most immediate task is, therefore, to establish democratic control over economic decision-making and management — through democratic soviets, consumer organizations, committees of people's control, worker collectives. This control must be reasserted at *all* levels of economic decision-making. The reform so far has not even looked at this issue above the enterprise level, while it is the higher levels that need it most of all.

The socialists are strong advocates of enterprise self-management. Some propose the use of leasing arrangements as a potentially flexible and efficient way of combining economic autonomy of the enterprise collective with renewed national planning and regulation of the economy. The broad autonomy afforded by these arrangements, though with strict observance of contract terms, even in the absence of full property rights of the collective, would permit the development of entrepreneurial initiative, market relations and competition.

But to limit self-management to the enterprise in conditions of *de facto* bureaucratic domination does little to change the basic problems of shortage-creating monopolism and the dictate of the producers. Popular economic sovereignty over the national economy must be restored as a first step of the reform. This requires the radical democratization of the central economic authorities in order to subordinate the administrative hierarchy to the will of the owners. The slogan of destatization is based on the false identification of the state with the administrative apparatus.

The socialists' similarly reject the liberals' identification of nationalized property with "nobody's property," with a generalized irresponsible attitude. "Human nature" does not require that property be individual for there to be a commitment to its fate. (It is certainly not the case under capitalism that private property always fosters a commitment to a specific property, if its destruction stands in the way of greater profit.) The irresponsibility which exists on all levels in the "command system" is the consequence of the bureaucratic usurpation of popular economic sovereignty, without the bureaucrats, however, themselves becoming owners. Democracy is, therefore, the very essence of a socialist economy. Without minimizing the complexity involved in creating the mechanisms of such a democracy, the socialist argue that it can create a basis for an effective sense of commitment to common goals. But this democracy must be more than the present practice of "popular consultations."

The alternative advocated by the socialists would not be an easy one to get across even if they enjoyed the liberals' privileged access to the public through the media. A major ideological handicap is the absence of a working model. The liberals, on the other hand, can point to the "whole world" as proof that their programme corresponds to human nature and natural economic laws and they can cite the higher living standards and well-stocked shops of the West: "And if you find the American model a bit rough on workers, then all you have to do is choose the Swedish." The socialists' are honest enough to admit that they have no ready-made formula for combining market and plan, which cannot be abstract, nor have they a fully elaborated concept for the mechanisms of democratic control of the economy. This stands in contrast to the apparently coherent, worked out, simple model of the liberals — which, of course, does not and could not exist in real life. Moreover, in the prevailing ideological atmosphere, when it is impossible to pick up a newspaper without being told several times that the whole country agrees that there is no alternative to the market, the socialists appear to be taking a defensive position: "We are not against the market, but..."[51] In such conditions, and given the strength of anti-bureaucratic sentiment, anyone defending centralized economic power risks being tarred as a reactionary.

On the other hand, the socialists have in their favour basic working class values and attitudes, which are compatible only with socialism. These, of course, are not fixed in stone — much can change under the impact of a deteriorating, increasingly hopeless economic crisis and a constant barrage of liberal ideas. Nor does the mere existence of these attitudes mean they will be translated into political action in favour of a socialist programme. A Polish scenario is possible: the workers' block the government's reform, or crucial parts thereof, the economy continues to deteriorate, and the liberals step in as offering a seemingly coherent,if painful, programme that at least offers some hope.

Despite this, there are grounds for guarded optimism, though the workers will probably have to experience a more "full-blooded" market than exists now before the socialists can become a real mass force. Socialist values have deeper roots in the Soviet, especially Russian, working class, than in Eastern Europe. ("We are the only country in the world where strong anti-market attitudes exist," complained O. Latsis, "except maybe Albania.") Even more important is the workers' democratism, which will not change easily. For the socialist alternative is the only genuinely democratic alternative for the Soviet Union.

June 1990

NOTES

1. *Sobesednik,* no. 49, 1989, p. 12.
2. Stenographic report of conference on "Economic Consciousness and Economic Behaviour in Conditions of the Perestroika", Zvenigorod, November 20-5, 1989.
3. *Gazette* (Montreal), Mar. 22, 1989, p. A-15.
4. *Moskovskie novosti,* No. 33, 1989, p. 7.
5. Interview with Yu. Boldyrev, *Rubikon* (Leningrad) no. 10, 1989, p. 40.
6. Photocopied document.

7. *Izvestiya*, Dec. 12, 1989.
8. E. Bérard-Zarzicka, "Pour une perestroika authoritaire," *Les Temps Modernes*, no. 523, Feb. 1990, pp. 11-22.
9. *New York Times*, Mar. 13, 1990, p. A-17 and Mar. 14, 1990, p. A-18.
10. *Nedelya*, no. 23, 1990, p.3.
11. *Moskovskie novosti*, June 3, 1990. p.4.
12. *Manchester Guardian Weekly*, June 14, 1990, p. 8.
13. See V.Z. Rogovine, "La perestroika et la différenciation socio-économique," in D. Mandel, ed., *La perestroika: économie et société*, PUQ, Montreal, 1990, pp. 138-139.
14. *Nedelya*, no. 17, 1990, p. 3
15. *Nedelya*, no. 23, 1990, p. 12.
16. *Argumenty i fakti*, no. 13, 1990, pp. 1-2.
17. *Nedelya*, no. 23, 1990, p. 13.
18. *Trud*, Apr. 27, 1990.
19. See Prime Minister Ryzhkov's interview in *Pravitel'stvennyi vestnik*, no. 8, 1990, p. 3.
20. *Moskovskie novosti*, no.25, 1990, p. 16.
21. *Trud*, Dec. 14, 1990.
22. *Rabochaya tribuna*, Mar. 16, 1990
23. *New York Times*, Mar. 20, 1990.
24. *Pravda*, Apr. 19, 1990.
25. *Trud*, Mar. 34, 1990.
26. See R.W. Davies, "Gorbachev's Socialism in Historical Perspective," *New Left Review*, spring 1990, pp. 22-3.
27. C. Samary, *Le marché contre l'autogestion*, Publisud/La Brèche, Paris, 1988.
28. *Trud*, Apr. 27, 1990.
29. *Trud*, May 25, 1990.
30. *Pravitel'stvennyi vestnik*, no. 25, 1990, p. 1.
31. *Rabochaya tribuna*, Mar. 27, 1990.
32. Bérard-Zarzicka, "Pour une perestroika autoritaire," p. 16.
33. Photocopied document.
34. *Rabochaya tribuna*, June 19, 1990.
35. *Trud*, June 16, 1990.
36. Cited in *Komsomol'skaya pravda*, May 1, 1990.
37. T. Zaslavsakaya, ed., *Sotsial'nye orientiry obnovelniya*, Politizdat, Moscow, 1990, p. 242.
38. *Rabochaya tribuna*, Apr. 18, 1990.
39. *Nedelya*, no. 52, 1989, p.5.
40. *Rabochaya tribuna*, Jan. 1, 1990.
41. *Nedelya*, no. 20, 1990, p. 5.
42. *Vesty iz SSSR*, no. 12, 1989, p. 11; *Izvestiya*, Dec. 12, 1989. One of the theoreticians of the UFT, as well as of the Russian Communist Party, is A. Sergeev, an economist at the Higher Trade-Union School. Some of his ideas can be found in the following articles: "Iz segodnya v zavtra ili pozavchera," *Ekonomicheskie nauki*, no. 9, 1989; "Sotsializm i tovarnove proizvodstvo: o chem stoit i o chem ne stoit sporit'," *Ekonomicheskie nauki*, no. 1, 1989; "Problemy obnovleniya ekonomicheskoi teorii sotsializma i kontseptual'nye varianty radikal'noi perestroiki," *Ekonomicheskie nauki*, no. 3, 1989.
43. *Rabochaya tribuna*, Apr. 27, 1990.

44. *Trud*, Dec. 16, 1989.
45. *Trud*, Mar. 31, 1990.
46. *Trud*, June 16, 1990.
47. *Trud*, June 15, 1990.
48. *Trud*, June 16, 1990.
49. Interview with M. Malyutin, *Dialog*, no. 7, 1990; *Pravda*, Apr. 16, 1990. See also *Inprecor* (Paris), Mar. 9, Apr. 20 and June 1, 1990.
50. This summary is based upon conversations and published materials, some of which are: *Sotsial'nye orientiry obnovleniya*, Moscow: Poltizdat, 1990 (I have leaned especially heavily on the sections written by Yu. Sukhotin, in particular pp. 234-245.); *La perestroika: économie et société*; Yu. Sukhotin, "Efficacité économique ou éthique socialiste?" *Interventions économiques*, nos 22/23, 1989/90. pp. 255-70; V. Bogachev, "Polnyi khozraschet i tsentralizovannoe khozyaistvennoe upravlenie," *Voprosy ekonomiki*, no.5, 1988; A. Buzgalin, *Protivorechiya samoupravleniya, tsentralizma i samostoyatel'nosti v planovom khozyaistve*, Moscow, 1988; V. Dement'ev et Yu. Sukhotin, "K obnovleniyu orientirov ekonomicheskoi teorii," *Ekonomika i matematicheskie metody*, no. 3, 1989; Yu. Sukhotin, *Potentsial ekonomicheskoi teorii*, Moscow, 1989. For the "New Socialists", see "Declaration of Moscow Committee of New Socialists," *Nevskie zapiski*, (Leningrad), no. 8, 1989. One of its leaders is B. Kagarlitsky, author of *The Thinking Reed*, London: Verso, 1989.
51. *Rabochaya tribuna*, June 19, 1990.

Chapter 6

"Destatization" and the Struggle for Power in the Soviet Economy: A New Phase in the Labour Movement

> *It is now our turn to reject that which has not withstood the test of history. They often try to frighten us that the market is exploitation, the restoration of capitalism, the rule of the shadow economy. In reality, we are talking about the transition to a civilized, cultured market, open to all honest and industrious people.*
>
> (From the appeal of the Russian Parliament to the population to support the "500-Day Plan for the Transition to the Market")[1]

> *I recently read in your paper: ... "Employees of the state sector are prepared to become hired workers only on condition that their wages rise significantly."...I don't know of any workers in the state sector who would be prepared to become hired slaves. And what can a "significant" increase, say a doubling, of wages give them if prices rise 5-10 times and if mass unemployment sets in? Criminals, who have amassed capital, are becoming a class of owners and rulers of the destiny of the state.*
>
> (From the letter of a worker of Kharkov region)[2]

This chapter treats developments in the Soviet labour movement as they relate to the issue of power in the economy. The first section presents certain elements of the current economic situation that have brought the issue of power to the fore. There follows an examination of the forms, spontaneous and organized, through which workers have responded to it. A final section evaluates the significance of the self-management current in the labour movement from a socialist perspective.

Of Markets and Mafias

In early December 1990, a journalist at the liberal daily *Komsomol'skaya pravda* purchased a pig from a farmer and brought it to the kolkhoz (private) market to sell. The market price of meat had doubled over the last half year to 30-35 rubles a kilo[3] (with a 33-66% rise over the past month alone), and he wanted to understand why. He made the rounds of sixteen of Moscow's 33 markets but everywhere was refused access to the counters where he would have been able to offer his meat for sale to the public. Finally, at the Riga market, Moscow's largest, after paying a "crazy" bribe to the butcher and inspector, he was given a counter among the egg dealers. He posted a sign: "Cheapest Meat at the Market" and started to sell at five times below the going price. The reaction was swift. A man purchased a very large piece of meat only to run back a few minutes later shouting that the meat was infected. When this false accusation failed to deter the other customers, our journalist was denied access to the scales, under the pretext that his meat was dirty. He then began to sell the meat unweighed, upon which four large men attempted to drag him away. "The markets of the capital," he concluded, "where, in principle, free economic laws should hold sway, are today completely monopolized. ...The mafia structure of a single market rakes in several tens of thousands of rubles a day. The whole path is thickly paved with bribes."[4]

73% of the respondents in a survey conducted in sixteen regions of the Soviet Union in the summer of 1990 stated that their ability to influence political life had not increased over the past two years.[5] In another survey in Moscow in the fall of 1990, 60% claimed that "power in the localities belongs not to the soviets but to the chiefs of the mafia."[6] In the sixth year of perestroika, people are waking up to the realization that despite the increased freedom of speech, the competitive elections, and the removal of the party apparatus from the levers of political power, they themselves remain almost as powerless as ever. People, who only a year ago were fervent supporters of the schemes of the radical marketeers, now typically express fear that the elimination of state control over the economy means that "it will all fall into the hands of the mafia." The term "mafia" reflects the popular perception of a growing fusion of the bureaucracy, especially the economic administrators, with the "affairistes" of the private sector.[7] These are the people who hold power in the economy, and so, to a large degrees also in society as a whole.

Any Soviet citizen can readily offer a list of examples drawn from personal experience to support this view. The "mafia" has lately also become a major theme of the press, liberal as well as conservative (there is no mass socialist press). As a social phenomenon, its contours are illusive and fluctuating — its shadowy character is in the nature of the beast. But the term most often refers to two principal kinds of related activity: the creation and maintenance of shortages by monopoly structures[8], and the illicit transfer of state resources and funds into private business. Both involve the collusion of administrators of the state sector with the "shadow" [tenevaya] economy, itself often indistinguishable from the legitimate private sector. The "mafia" was not, of course, born under Gorbachev, as the trials at the start of perestroika surrounding Rashidov's reign in Kazakhstan amply showed. But with the further weakening of central control and the legalization of the private sector, the "Rashidovshchina" has become much more generalized. The following are some additional examples of "mafia" activity; these could easily be multiplied.

In September 1990, a deputy of the Moscow Soviet travelled to Astrakhan' to find out why tomatoes and watermelons were arriving from this southern region in such small quantities. The local Astrakhan' authorities showed him a pile of telegrams sent by administrators of Moscow's produce wholesale-retail network instructing them to stop shipment because of an oversupply in Moscow, which, of course, did not exist. "Prices are now mostly 'by agreement'," explained the deputy. "The less goods, the higher their price can soar. Who profits from this reduced supply of vegetables? Those who sell them. I consider that mafia links along the lines warehouse-shop-speculator are real!"[9] As for dry goods, the director of a Moscow department store chain estimates that only 18% of the goods in high demand that are produced and imported actually reach the ordinary consumer.[10] Enormous lines stretch around state shops, while at the private markets — and sometimes only a few yards from the door of the state shop itself — one can purchase the same goods without any wait for several times the state price.

The Soviet Union has imported hundreds of millions of dollars worth of medicine over the past two years. Yet even simple aspirin has become a rare find in the pharmacies. According to the director of a Moscow pharmaceutical trading firm, most of the imported drugs are not those that are in most demand; no one consulted her about this.[11] But someone surely made a bundle in pay-offs from the exporters. On the other hand, anyone with enough money can obtain needed drugs by bribing the pharmacy or warehouse manager, or at the black market or at Moscow's little-known, but now quite legal, foreign currency drug store. According to one report, the volume of illegal trade in medicine is already approaching that of the state pharmacies.[12]

Besides economic gain, shortages also play a useful political role for those interested in maintaining popular quiescence. People are so preoccupied with the material struggle for survival that they have little time or energy for sustained political activity. (This is, of course, not to claim that the shortages are the result of a political conspiracy, though in some cases even this hypothesis should not be dismissed. In any case, one can argue with confidence that, were it not for the political role played by the shortages, efforts to deal with them would be more intense and successful.) And when political tensions rise dangerously, "defitsit" (scarce goods — literally "shortage") is suddenly "thrown out" onto the market. According to a resident of the industrial town of Sverdlovsk, soon after a mass political demonstration, the authorities "began to 'throw out' Austrian boots, Rumanian blouses and deodorant from somewhere or other. Naturally, lines sprang up, then lists, guardians of the lists and guardians of the night lines. The people are busy, they have become active." The committee elected at the demonstration soon found itself isolated from the rest of the population.[13]

As shortages grow more serious, the practice of selling "defitsit" directly in the enterprises has expanded. This is a common and quite effective tool in the hands of the administration for reinforcing the workers' dependence. A worker who speaks up against management might miss out. At the same time, there are never enough goods to go around, and the squabbling over who is to receive what can seriously undermine solidarity within the collective. This practice also has a deeply corrupting influence on workers, since the goods that are sold are often not scarce basic consumer goods but items such as cars, electronic equipment, video cassettes and French perfumes, which the workers then resell at a large profit. Management is, of course, perfectly aware of this.

Shortages also serve as a political football for conservatives and liberals who want to discredit each other. With the potato crop rotting in the fields, party officials accused the "democrats," elected to the soviets in the spring of 1990, of doing nothing to mobilize their constituents for the harvest. (This used to be the role of the party apparatus until it was stripped of its administrative functions in the economy.) The liberal press, in its turn, blamed the conservatives for sowing panic in order to discredit the "democrats." The "democrats" pointed their finger at the central economic apparatus for failing to take measures in time, when the problem was foreseeable even a year ago. Indeed, the first reaction of Gavriil Popov, Moscow's liberal mayor, was to refuse to mobilize his constituents, suggesting instead that the incompetent ministerial apparatus be sent to the fields.

Leonid Sukhov, a taxi driver from Kharkov and member of the USSR Parliament, expressed a widespread view when he suggested that "someone" is consciously creating a desperate situation with the aim of preparing the workers psychologically to accept any reform, including the market.[14] The "democrats" argue that they lack real power to change the situation. And while there is much truth to this claim, they have done little to mobilize the population in order to change the correlation of forces. There is a general reluctance on the part of liberals, stemming from their ideological orientation as well as from more concrete political considerations, to apply "administrative" methods — the only ones that could be effective against monopoly — to reign in the "mafia." For, as the Russian-born American economist Vasily Leontief has argued, today's mafia is tomorrow's class of "civilized" capitalists.

Direct robbery of the consumer is only one source of "mafia" profits. Parallel to this, and sometimes overlapping, is theft from the state. This also takes many forms. Workers tell of the "pocket" co-operatives[15] and joint ventures set up by enterprise management for the illicit sale abroad or to the private sector of raw materials and semi-manufactured goods. For example, the director of the state research and manufacturing association Gidrolizprom authorized the creation of the co-operative Khimtekhnika and transferred to it — free of charge — the association's large store of defective titanium hydrolysis apparatuses. Khimtekhnika, which began with no assets of its own, traded the titanium for from six to nine million rubles worth of computers and video players, of which Gidrolizprom itself saw none. After several narrow escapes from the police and tax inspectors, Khimtekhnika's directors transferred these assets to a joint Soviet-Swiss venture, Intercomplex, created specially for that purpose. (Joint ventures enjoy a two-year tax holiday.) Since then, the Gidrolizprom association has been disbanded. Its former institutes and factory, now independent, face large debts and bleak futures. Not so the former director of Gidrolizprom, who now stands at the helm of Intercomplex.[16]

Subcontracting work to co-operatives is a common way of turning non-cash credits into cash. In the Soviet economy, monetary exchanges between state enterprises take the form of bookkeeping transactions between the State Bank accounts of the different enterprises. In such exchanges (po beznalichnomu raschetu), no cash changes hands. On the other hand, in transactions between state enterprises and co-operatives, which are non-state enterprises, cash is paid out of these accounts, allowing state managers to receive kickbacks or salaries as members or employees of the co-operative. There are also fortunes to be made in foreign dealings. Most of the Moscow's "joint venture" construction companies are too busy importing and selling computers to put up any buildings. And why should they, when their profits can reach 4,000%.[17] As a minister in the Latvian government put it, "cooperatives and joint enterprises are often oriented not toward the production of consumer goods but toward their redistribution. From the state's pockets into their own. That is, if we are to call things by their name, they are involved in speculation on a very large scale."[18] Under Brezhnev, a "gift" of jeans or whiskey helped to seal foreign export deals to the Soviet Union. Under perestroika, when foreign dealings have been decentralized, large cash sums of foreign currency have become *de rigueur*.[19]

Mention must also be made of the party apparatus, many of whose former and current members are using their connections and illegally accumulated wealth to go into business. In Leningrad, for example, the once mighty regional party apparatus has been reduced to 37 people. But they keep busy renting out offices to co-operatives, private banks and foreign companies in the Smolnyi Institute, an historic landmark and prime piece of real estate that rightfully belongs to the people. They have also turned one of the committee's hotels into a joint venture.[20]

But it is not only members and former members of the bureaucratic clans who are involved in these activities. A scandal broke out in the Moscow Soviet when a deputies' club by the name of "Stolitsa" (capital) tried to oust the local temperance society from its premises on Chekhov St. It was discovered that this club's goals are "production and commercial activities." Further inquiry revealed that its founders work in the Soviets' Commission on Economic Policy and Entrepreneurship. *Komsomol'skaya pravda* remarked: "The example of 'Stolitsa', unfortunately, is not unique but is even typical of the existing structure of soviets: different commissions of local soviets often create various commercial organizations and pay part of their profits, not to the local budget, but directly to their founders. And the founders, of course, repay the kindness."[21]

In December 1990, 35 members of the Oktyabr'skii District Soviet in Moscow publicly accused its chairman, Ilya Zaslavskii, a liberal luminary, of "organizing monopoly structures, as similar to classic 'shadow' formations as two peas in a pod... Judge for yourselves: the chairman of the District Soviet, the chairman of its executive committee, and almost all his deputies, having become heads of the district's political structures, are at the same time directors of co-operatives, commercial banks and firms. [There follows a long list of these enterprises.] Exceptionally favourable conditions are created for the activity of all these firms, and tens of thousands of rubles are being pumped at an intensive rate into their financial accounts from the basic budgetary funds of the district executive committee, that is, they are openly robbing you and me of funds intended for the socio-economic development of the district." The deputies went on to accuse the executive, busy with realizing Zaslavskii's conception of "the market economy and financial independence of the district," of sabotaging the district's vegetable harvest campaign. The housing programme, they argued, was also failing: while the executive was selling state apartments primarily to occupants who openly stated their intention of leaving the country and reselling the apartments for foreign currency or renting them out to foreign companies, 60,000 people in the district still lived in communal apartments.[22]

These developments, the "transition to the market" as the uncontrolled sway of monopoly formations and the illicit transfer of public wealth to private hands, popularly termed the "mafia-ization" of the economy, do not come as a surprise to Soviet Marxists, who are among the rare analysts even to attempt a serious examination of the underlying causes of the "command" system's failure.[23] They have always insisted that the basic issue in economic reform is power, that is a social issue, and that the market-versus-plan debate is about mechanisms of regulation that in and of themselves do not determine the nature of a social system. The failure of the "command" system cannot be explained by simply citing the allegedly "utopian nature of a planned economy," though the Marxists themselves call for a revision of the old socialist model of "one big factory," including a significant expansion of the role of market relations in the Soviet economy. But this task, however important, cannot be resolved successfully in the interests of the great majority without directly confronting the issue of power.

For these analysts, the underlying social cause of the crisis of the old system is the absence of control over the economy's administrators, who, after the revolution usurped the power of the economy's official owner, the people, without becoming full owners themselves. Under Stalin, at the origins of the "command economy," some control from above did exist. A manager who failed to carry out assigned tasks knew that he or she would be sanctioned, often in a drastic manner. Khrushchev eliminated the terror but did not replace it with democratic control from below. He merely played with democracy. But even his timid reforms provoked the opposition of the bureaucracy that was able to find allies in the majority of the political leadership. Brezhnev thus came to power as the candidate of the bureaucracy. What Soviets today call "the period of stagnation" was probably the purest expression of the rule of a bureaucracy increasingly free of outside political control. During this period, administrators (especially at the top and middle levels) did not need particularly to fear punishment for failure to carry out offical duties. Real sanctions were reserved for those who violated the informal rules, the *esprit de corps,* of the bureaucratic caste mired in corruption.

From this point of view, Gorbachev, though himself a reformer, has favoured the process that he inherited from the Brezhnev régime: today the centre has become almost as powerless as the people themselves against the economic bureaucracy, which is free to exploit its monopoly positions in perfectly predictable ways: restricting the volume of goods put on the market, cutting quality, and raising prices. This is the inevitable consequence of an attempted "revolution from above" which has entrusted the economic reform to the bureaucracy itself. Its aim is to preserve the power and privilege of at least a part of the bureaucracy by transforming the mode of domination and exploitation. This, of course, requires bringing new elements into the ruling class and sacrificing some of the old.

The developments in the Soviet economy described above are forcing the liberals to come to terms with the unpleasant reality. Their standard argument that the deepening economic crisis and the "debauch of the mafia" are due to the absence of "real" reform has lost much of its force, since ordinary citizens have already experienced enough of the market to form a quite clear picture of what a "real" transition to the market probably holds in store for them. In the words of the then USSR Minister of Finance: "One can argue whether we are prepared or not for the transition to the market, if competition has been established among producers or if that still remains a very distant goal, but the reality is such that the market is already imperiously intruding into our lives. Over 60% of prices are not under the control of the state. That means that they are rising, and very significantly. ...Monopolism in industry, agriculture and transport has very strong positions."[24] (This is quite an admission, in view of the fact that there has not yet been an official price reform. In the spring of 1990, Gorbachev solemnly promised that there would be no price reform without first consulting the population, itself overwhelmingly opposed to price rises.)

Liberal Journalist Leonid Radzikhovskii argues that the Soviet economy is dominated by a "lumpen-bourgeois ethic: the desire to increase one's own property at the expense of state property, which is 'no one's' property." This has yielded "a unique, historically unprecedented monster — a completely mafia-ized economy." All this he attributes, of course, to the socialist revolution itself. But he is not far from the Marxists' analysis when he describes perestroika as the "privatization of the bureaucratic-mafia structure: the ministry becomes a monopolist concern and the city trade administration — an assocation of private shops." Nevertheless, he warns that it would be silly to believe that anything else is possible, since the "mafia-nomenklatura" is where the power is. And so, however distasteful, one must hold the course since "only in conditions of open private property will it be possible to begin, drop by drop, to crush monopoly and the mafia,...millimeter by millimeter to restore the common human ethic[25] and to get rid of the lumpen bourgeoisie."[26]

In essence, Radzhikhovskii is proposing to hold one's nose and support the revolution from above. He does not even mention the possibility of a popular revolution as an alternative. For the wresting power from the "mafia-nomenklatura" by the people itself might jeopardize his goal of a capitalist restoration.

Leningrad's social democrats, advocates of a "mixed" (but predominantly capitalist) economy, have also recently come to the realization that "privatization will mean the transfer of property into the hands of the directors; and the introduction of a market economy — their freedom from any limitations whatsoever." The following are only the most striking of the developments along these lines in their city: "The 26 largest enterprises, having formed the 'Association of Industrial Enterprises', have now founded the bank 'Rossiya', in which they are investing millions of rubles. They have also created the firm 'Nevskaya perspektiva', through which they will buy up...the consumer goods and food industry of the city along with the trade network — all this, naturally, to help the citizens and Leningrad Soviet. At the conclusion of these operations, the city will still be run by the same old administrative structure, only its elements will enjoy new opportunities, which hitherto were considered criminal."[27]

While this in itself is worrying to the social democrats, who want a "normal" Western-style economy for the Soviet Union, they clearly fear even more the "political instability" and "social unrest" will result. "People in the factories will not wait for long when they discover that society is being ruled by the same actors, leading the same kind of life, along with all their relatives and friends and with a part of the most amenable democrats, the only difference being that they will have exchanged their black Volgas for black Mercedes." The Leningrad social democrats are fervent partisans of what they call the "parliamentary path." "There are two alternatives: try to use the extreme instability of the situation to destroy the remaining conservative structures and on the wave of the mass actions hope to become political leaders 'expressing the interests of the people'; or try to prevent the social explosion by any methods available, preserving the parliamentary path of development of events. The Bolsheviks of 1917 were the most consistent partisans of the first option....We know the consequences of trying to make a social revolution." Consequently, the social democrats see the bureaucrats' move from Volgas into Mercedes as virtually inevitable. All they can think to propose is to invite Western capitalists in the hope that they will introduce a "civilizing" element into Soviet business. Another proposal is for the Lenigrad Soviet itself to go into business, as a counterweight to the "mafia." But, they sadly note, in that case there would be no guarantee against the Soviet itself becoming "mafia-ized."[28]

The Struggle For Power in the Factories

The growing prominence of the question of power in the economy, as well as the accelerated decline in the general economic situation, have had a direct impact on the labour movement. Labour conflicts in the first years of perestroika centred around issues of wages and work conditions, with demands addressed to the enterprise management and sometimes to the ministry. Although wages and conditions still remain central issues, a new type of conflict has emerged over the past year. Rather than putting forth economic demands and pressuring management to meet them, workers are themselves seeking an active role in the management of their enterprises. These conflicts, which are more offensive in nature and pose directly the issue of power in the enterprise, have been especially prominent in the crucial machine-construction industry, which unlike coalmining, has not seen any co-ordinated, inter-enterprise strike movement.

At the start of 1990, Moscow's AZLK auto factory, which makes the "Moskvich," seemed even to its handful of activists an unlikely place for an "uprising." Like many of Moscow's factories with large semi-skilled and unskilled labour forces, about two-thirds of the workers here are "limitchiki," workers from the provinces with temporary Moscow residence permits that can be revoked upon dismissal from the factory. They are, therefore, especially vulnerable and generally quiescent. But even the settled Muscovites felt the pressure and corrupting influence of the internal distribution system, which expanded as shortages in the state shops worsened.

True, the year before, something unheard of had occurred at the factory's trade-union conference: someone complained about the purchase of useless machinery in Western Europe. Some speakers blamed this on management's decision to send the director's son (travel to the West is a coveted privilege) rather than workers and engineers who had first-hand knowledge of the specifications. AZLK's workers also remembered how the previous year the director had ignored the decision of the work-collective (self-management) council and adopted a 120,000-car plan target. He went so far as to dismiss his popular assistant director, who had insisted that the plant's capacity was only 80,000. In fact, only 74,000 cars were made in 1989, but the workers received their bonuses anyway, since the director is well-connected and was able to persuade the ministry to "correct" the plan. The adoption of the original plan had allowed him to obtain additional funds, some of which went to buy the machinery that was lying about uninstalled. 1989 also saw the workers' reject management's proposed schedule of fifteen "black" (working) Saturdays, when the director, in a nod to the current fashion (since then abandoned, as we shall see), foolishly decided to consult the workers.

But otherwise, the workers looked on in their usual gloomy silence at management's inability to rationally organize production and provide normal work conditions as well as at its deepening corruption. (The huge sums involved in the "shadow" economy and the great demand for the attractive new "Moskovich" have opened up new vistas in this area.) Then came an article in *Komsoml'skaya pravda,* written on information provided by factory activists, describing the poor management at the enterprise. If in 1985, 17,500 workers produced 175,000 cars, in 1989, 16,900 workers made less than half as many. This was followed by a television report that the factory was being fined one and a half million convertible rubles for non-fulfillment of a contract to build a sports car for a West-German firm. The final piece of tinder was provided by the news that the retail price of the "Moskvich" would be raised 50% to 13,500 rubles, even though no substantial improvements had been made to the model. The factory would be allowed to keep 1,000 extra rubles for its needs.

In January 1990, the work-collective council of the assembly shop, led by a group of activist workers (who are also party members), called a shop meeting to discuss the situation. To the surprise of the initiators, workers streamed in from all over the factory and filled up the 800-seat hall and adjacent corridors to overflowing. The following demands were put forward: dismissal of the director and election of a new one; reinstatement of the dismissed assistant director; new elections to the enterprise work-collective council, since the present one was subservient to the administration; no price rise (speakers explained that it might permit the factory to raise wages, but if all enterprises made unjustified price rises, wage gains would soon be wiped out); equalization of the rights of the "limitchiki" with those of permanent residents; a regular work process, without idle time, "storming," and violation of internal supply schedules; real cost-accounting; and wages paid according to labour (wage differentials exist from shop to shop for the same kind of work). Some speakers demanded that supervisory and technical personnel be cut and the savings be used to raise the salaries of the remainder in accordance with results.

In a letter to *Pravda,* Sergei Novopol'skii, chairman of the assembly shop's work-collective council and head of a brigade of mechanic-assemblers, explained the underlying impulse behind the explosion: "The main thing is that we are convinced that perestroika does not need silent workers of the kind the present management would like to see but workers who think, who understand, and who know how to work in a way that is useful for the country."[29] But the director, on his part, attributed it all to "intrigues of the apparatus," which he accused of abusing the new democracy and glasnost'. He agreed to hold a referendum on his administration, which he won.[30] The main results of the meeting were new elections to the work-collective council and a halving of the proposed price rise.

The workers were obviously not prepared for sustained activism. In part, this can be attributed to the influence of the economic crisis and the internal distribution system. However, the latter's arbitrary and corrupting nature, while effective in the short run, is particularly degrading to the workers and eventually adds fuel to the explosions, when they finally occur. And most Soviet observers expect these to occur soon. More importantly perhaps, the auto workers' demands were addressed to the enterprise management, but many of their problems could be resolved only at higher, essentially political, levels. Any new movement will have to link up with workers in other enterprises if it is to be effective and take on stable, organized forms.

Only a few weeks after the AZLK meeting, a similar gathering took place several thousand kilometers away at the Sibelektrotyazhmash plant in Novosibirk which makes large electric generators. Here too workers had never shown much concern for the economic fate of the enterprise. Their complaints were traditionally about the cafeteria's food, bad ventilation and heating, the periodic absence of hot water. In short, it was a typical machine-construction enterprise, except perhaps for the shiny new Toyotas parked in front of the administration building, though these too were becoming a familiar scene in the fifth year of perestroika. The initiative for the meeting here too came from a group of activists. A few days before, the head of a bridgade of turners, himself a member of the factory's party committee, sounded out the shops and met with an enthusiastic response from the workers. The main issue at the meeting was poor management. The director had been elected a year ago but had not carried out his programme: no new forms of work organization had been introduced. Output was half of what it had been twenty years ago, but the work force was the same size. The assembly brigade stood idle for weeks, while workers in the adjacent shop put in ten hour shifts for the same wage. Copper wire worth thousands of rubles was cut up because there were no reels. Technical and production discipline had declined catastrophically. While the director blamed all this on the middle levels of management that he accused of sabotaging his initiatives, the workers complained that they rarely saw him at the factory and never on the shop floor. While the collective was seething and with the conference already in preparation, he took off to Moscow to attend a branch conference of directors. The chief engineer's assertion that things were not so bad since profits had risen 400% over 1976-88 made no impression on the workers.

But the most insistent accusation against management concerned the co-operatives. These had been created to help the enterprise fulfill the state's directive to increase its production of consumer goods. "Where are these goods?" asked the workers. "We don't see any more [on the market] than before. Whom are we fooling?" "The managers are coddling the co-operatives, and the co-operatives are robbing the enterprise blind. Transformer copper is going to the co-operatives, but who signs it out? We produce no copper waste." "The superintendent of the first department received 1500 rubles from one of the fifteen co-operatives organized at the factory to produce consumer goods. ...In essence, this is payment for his having ruined the shop — let's tell things as they really are. The shop is now working to meet the needs of the co-operative, not the factory. Forty welders left the shop for the co-operative, forcing other shops to send their people to help it out. One of the assistants to the chief engineer received 2700 rubles for the construction of a trestle bridge in his spare time. Where does he get it, if he doesn't have a fixed workday!? The party organizer has also dirtied his hands in the co-operatives. He has passed all his work to his assistant and himself is nowhere to be seen. People are sick of all this. It angers us to the bottom of our souls. What is going on around us!? We have to change our life, we cannot go on living like this."[31]

The meeting elected a workers' committee (representing only the blue-collar workers) to take power in the factory and decided to hold new elections to the work-collective committee (which represents all employees: workers, office employees, engineering and technical personnel as well as management), which had been doing little more than distributing "defitsit." The factory's newspaper was removed from the control of the administration, the party and trade-union committees and made responsible to the workers' conference. Managerial, engineering and technical personnel were to be cut in half, and a new director elected. (The workers' committee later decided to give him six more months, after which he would report back to the workers, who would take a final decision.) Characterizing as one-sided the enterprise's relations with the ministry, regional and union governments (it paid them 70% of its income, leaving little for the collective's social development), the meeting decided to negotiate a reduction in its payments. The workers' committee was instructed to study, with the aid of economists, the question of gradually leaving the ministry. (The workers were aware that they might be worse off without the ministry playing its redistributive role within the branch.)

The co-operatives, accused of "pillaging the enterprise's resources and fostering the moral decay of the collective," were ordered off the enterprises's territory, and administrative personnel as well as employees in the financial and accounting departments forbidden from working in them. Full reports on their activities and finances were ordered from the co-operative chairpersons. The meeting also turned its attention to the nefarious effect on the collective of the internal distribution system and decided that henceforth, the sale of scarce consumer goods, food, cars etc. would take place only after this had been approved by a workers' conference. Finally, on the issue of the Toyotas, a report was demanded of the superintendent of the transport department on the cost of maintaining the enterprise's fleet of cars and vans and on his budget in 1989.

The election of a workers' committee is characteristic of many of these conflicts. As one observer put it, "in the majority of cases the work-collective committees fail to show any independence vis-à-vis management. The work-collective committees were basically created on order from above. [Until the government issued a special instruction, they were often headed by the director.] The workers' committees [representing only the blue-collar workers], on the other hand, are not obligated to anyone at their birth, i.e. they are not the result of initiative from above but of the realization that we are all responsible for changing things and that if we do not, who will?"[32] The formation of workers' committees reflects in part the deepening hostility between workers and "white blouses" in the enterprises — the reduction of administrative and technical personnel is a very popular demand.[33] But it also is a response to the fact, that technical, like administrative personnel, have no right of appeal against dismissals and are therefore more dependent on the director. One of the workers' leaders explained: "The shop engineers are our brothers; they work in the same dirt and face the same difficulties. ...We aren't against them. They should be with us. Our level of knowledge does not allow us to really spread our wings, especially when it comes to economic questions. But for the time being, we have decided to create a workers' committee with representatives only from the working class... We have a good lever... — the strike. Management has to consider that possibility and take the proletariat into account. ...But we do include the engineering and technical personnel in the work-collective committee."[34] Another interesting aspect of these conflicts is the initiating role often played by worker party activists. This occurs against the general background of the party's unpopularity among workers, who are leaving it in significant numbers.

At a Vilnius trucking enterprise, whose existence was threatened in the spring of 1990 by Moscow's oil embargo and the republican government's proposed economic reforms, the workers dissolved the work-collective committee and elected a workers' committee, assuming full control of the enterprise. The committee was instructed to take "all measures to organize the enterprise's complete, normal functioning, which has been undermined of late." Among other things, it independently concluded a contract with the Ministry of Transport of Byelorussia (just across the border from Lithuania), which agreed to supply the enterprise with fuel and parts. "I would never have believed it," commented a member of the administration. "I always thought that the main thing for them was their 19 rubles a day, and to hell with the rest."[35] At a Voronezh machine-construction factory, the director was misappropriating the factory's equipment and materials for his personal benefit. A small, poorly organized enterprise that was in bad economic shape, it nevertheless maintained seven well-paid assistant directors. Spurred on by the party committee, a bare majority of the work-collective committee called a workers' conference. It elected a workers' committee, which it mandated to investigate and restore order in the factory. The director was replaced through competitve elections, and affairs began quickly to improve.[36] At a Novosibirsk machine-construction factory, the workers shut down a co-operative that management had entrusted with the enterprises's supply and transport services. This occurred after a group of workers forced open the assistant manager's safe and found a contract showing him to be an employee of the co-operative which had been selling the factory's raw materials on the side at two and three times the state price.[37] At the VAZ auto factory, the workers first learnt from an interview by the assistant general director in the enterprise newspaper that, as one worker put it, "our clever managers had already prepared a packet of documents for the conversion of VAZ into a concern." In response, the work-collective committee declared VAZ and all its production the property of the work collective.[38]

Conflicts over power in the enterprises, that is over workers' self-management, are destined to grow as the economic and political disintegration of the country continues and factory and ministerial administrations, behind the backs of the workers, who typically suspect the worst, transform enterprises into joint-stock companies, enter them into "concerns" (independent association of enterprises), transfer departments to co-operatives, establish joint ventures and commercial banks with enterprise resources and funds.

The Limits of Trade-Unionism

Until recently, however, one could not speak of a self-management movement in the Soviet Union. There were only isolated conflicts over power and committee activity in the enterprises. The organized labour movement, which began with the miners' strike of July 1989, has been characterized by a basically, though by no means exclusively, trade-unionist orientation. After the 1989 strike, the miners transformed their strike committees into workers' committees, which united on a regional basis. Their main function was to monitor fulfillment of the accord with the government, Resolution 608 that ended the strike. The miners have also held two national congresses, in June and October 1990. These resulted in the founding of an independent trade union. Unlike the official union, which embraces all the employees of the Ministry of the Coal Industry, the new union limits its membership to non-managerial personnel employed directly by the coal mines or the coal-enrichment factories. The Fifth Conference of Workers' Committees of the Kuzbass, which (along with the much smaller Pechora basin), has been the most militant and politicized region, in September 1990 also set as its central goal the formation of a "normal" trade-union movement.[39]

For a movement that arose out of nothing after almost 60 years of very effective repression, these are impressive organizational gains. Nevertheless, this movement is today in crisis. It has not really succeeded in spreading outside of the mines and mining regions. The unions of workers' committees that have arisen in other regions consist mainly of small groups of activists, who emerge out of their isolation only when serious conflict arises in their enterprise. None of the organizations from outside the coalmining areas that attended the Congress of Independent Workers' Organizations and Movements in May 1990 in Novokuznetsk (which founded the Confederation of Labour) has anything resembling a mass base.[40] In the mining areas themselves, rank-and-file activism has declined, and the ties between the unions of workers' committees and the rank-and-file have weakened.[41] Many delegates to the Second Congress of Coalminers in Donetsk at the end of October 1990 were not at all certain that the congress's decision to found a new trade union would meet with an active or enthusiastic response back home in the mines.[42]

This is essentially a crisis of political orientation against the background of the deepening economic crisis. The attempt through strictly trade-unionist activity to protect living standards and labour conditions in a collapsing economy has reached its limits. The miners themselves have recognized that the government lacked the means to carry out certain parts of Resolution 608 and that many of those economic gains realized were soon lost to inflation. Moreover, in existing Soviet conditions, a trade-unionist orientation often leads to solidarity between workers and their own administration, generally at the expense of the rest of the population that ends up with a bill it can ill afford to pay. For example, the one-day mail carriers' strike on June 15 1990 was organized by the Minister of Communications itself.[43] And the second Congress of Miners was financed by the Ministry of the Coal Industry, which had its representatives on the organizing committee. This surely must raise questions about the interests being pursued by the various bureaucratic clans in supporting these movements.[44]

The miners' movement did, of course, put forth important political demands relating to the democratization of the state. But the basic question remained unanswered: what to do with this democracy if and when it was won? The most politicized elements (often those most strongly under liberal influence) have tended to advocate a trade-unionist orientation for the labour movement and, to the extent that they put forth a positive economic programme, a market reform borrowed from the liberals. But this is running up against the same reality that the liberals are now being forced to confront.

Representatives of the Kuzbass Union of Workers' Committees, which under the presidency of Vyacheslav Golikov has had the strongest pro-liberal orientation, participated in the work of the Shatalin-Yavlinskii commission that drew up the 500-Day Plan. This is a programme for the wholesale privatization of the economy and the establishment of a market system in which state regulation plays a subordinate role.[45] The Kuzbass union has been a strong supporter of Boris Yeltsin and the Russian Parliament, with whom it concluded a social peace accord in exchange for the parliament's support in creating a "zone of joint entrepreneurship" (free-trade zone) in the Kuzbass. But Golikov, in his report to the union's fifth conference at the end of September 1990, was forced to recognize the "deformations" (of the type described here in the first section) that were already occurring in the Kuzbass with the expansion of the private sector and market relations in the region. He appealed "not to leave these processes to themselves without the participation of the toilers. While defending market relations in the economy, we do not intend to allow it be bought up by existing structures and their functionaries." Yet he offered no practical proposals for preventing this. Similarly, the conference's "Appeal to the Toilers of the Kuzbass" observed that "the programme of transition to market relations and, in the Kuzbass, also the creation of a zone of joint entrepreneurship are on the whole seen positively by the toilers of the region. But at the same time, the shift of the enterprises to cost-accounting and self-financing is already causing job cuts and the closure of unprofitable factories. The transition to market relations will intensify this process by many times." But rather than question the wisdom of this reform, the document merely calls for the creation of "genuine trade unions" to defend the workers.[46]

The liberal orientation of the Kuzbass leaders is to a large extent premised upon their their understanding that the region is well-situated to benefit from the market. The cost of extracting coal in the Kuzbass is relatively low, since the industry here is comparatively new and the coal close to the surface, often allowing open-pit mining. Export contracts have already been signed with Japan. (Some economists, however, argue that Kuzbass optimism will be short-lived. The region is 6000 kilometers from a port, and the exports are being subsidized by cheap Soviet freight rates. If these rates were raised to the same world levels at which the coal is being sold, there would be no foreign contracts. How long will the railroad agree to subsidize the foreign-currency earnings of the Kuzbass coal industry?) The future, however, does not look so rosy to the Donbass miners. Their mines are old, deep — many are virtually mined-out — and their production costs are high. The transition to the market here threatens the region with mass unemployment and the extinction of entire towns and villages.

It is not surprising, then, that outside of the Kuzbass and the Pechora basin (which has export contracts with Sweden though Arctic ports), the miners' movement has been rather less enthusiastic about the market. As the inevitable consequences of a transition to the market, as envisaged by the liberal reformers, become clearer, their lack of enthusiasm is turning into alarm. After the publication of the 500-Day Plan, which calls for an end to subsidies and the eventual freeing of prices, dozens of mining associations and enterprises sent angry telegrams to the government.[47] A delegation of miners from the Yakutugol' Association came to Moscow to protest against the intended dismantling of the industry's central administration and the ending of subsidies. "Natural and geological conditions vary from mine to mine," they explained. "Therefore, they cannot all be equally profitable. In our association the average cost of coal is from one to eighteen rubles, but in Donbass it is 40 to 120 rubles. Without the centralized redistribution of funds, without subsidies, Donbass will not survive. ...Without centralized management, all sorts of misfortunes and shocks await the branch."[48]

Taking note of these concerns, the organizing committee of the Second Congress of Miners decided against endorsing the plan. One of its members, a miner from Karaganda, explained: "There are disputes in the collectives and in the organizing committee [about the transition to the market]. The interesting thing is that we ourselves participated in the creation of one of the programmes — that of Shatalin. ...But we wavered. Why? First of all because the hardest blow will be struck against the extractive industries, and we wanted first to see a separate programme of transition to the market for our branch. Of course, a part of the people understand that it will be necessary to accept certain sacrifices, but there are also many who say: why do I need that market if my interests are violated, if I lose benefits and job seniority? ...We are also worried by the fact that the realization of the Shatalin programme calls for a strong presidential power. Yet just yesterday, we proclaimed the democratization of society and self-management."[49] The organizing committee demanded the maintenance, at least for the transitional period, of the industry's central administration and subsidies.[50] Even the Council of Representatives of the Confederation of Labour, which was subject to strong liberal influence at its founding, also balked at endorsing the 500-Day Plan at its September 1990 meeting in Donetsk.[51]

The differences in orientation among the mining regions manifested themselves from the very start of the Second Congress of Miners at the end of October 1990 in the debate over the agenda. There were three main items: a report on how the decisions of the first congress had been carried out, the transition to the market in the coal industry, including a report by the Minister, and the establishment of an independent trade union.

Delegates from the Donbass insisted on allotting an unlimited amount of time to the second question. They felt their region was at stake and that trade unions would be of no use if the mines were closed. Delegates from the Kuzbass, on the other hand, insisted on unlimited time for the third point, since, they argued, whatever system the workers lived under, they would need strong trade unions to defend them.[52]

Though the vast majority of delegates were in favour of a new independent trade union (a significant minority wanted to democratize the old one), a split over these differences in orientation was narrowly averted only at the very end of the congress, when the new trade union was established. But the delegates remained extremely dissatisfied with the report on the transition to the market, even though the minister had assured them there would be no layoffs in 1991. ("If even one miner is dismissed," he declared, "you won't have to ask me, I will resign myself.") The discussion made it amply clear that although many miners fear the market, they certainly do not want to retain the old system. But the minister offered no new vision, only the need to ask the government for additional subsidies. The delegates responded with the decision to create their own commission of experts to develop a plan for the industry.

This decision was implicit recognition of the limits of the strictly trade-unionist approach that some of the Kuzbass delegates, like Golikov, were advocating. These delegates argued that the congress's basic task was to create a trade union whose principal function would be to obtain the highest price for the labour power the workers were selling to the "employers" (rabotodateli). But most of the delegates obviously felt that the new union could not leave the tasks of managing and restructuring their industry outside of its purview.

The Emergence of a Self-Management Movement

Although self-management has not played a prominent role in the miners' movement, even those leaders closest to the liberals say that they support the idea. One often has the impression that their alliance with the liberals is in no small part based upon a misconception (fed by liberal rhetoric about "people's enterprises" and "returning property to the people") that the market proposed by the "democrats" is a necessary condition for real self-management. In fact, the history of market reform in

Yugoslavia, which has had the richest experience in this area, shows that self-management poses severe limits to the free circulation of capital and labour, and as such is incompatible with the efficient functioning of the kind of "full-blooded market" that Gorbachev has said he wants to introduce in the Soviet Union. In Yugoslavia, as well as in the rest of Eastern Europe and the Soviet Union, the "radicalization" of the market reform is being accompanied by a retreat from the self-management idea and the restoration of full private property rights, including the right of owners to manage and sell their enterprises.

But although the self-management orientation has until recently been a minor note in the organized labour movement in the Soviet Union, it was never completely absent. At the May 1990 Congress of Independent Workers' Organizations and Movements, where the influence of certain liberal Moscow intellectuals was strongly felt, a minority "Block of 33" delegates (mostly from outside the mining areas and in particular from the industrial centres of the Urals), argued an independent labour movement within the broader democratic movement (a position firmly opposed by the liberals[53]) and proposed the following platform as a response to what they described as an offensive against labour's social and political rights: "In no circumstances to deprive the workers of the right to manage their enterprises and to realize the principles of self-management; not to allow the economic reform to be carried out at the expense of workers' interests, the reduction of their real wages and the spread of unemployment; to oppose the democratization of property relations through the sale of state enterprises to private individuals."[54]

The conflicts over power in the enterprise and the deepening suspicion among workers that destatization will in practice mean the transformation of their enterprises into the property of bureaucrats and "affairistes" formed the background for the emergence of an organized self-management current in the labour movement in the late summer of 1990. But the immediate impulse was provided by the passage in the USSR Supreme Soviet of a new "Law on Enterprises in the USSR" at its spring 1990 session. This law, adopted with suspiciously little publicity, supersedes the 1987 "Law on State Enterprises" that had granted broad self-management rights to the work collectives, including the right to elect managerial personnel and to participate in and monitor the administration of the enterprise through their elected work-collective councils. The new law was explained at the time by the need to facilitate the process of democratization and the shift to the market. But the activists who managed to learn of it described it as "depriving the work-collective councils of any real functions in management and in practice reducing them to nothing."[55] Under the new law, which said nothing about self-management, enterprises are to be managed according to their charters, which are to be established by the owners.

A week after the law's adoption, the workers of the main assembly line of the VAZ factory declared: "[We] are deeply angered by the fact that the Supreme Soviet of the USSR, on June 4 1990, passed a 'Law on Enterprises in the USSR', in secret from the people, without first even publishing a draft in the press and submitting it to the collectives for discussion. In essence, a gross provocation has been committeed against the toilers of the country. A law affecting the interests of every work collective has been adopted without any consideration for the opinion of the toilers themselves."[56]

In fact, the offensive against self-management, which had never become much of a reality anyway, had begun months earlier with the government's instruction to end the practice of electing managerial personnel. "The absurdity of these elections does not require discussion," wrote the management-oriented journal EKO. "This has already been recognized by N. I. Ryzhkov. M.S. Gorbachev, who first proposed them, has not expressed any opinion, but his silence speaks loudly."[57] The liberal ideologues have also participated in this offensive, though often hiding behind self-management rhetoric. Thus, Gorbachev's personal advisor, economist Nikolai Petrakov, has described the creation of councils of stockholders (who are not limited to the enterprise's employees), which will appoint the directors and make key decisions on investments, dividends and profits, as "a sort of step toward self-management free of higher-standing links."[58]

The convocation of the First All-Union Conference of Work-Collective Councils and Workers' Committees in Togliatti on August 31-September 4 1990 was a direct response to the passage of the new law. Attended by about a hundred delegates from enterprises employing some two million employees, it was almost completely ignored by the national media. *Rabochaya tribuna* (Workers' Tribune, published by the Central Committee of the CPSU) was the only central paper to give it any coverage, and this was really incidental to its main interest in responding to the challenge of Nikolai Travkin, leader of the Democratic Party[59], who said he would eat his hat if the paper published the conference's resolution critical of the government. The crew of the national news programme "Vremya" also came, but its purpose was to film Venyamin Yarin, an "honorary" worker-member of Gorbachev's Presidential Council. Yarin told the conference that the President had entrusted him with the mission of organizing the representatives of the work-control councils around himself and the Presidential Council.[60] Apparently, the conference's failure to respond to this offer explains why no news about it appeared on Soviet television screens.

While the conference approved of the new law's intention of increasing the economic autonomy of enterprises, it otherwise assessed it as anti-democratic, directed against self-management, favouring the arbitrary power of the administration and the ministries and holding back the processes of demonopolization and destatization. Some did argue that the work-collective councils had been subservient to management and, in any case, they were outmoded now that the government had adopted a policy of privatization[61] that allows for more "progressive" forms of enterprise management. The new law states that enterprises are to be administered according to their charter established by their owner or owners. Since, it was argued, the work collectives are about to become the owners, why make a fuss? If they judged the council to be useful, they could decide to retain it.

But that was the rub: the majority of delegates were not at all certain that the work collectives would inherit the destatized factories. Certainly this was as far from clear in the 500-Day Plan as it was in the USSR government's Basic Orientations for the Stabilization of the Economy and the Transition to a Market Economy. Both allow for all forms of property and neither makes specific provision for self-management, let alone for ownership or control by the work collectives. Indeed, if one goes beyond the rhetoric and deliberate fuzziness of sections relating to property and management, their entire thrust is against self-management and for the introduction of full private property rights.[62]

Accordingly, the conference demanded that the work-collective councils themselves choose the appropriate form of property for their enterprises. Specifically, they should have two options: they could either become collective owners, without any payment for the enterprise, or they could decide that the enterprise remain state property that would be managed by the councils. In discussing the first option, some argued for payment, since the enterprises were built, not by the collectives, but by the entire society. Others said that property that was obtained for free would not be valued by the collective. But the majority rejected these arguments, not least because the workers simply lack the means to purchase their enterprises. As for management of the enterprises, all were agreed that under both options the administration should be hired employees of the collective and work under its supervision. The meeting declared "impermissible the transformation of ministries into concerns playing the role of leasors or into joint stock companies." It called on the Supreme Soviet to suspend the law until it could be revised to take into account the decisions of the conference and it asked republican parliaments to ignore those provisions that contradicted the self-management provisions of the 1987 law. A new draft law should be submitted to a national discussion. The conference elected an organizing committee to co-ordinate the activities of the work-collective councils and workers' committees throughout the country and to act as their spokesperson. It was instructed to participate in revising the law and to convoke a full congress of self-management committees in December that would establish a permanent organization.[63]

This was the first organized expression of how at least a significant part of the workers see "destatization." It made clear the underlying differences between of the workers' support for market reform and that of the liberals. As noted earlier, rhetoric aside, a "full-blooded market", the liberals' ultimate goal, requires full private property rights. The workers, on their part, support market reform and the enterprise autonomy that it would provide as conditions for a more efficient economy and real self-management by the collectives. Although the conference was silent on this, it was implicit in its position that enterprises that become the property of the collectives (there is no question for those that remain state property) could not be sold.

Despite the organizing committee's meager resources and the difficulty in finding a large enough hall, 700 delegates and 300 observers, mainly workers and engineers, self-management activists from large enterprises that together employ about seven million workers, attended the Founding Congress of Work-Collective Councils and Workers' Committee in Moscow on December 8-10, 1990. Many of the delegates had to pay their own way, and some had even to brave threats from management.[64] But the main purposes of the gathering, to create a permanent organization of self-management committees, to reaffirm the Togliatti conference's position on the "Law on Enterprises in the USSR" and on destatization, and to develop a plan of action were achieved.

The congress founded the Union of Work-Collective Councils and Workers' Committees and elected a council of representatives from the major regions, with three co-chairpeople.[65] A heated debate took place over the issue of a warning strike at the start of January to support the congress's programmatic demands. Although a strike was not ruled out, it was decided first to try other means, in particular to act through the republican parliaments. The chairman of the USSR Supreme Soviet, A. Luk'yanov, tried to reassure the delegates that the the Soviet parliament agreed that the self-management councils should have the right to decide all the matters that affect the vital interests of the workers. He invited them to work with the parliament in revising the Laws on the Enterprise and on Property, which, he admitted, had already been overtaken by events. But not all delegates were reassured. Sergei Novopol'skii of the AZLK factory explained that "It does not depend on promises and declarations and not even on the intentions of the other side, but on our decisiveness. If they do not carry out our demands, we will declare a strike."[66]

A dominant theme of the discussions was the danger of quiet appropriation of state property by bureaucratic clans who are adapting the market to their interests. Much evidence, along the lines cited earlier in this chapter, was brought to support that fear. The Union's programme took note of the "critical situation in the country linked to the attempt by the administrative-command system to consolidate its power through the appropriation of the property belonging in common to the people and to leave the toilers in the situation of hired labourers deprived of rights." It called on the councils to convene their collectives to hear reports from the administration on its activity "including [that relating to] joint enterprises, small enterprises, co-operatives, as well as its participation in associations and concerns...and to stop any attempts to transform enterprises behind the back of the collective into concerns, joint stock companies, etc."

The Union's basic goals are the achievement of "legal guarantees and the realization in practice of the voluntary and free choice by the work collectives of forms of property and management," as well as the "drawing of work collectives into the process of managing their enterprises, as one of the main ways of fighting against the totalitarian system in the aim of overcoming the alienation of the toilers from power and from property and the liquidation of the cruel exploitation of the people by the barrack-bureaucratic state." Finally, the "Union unites the labour collectives in the aim of mobilizing their civic activity as a factor for the general improvement of the situation in the country, as a factor of constant positive pressure from below on legislative and executive organs, and, finally, as a factor that will block anti-popular actions and facilitate the precise and swift execution of plans and decisions in the interests of the toilers."[67]

The Self-Management Movement and the Socialist Alternative

From a socialist point of view, the programme of the new Union is not unambiguous, and it is worth looking first at some of the potential dangers it presents. As already noted, although the inalienable nature of the collective's property flows logically from the programme, this is not made explicit. More importantly, there is no overall economic conception. The Union clearly supports market reform (although this too is not really spelled out), but is this reform to lead to a system defined by market relations, i.e. one in which the market dominates and dictates its logic to society, or to one where market relations are a mechanism of economic regulation and co-ordination subordinated to the collective will of the society? It could be argued that the movement's emphasis on enterprise autonomy and on ownership by the collective can serve as a basis for an eventual restoration of capitalism as well as for the construction of a socialist economy based upon self-management, depending on whether the accent is on the market or on the collective power of the workers. If it is on the former, there seems little more reason to welcome monopolism based upon workers' self-management than bureaucratic monopolism; both involve the pursuit of particular, corporatist interests at the expense of the collectivity.

With Gorbachev moving to the "right" (in particular his attempt to shore up the Union and the disintegrating economy through extraordinary presidential powers based upon a greater reliance on the army and KGB and his appointment of conservatives to certain top posts) and the realization among liberals that "destatization" is not proceeding as they would like (that is, in a way that would give ample influence and rewards to the intellectual élite and to a private sector not dependent on bureaucratic whims), some liberals are already proposing the idea of an alliance with the self-management movement, hoping to dominate it. Gavriil Popov has publicly warned of two possible variants of privatization: "the transfer as property to the bureaucracy (along with the trade mafia) of that which they have, so to speak, already been 'managing' so successfully; or democratic privatization, with transfer of the enterprises to the toilers."[68] (A supporter of the "500-Day Plan," Popov no more really wants to see the second option realized than do the bureaucrats he is attacking.) Publicist Igor Klyamkin, has now also come around to seeing in Gorbachev the leader of the "revolution from above." Yelstin, on the other hand, represents for him "new [unnamed] forces"; Yeltsin wants a "different [unspecified] kind of market." Klyamkin laments the fact that nationalism cannot serve as a basis for "democracy" (i.e. for the liberal intelligentsia and its restorationist project) in Russia, as it does in the other republics. He suggests, however, that such a basis might be constructed from the struggles provoked by destatization, and he calls for "a broad bloc of employees and entrepreneurs."[69]

The hopes pinned on this tactic of harnessing the popular movement to the liberal programme in the Russian Republic by playing up the opposition of a supposedly democratic republican parliament led by Yel'tsin to the undemocratic central government and parliament led by Gorbachev have some basis. The tactic has a major trump in Yeltsin's personal popularity as an outspoken opponent of the establishment. Thus, the workers of the VAZ assembly-line, whose resolution was cited above, appealed to Yeltsin and the Russian parliament to defend their self-management rights against the central government. The programme of the December Congress called on the collectives to work through their republican parliaments and to push for the transfer of their enterprises from Union to republican jurisidiction.

Nevertheless, the liberals' attempt to win the self-management movement to their cause has slight chance of success: their market reform is no more compatible with a revolution from below and genuine self-management than that of the reformist wing of the bureaucracy. And these two groups need each other to realize their programmes, which are really not that different.[70] It was only a little over a year ago that Klyamkin himself wrote that the transition to the market could not be achieved democratically, since the workers are too attached to the idea of social justice.[71] Now, after suddenly "discovering" that Gorbachev, in contrast to Yeltsin, has embraced the "revolution from above," he nevertheless still concludes (not at all disapprovingly) that a Gorbachev-Yeltsin alliance is inevitable, though for good measure he adds that it will be a stormy union of convenience. As Sergei Stankevich, deputy mayor of Moscow and one of the leaders of the liberal Interregional Group in the USSR Parliament put it in the closing days of 1990: "The situation in the country is critical and by ordinary parliamentary methods, using only our newly-born and still ineffective democracy, it will be impossible to resolve our problems. Therefore, we need a more authoritarian leadership of the reform process."[72]

The liberals' feeble reaction to Gorbachev's shift to the "right" indicates that Stankevich's views are widely shared by his colleagues, or that, in any case, they can find no acceptable alternative to Gorbachev.

Of course, few would deny the need to restore some semblance of order in the economy. The Presidential decree reactivating and strengthening "workers' control" of trade (to be aided by the KGB!) should be seen as a populist gesture on Gorbachev's part.[73] But this measure is not really intended to change the relations of power in the economy. The unmistakable thrust of Gorbachev's latest shift (certainly not his last — the "revolution from above" has only one possible programme: the market) is toward bureaucratic recentralization, which in practice necessarily means strengthening the power of the economic managers vis-à-vis the workers. The All-Union Meeting of Managers of State Enterprises that took place at almost the same time as the self-management congress adopted a strong law-and-order resolution. In contrast to the workers' congress, this gathering, held in the Kremlin's Palace of Congresses, was addressed by Gorbachev himself and received broad press coverage.[74]

As the liberal-apparatus alliance becomes more explicit, so the liberals' chances of winning popular support by posing as the only real democrats and the most fearless enemies of the bureaucracy will decline. On the other hand, socialists, who so far have remained relatively isolated from their potential social base, are the only ones who embrace the revolution from below and put forth a consistent democratic programme. The self-management movement thus offers the potential for breaking their isolation. Summing up political developments in 1990, Pavel Voshchanov, political observer for *Komsomol'skaya pravda,* lamented "a mass shift to the right in consciousness ...The discrediting of the democratic idea is one of the political outcomes of this last year." By "democratic idea," Voshchanov, of course, means "liberalism." His use of the term "right" is more ambiguous, since it can refer to conservative "defenders of socialism" as well as to genuine socialists (these two groups are indistinguishable to liberals, who are in complete agreement with the conservatives that socialism has already been constructed in the Soviet Union). But there is no evidence of a shift in mass consciousness toward the conservatives, either of the Stalinist or of the Pamyat' (Great-Russian chauvinist) type. On the contrary, the emergence of an organized self-management current demonstrates the continued strength of democratic sentiment among the workers.

The creation of the Union of Work-Collective Committees is itself a sign of the weakening of liberal ideological influence in an important sector of the labour movement. The recognition of the need for co-ordinating their activities indicates that self-management activists are beginning to understand the limits of a corporatist approach to their struggle for enterprise autonomy. Such an approach, which has received strong encouragement from liberals, was to a large degree a spontaneous reaction on the workers' part to their experience with bureaucratic centralism. But this may be changing under the impact of what they have already experienced of the market and the threat posed by the growing economic dislocation. "Certain elements very much would like to split up the workers as potential owners," explained a delegate to the Congress from the Elabuga auto factory. "When they are isolated from each other, it will be easier to manipulate them in the service of alien interests. This is one of the reasons we called the congress."[75] Much was said at the congress of the need for a strong central authority capable of restoring respect for laws and harmony among the republics, uniting regions and establishing stable economic relations in a unified economic space. But the congress rejected Gorbachev's authoritarian solution. According to V. Kataev, a delegate from Cheboksar:

> Such an authority cannot be established from above with the aid of a club and decrees. It will be established by the work collectives themselves if they become the complete masters of the socialist property. In that case, as the resolution of the Congress states, the work-collective as owners are prepared to bear full responsibility for the results of the economic activity of their enterprises and for order in the country.[76]

V. Adrianov, co-chairman of the Union and a mechanic on the VAZ assembly line, expressed the outlook of the self-management movement in the following terms:

The work-collective councils in the enterprises were born of perestroika. But from the very start, they were separated from each other. Today the time has come to unite. Why? We are standing on the threshold of the market. We are not indifferent when it comes to who will get that part of the national property that will undergo destatization. The aim of our union is, through common efforts, to win the possibility for every collective to itself choose the form of property, to itself become, if it so desires, the owner of its enterprise without payment. Only the workers, having become the master, the owners of the property, are capable of stopping the advancing chaos in the economy.

The programmes of transition to the market that have been adopted contain within them the danger of violation of the workers' interests. Exploiting the confusion, the administrative-command apparatus is attempting not only to hold onto the reins of management, but to become in fact the owners of the means of production, creating concerns, associations, joint-stock companies. As for us, we are left the role of hired labour, the draught force of the economy. We cannot and simply do not have the right to allow that.[77]

If the workers are really going to prevent this, they will have to take up the fight for a socialist path of development. For it alone holds out the prospect of genuine democratization of economic and political relations. While the liberals form alliances with the apparatus in order to push through by authoritarian means a reform that would leave economic power in the hands of a small élite, the socialists emerge as the only real democrats. In a joint declaration at the end of September 1990, a coalition of left parties and groups in Moscow condemned the official reform programmes as:

> One more social experiment that would maintain power and property in a new form in the hands of the party-state bureaucracy and the "affairistes" of the shadow economy. The bosses of the [Brezhnev] period of stagnation want to change the form of their domination. ...And once again, the

burden of these transformations will fall entirely upon the shoulders of ordinary people. ...Yesterday's "irreconcilable" fighters against the privileges of the partocracy are prepared today to defend the power of the same nomenklatura, with the only difference that now transactions will occur in cash [pod nalichnyi raschet]. ...The slogans of justice, humanism, and charity, under which the democratic movement of the perestroika period developed, have been replaced by calls for a cruel economy, a firm hand, and the auctioning off of the nation's wealth. ...It is necessary to overcome the false alternative between totalitarianism and a monopoly-dominated capitalist market and to take our own path, determined by the creative activity of the people where they live and work and by the unity of their actions as a people. In this work, our sympathies lie with social, production and territorial self-management, though this too cannot be imposed from above.

Among the immediate measures proposed in the declaration are: the right of work collectives to determine independently, without purchase, the forms of property, management and self-management in their enterprises; the right of local soviets to manage land and natural resources, monitored by public organizations; the right of republics and other territorial formations to independently determine their status as well as the powers they voluntarily delegate to superordinate organizations; the abolition of presidential power; democratic opposition to the creation of authoritarian national states that refuse national and civil rights to their own minorities; the consistent introduction of full human rights, in particular the abolition of the death penalty, of anti-strike legislation, of all forms of forced labour, of the internal passport régime, and of the political police; the right of the local population through their soviets and through referenda to veto the construction of enterprises on their territory.[78]

Such is the state of glasnost' that none of the mass newspapers would agree to print this declaration. But despite the obstacles posed by the liberal quasi-monopoly of the mass media (tempered only by the minority conservative media), the profoundly democratic nature of the labour movement, and more particularly, the appearance of an organized self-management current within it, give new grounds for optimism about the eventual development of an active, mass base for socialism in the Soviet Union.

December, 1990

NOTES

1. *Sovetskaya Rossiya*, Oct. 10, 1990.
2. *Rabochaya tribuna*, Sept. 4, 1990.
3. The average industrial wage is about 260 rubles a month.
4. *Komsomol'skaya pravda*, Dec. 12, 1990.
5. *Trud*, July 11, 1990.
6. *Sovetskaya Rossiya*, Sept. 30, 1990.
7. A related term, less frequently used, is "bandokratiya" (from the word "banda" — gang), which one economist has defined as "organized crime that has grown up on the basis of bureaucratism and merged with it economically, socially and even politically." A. Buzgalin, "Est' li u nas ekspluatatsiya," *Sovetskie profsoyuzy*, no. 17-18, 1990, p. 26.
8. Many factors, of course, contribute to the shortages, but among these, monopoly behaviour occupies a special place. For an analysis of the role of monopoly in the Soviet economy, see V. Bogachev, "Monopoliya v sovetskoi ekonomike," *Ekonomicheskie nauki*, no. 6, 1990, pp. 11-22.
9. *Kuranty* (Moscow), Oct. 4, 1990.
10. *Rabochaya tribuna*, Oct. 9, 1990.
11. *Vechernyaya Moskva*, Sept. 27, 1990.
12. "Apteka gde est' vse," *Nedelya*, no. 41, Oct. 8, 1990, p.5.
13. G. German, "Ochered'," *Rabochii vestnik* (Perm'), no. 5, May 1990, p. 3.
14. Central Soviet television, Sept 21, 1990. At the same session, Sukhov also called on the leadership to be honest enough to admit that the better life they are proposing is one that will take place under capitalism. In that case, he suggested, the Communist Party's name should be changed to the Capitalist Party.
15. Soviet co-operatives are often ordinary private enterprises that employ hired labour. Asked in September 1990 what would happen if the state legalized private property, Artem Tarasov, vice-president of the Union of Co-operators, answered: "Nothing. We would simply get rid of the camouflage and call things by their names. [...My co-operative would become] a company with private capital." *Rabochaya tribuna*, Sept. 4, 1990.
16. T. Bogacheva, "Rasgosudarastvelenie — ne razgrablenie," *Pravitel'stvennyi vestnik*, no. 50, Dec. 1990, p. 6.
17. Such is the finding of a Moscow research institute. Personal communication by M. Malyutin, director of the sociological service of the Moscow Soviet.

18. I. Litvinova, "Zaslon spekulyatsii," *Nedelya*, no. 42, Oct. 15, 1990, p.4.
19. Private communications from German and Italian businessmen.
20. From Leningrad television, Nov. 5, 1990. Smolnyi, once a school for girls of the nobility, was seized by the Bolsheviks and other revolutionary organizations in 1917.
21. *Komsomol'skaya pravda*, Oct. 3, 1990.
22. *Rabochaya tribuna*, Dec. 9, 1990.
23. Non-Russian readers will find Soviet analyses that share this basic framework in the review *Socialist Alternatives* (Montréal) no. 1, fall 1991 (articles by K. Lemeshev and Yu. Sukhotin).
24. *Trud*, Dec. 30, 1990.
25. Soviet liberals oppose "common human values", that supposedly predominate in "normal" (capitalist) societies, to the "class values", which allegedly inspired Stalinism. This has prompted one Leningrad cynic to quip that the "common human values" of the liberals must surely be dollars.
26. L. Radzikhovskii, "Kapitalizm v otdel'no vzyatoi kvartire," *Nedelya*, no. 48, 25 Nov. 1990. p. 7.
27. V. Dudchenko and A. Karpov, "O vozmozhnykh posledstviyakh naibolee ochevidnogo i pryamogo puti k privatizatsii." Sept. 2, 1990. (unpublished document) The author's are leaders of the Leninigrad social democrats. Karpov is a delegate to the Leningrad Soviet and a member of its economic reform commission.
28. O. Savel'ev, "Politicheskaya situatsiya v Leningrade," Aug. 25, 1990 (unpublished document); O. Savel'ev, "Obsluzhivanie demokratii," *Informatsionnyi byulleten' Sotsial-demoraticheskoi assotsiatsii* (Leningrad), no. 24, Sept. 1990. This account is also partly based on conversations with social-democratic leaders.
29. *Pravda*, Feb. 8, 1990. This account is based mainly on interviews and a recording of the Janaury meeting.
30. *Za sovestskuyu malotirazhku* (Moscow), Feb. 5, 1990.
31. "Demokratisatsiya na proizvodstve: vlast' dela i vlast'...ch'ya?, *EKO* (Novosibirsk), no. 8, 1990, pp. 85-102.
32. *Rabochaya tribuna*, June 15, 1990.
33. The view is widespread among workers that "those people" do not work. Another contributing factor is the wage reform that began in 1987 and under which the salaries of technical and administrative personnel have risen significantly faster than wages. V. Pavlov and I. Yurchikova, "Novye usloviya oplaty truda," *Sotsialisticheskii trud*, no. 8, 1990, p. 89.
34. "Demokratizatsiya na proizvodstve...", p. 96.
35. *Rabochaya tribuna*, Aug. 15, 1990.
36. *Rabochaya tribuna*, June 15, 1990.
37. A.N. Shkulov, "Na potustoronnnei traektorii," *EKO*, no. 8, 1990, pp. 108-9.
38. *Rabochaya tribuna*, Dec. 8, 1990.
39. *Nasha gazeta* (Novokuznetsk), no. 33, Oct. 2, 1990.
40. P. Funder Larsen, "La Confédération du travail," *Inprecor* (Paris), no. 312, June 26, 1990, pp. 9-12 and B. Ikhlov, "Neklassovyi vrag," *Rabochii vetsnik* (Perm'), no. 5, May 1990, pp. 4-7.

41. This was noted, for example, by V. Golikov, chairman of the Kuzbass Union of Workers' Committees, in his report to the Fifth Conference on Sept. 29-30, 1990. See *Nasha gazeta*, no. 33, Oct. 2, 1990.
42. This is based upon conversations and on the unpublished proceedings.
43. *Kazanskii rabochii* (Kazan'), no. 2, July 1990.
44. People close to the (official) Union of Workers of the Coal Industry claimed that the minister favoured the creation of a new trade union in order to split the workers. While there is probably some truth to this, most of the delegates to the Miners' Congress that founded the new union were of the opinion that any further attempts to reform the old union would be futile.
45. A summary of this programme appeared in *Komsomol'skaya pravda*, Sept. 29, 1990. For an analysis of this programme and a comparison with the USSR government's "Basic Orientations for the Stabilization of the Economy and the Transition to a Market Economy," see A. Kolganov, "Doloi nomenklaturnyi kapitalizm!" *Dialog*, no. 17, Nov. 1990, pp. 41-8.
46. *Nasha gaezta*, no. 33, Oct. 2, 1990.
47. The editors of the popular weekly *Argumenty i fakty* rejected, without any explanation, an article by one of their journalists about these telegrams. This perhaps has something to do with the fact that five members of the editorial committee are deputies in the Russian parliament, which adopted the "500-Day Plan" with only one opposing vote, even though few of the deputies had seen more than a brief summary of it.
48. *Rabochaya tribuna*, Sept. 25, 1990.
49. *Komsomol'skaya pravda*, Oct. 4, 1990.
50. *Rabochaya tribuna*, Oct. 21, 1990.
51. Personal communication. The Confederation of Labour was founded by the Congress of Independent Workers' Organizations and Movements in Novokuznetsk in May 1990.
52. From the unpublished protocols and personal conversations. At one point, Golikov tried to reassure the Donbass miners, saying that Kuzbass had helped the British miners during their strike; why think that they would not help their Donbass brethren?
53. According to the bulletin of the Workers Group in the Yaroslavl' Popular Front, "Many intellectual democrats talk of the need for a union of the democratic intelligentsia and the workers. It sounds nice. But what they mean in practice can be seen from the example of the Yaroslavl' Popular Front. ...They rejected from the very start the idea that the Popular Front should seek a social base in the workers and they observed with gloomy apprehension from the sidelines the activity of the Workers' Group. The Popular Front not only did nothing for the organization of Yaroslavl's workers, but it simply does not want the creation of real workers and really independent workers' organizations. ...They mouth off about 'common human interests' and toss out stupidities from the tribune to the effect that 'the class approach leads to genocide'." From *Listok Rabochei Gruppy* (Yaroslavl') reproduced in *Rabochaya tribuna*, Nov. 7, 1990.

For analyses of the debates at the Congress of Independent Worker Organizations and Movement on this issue, see P. Funder Larsen, "La Confédération du travail," and B. Ikhlov, "Neklassovyi vrag."
54. *Rabochii vestnik*, no. 5, May 1990, p. 11.
55. *Rabochaya tribuna*, Dec. 6, 1990.
56. *Sobstvennoe mnenie* (Togliatti), no. 7, 1990.
57. "Demokratizatsiya na proizvodstve...", p. 85.
58. *Rabochaya tribuna*, Apr. 22, 1990.
59. Of the sundry liberal parties, Travkin's has made the most effort to court workers. Travkin himself, who rather dubiously claims he was once a worker (at present, he is a businessman and politician), regularly appears at large worker gatherings, spreading his message of primitive anti-communism. So far, he has had little success among the workers, who have generally been witholding their allegiance from all political parties.
60. In December 1990, Gorbachev disbanded this largely symbolic advisory council, one of whose main purposes seems to have been to co-opt potential opposition. Yarin, a metallurgical worker, had been co-chairman of the anti-liberal United Front of Toilers. He liked to say that after 30 years at the factory, all the property he had accumulated was what he was wearing. As member of the Presidential Council, Yarin enjoyed a spacious apartment, trips abroad, a generous salary, and, of course, much official honour. It did not take him long to come around fully to Gorbachev's policies. The United Front of Toilers, whose fortunes have been flagging since its foundation in the summer of 1989 (its worker support is quite thin), recently ousted Yarin. (According to Yarin, he resigned.)
61. "Privatization" and "destatization" (razgosudarstvlenie) are often used interchangeably in the Soviet Union. This confusion, of course, speaks loudly.
62. The "500-Day Plan" gives the work collective one month to propose a form of property for the enterprise, but the decision remains that of the state authorities. It also allows that 10% of the stocks "may be transferred" (this apparently also depends on the discretion of the authorities) to the enterprise for sale or transfer on preferential terms to members of the work collective (not to the collective as a group).
63. This account is based upon personal communications from participants and *Rabochaya tribuna*, Sept. 9, 1990.
64. *Rabochaya tribuna*, Dec. 8, 1990. Parts of this account are based upon personal communications. The still incomplete representation at this congress was explained by the organizational committee's limited resources. The original decision had been to invite delegates only from regional unions of work-collective councils. But since these had not yet been established everywhere, requests from individual councils were accepted. But the organizational committee still had no bulletin, and not all councils learnt of this change.
65. These are a mechanic-assembler from VAZ, an engineer from the new Elabuga auto factory and the chairman of the work-collective council of the Moscow Kauchuk rubber factory.
66. *Rabochaya tribuna*, Dec. 12, 1990.
67. Unpublished document.

68. Radzikhovskii, "Kapitalizm...". Of Popov, Moscow wags say that "he is capable, even very capable, indeed capable of anything."
69. I. Klyamkin, "Oktyabr'skii vybor prezidenta," *Ogonek*, no. 47, Nov. 1990, p. 7. Klyamkin uses the term "rabotniki" (very roughly translated as "employees"), which is even less socially defined than "trudyashchiesya" (toilers), the term usually preferred by liberals. Use of the word "rabochie", workers, is generally shunned, since it might imply the existence of separate working class interests.
70. In the view of A. Kolganov, a Marxist economist at Moscow University, "the '500 Days' are based upon a bloc between the 'new rich' and the party-economic bureaucracy on terms dictated by the 'new rich'. The Union programme calls for a smoother, less painful path of transformation of the bureaucracy into 'new rich', naturally, on its own terms, not forgetting to toss a little something to the people so that it, God forbid, will not interfere in this process." A. Kolganov, "Doloi nomenklaturnyi kapitalizm," *Dialog*, no. 17, Nov. 1990, p. 45.
71. E. Bérard-Zarzicka, "Quelques propositions pour une perestroika autoritaire," *Les temps modernes* (Paris), no. 523, Feb. 1990, pp. 11-22.
72. *Komsomol'skaya pravda*, Dec. 30 1990.
73. *Trud*, Dec. 2, 1990.
74. *Rabochaya tribuna*, Dec. 8,9, and 11, 1990.
75. *Rabochaya tribuna*, Dec. 6, 1990.
76. Ibid.
77. *Rabochaya tribuna*, Dec. 8, 1990.
78. For a French translation of this document, see *Inprecor*, no. 318, Nov. 9, 1990. The signatories included representatives of the Socialist Party, the Green Party, the Confederation of Anarcho-Syndicalists, the Marxist Platform in the CPSU (which has since split), the Committee to Aid the Labour and Self-Management Movements, the Social-Democratic Party of the Russian Federation, and "Moscow Memorial". (The last two organizations have socialist as well as liberal currents).

Chapter 7

The Strike Wave of March-April 1991

March and April 1991 witnessed the second major strike wave of perestroika, after the coalminers' strike of July 1989. These events give some measure of the distance travelled by the labour movement, indeed, by the Soviet Union as a whole, in the intervening 21 months.

A comparison of the two miners' strikes presents a number of paradoxes. When the 1989 strike began, there were no independent miners' organizations. Yet the strikers displayed a degree of solidarity that was remarkable for the circumstances. By the start of the 1991 strikes, the miners had already held two congresses and founded the Independent Miners' Union (IMU). Their workers' committees, successors to the 1989 strike committees, were organized into regional unions. Finally, even though the IMU itself counted only about 50,000 members, many official trade-union committees in the mines and mine associations had come under democratic, rank-and-file control (though the union at the national level remained quite bureaucratized). Yet despite this organizational progress, the 1991 strike began and evolved with almost the same degree of spontaneity as that of 1989. Moreover, its two-month duration and the stubborn determination of many of its participants contrasted sharply with the confusion and disunity that plagued it throughout. Indeed, the length and scope of the strike probably owed more to the government's stupidity than to any strategy on the part of the miners' leaders.

In 1989, the strikers shunned contact with the liberal movement and put forth mainly economic demands. Many, possibly a majority, of the strike committee members were Communists, including some of their most prominent leaders. 21 months later, there were hardly any party members left, while liberal political and ideological influence had become quite tangible in the miners' movement, particularly in the avowedly trade-unionist orientation of the IMU's leadership, who were fond of saying that the miners' basic concern as workers was to obtain from their employers, whoever they may be, the highest price for their labour.[1] Yet almost from the start, the strike became highly politicized, with its central demand the resignation of the entire political leadership of the Soviet Union. To add to the confusion, the miners returned to work essentially for economic concessions. However, these concessions were made to the miners, not as wage-labourers, but as *de facto* managers, if not owners, of their mines.

These contradictions ultimately have their source in the movement's failure to date to formulate a programme of socio-political transformation of its own that would correspond to the miners' understanding of their concrete short-term and intermediate interests. Although the conflict between the miners' interests and the liberal reform programme rarely plays itself out on an ideological level, that is, on the level of political consciousness (partly because of the sense of a lack of alternative among workers), it does manifest itself on the level of practice. The future shape of Soviet society to a very large extent depends on how this conflict works itself out.

The latest strike wave also marked an important, qualitative development of the Soviet labour movement. The price reform of April 2 provoked the first large-scale, intersectoral strike of perestroika and gave rise for the first time to the creation of an independent, city-wide and, to a degree, republican-wide, mass workers' organization outside of the coal regions. The economic and political strike in Minsk, that later spread to large enterprises all over Byelorussia, was the first such general strike since Novocherkassk in 1962. But it, too, was not without its paradoxes. Many observers had been predicting for months an explosion over price reform. But few would have guessed it would occur in a region where the political opposition (nationalist and/or liberal) was so weak and the state shops relatively well stocked. In contrast, attempts to raise the workers of Kiev, a centre of political turbulence with a much more difficult consumer situation, met with very limited success. Protest was even more subdued in other large cities like Moscow and Leningrad.

Background to the Strike

The deepening economic crisis dominated the period preceding the strikes. In 1990, the industrial production had regressed to the level of 1988, the first absolute decline in decades. Overall national income had fallen even more. Figures for the first quarter of 1991 showed that the decline was accelerating.[2]

But even much of what was produced was no longer available at fixed state prices. The shortages of consumer goods, already very serious, became even more dramatic in the fall and winter of 1990/1, although for workers in large enterprises, the problem was somewhat less serious thanks to the practice of selling consumer goods directly at places of work.[3] In the Urals, some factory cafeterias were forced to stop serving main dishes.[4] Of course, the scarce goods could generally be found in the private commercial sector, but only the well-to-do could afford its prices.[5] Moreover, since the fall, state sector prices themselves had begun to climb rapidly, as shops turned more and more (often illegally) to "contractual" prices.[6] The Trade-Union Federation of Kazakhstan, for example, reported a drop in real personal income of 6% in 1990, a trend that picked up speed over the winter months of 1990/1.[7] Meanwhile the official trade-unions' proposed law on the indexation of incomes to the cost of living had been "under study" for over six months, with no decision in sight.[8]

Supply problems in the area of producers' goods were also reaching crisis proportions, causing stoppages in several sectors, along with wage losses and even posing a threat to jobs themselves. In February 1991, telegrams began to pour into government offices from shops and entire factories on the verge of closing.[9] In addition, the government's decision at the start of the year to raise wholesale prices for a series of key producers' goods placed enterprises that could not raise their own prices, in particular coal mines, on the verge of bankruptcy and made it impossible for them to raise wages to compensate for inflation. In January, the administrations of the coal mines themselves brandished the strike weapon to pressure the government to raise coal prices.[10] (Whether they would have been able to raise the miners is another question.)

On top of all this came two very unpopular government measures: a currency exchange with outright confiscation of 20- and 50-ruble notes beyond a limit of a few thousand rubles and restrictions on withdrawals from savings accounts; and a 5%, virtually across-the-board, sales tax. The currency measures were not supposed to hurt people who could prove the legitimate source of their money, but the operation was so poorly organized (the government itself admitted that it largely failed in its avowed goals of reducing the monetary overhang and undermining the "shadow economy") that it was widely viewed as just another government deception, one, moreover, that further destroyed the credibility of the currency.[11] But if memories of currency reform began slowly to dim, the sales tax, popularly dubbed "the presidential tax" (though 70% of the revenue went to the republics), remained a constant source of irritation with the discredited central government.

All this occurred against the general political background of Gorbachev's conservative turn in the fall of 1990. The liberals accused him of having abandoned economic reform to make common cause with the hardliners. Gorbachev himself spoke of the need to halt the accelerating economic and political disintegration of the country — unleashed, it should be added, by his earlier policies, which, incidentally, owed much to the counsels of his now liberal critics, who had since crossed over to Yeltsin. But Gorbachev was indeed leaning more on the army, the KGB and the party bureaucracy (the first two being the only more-or-less intact national apparatuses). He made conservative top-level appointments, sanctioned military action in the Baltic republics, gave expanded powers to the KGB in the area of economic crime (a move interpreted by liberals as an attack on the private sector), introduced joint army-police patrols in the cities; and timidly reigned in glasnost', particularly on national television.

In this context, Yeltsin, appearing on national television on February 19, for the first time called for Gorbachev's resignation: "He has betrayed the people... In Gorbachev's character there is a striving for absolute personal power... I distance myself from...the policies of the President and call for his immediate resignation ...I have made my choice and will not turn from that path."[12] Until then, liberals dissatisfied with the centre's reform programme had demanded only the government's resignation, sparing Gorbachev. Even when Gorbachev rejected the "500-Day" programme in September, Yeltsin told the Russian parliament that Gorbachev differed with him only on tactics and timing. He blamed rather the bureacrats, led by the prime minister, intent on defending their economic power, as the cause of Gorbachev's wavering.[13]

This tactic (Prime Minister Ryzhkov had, in fact, always been a faithful subaltern of Gorbachev) was dictated by the liberals' need for Gorbachev as the person who could cement an alliance between them and the reform bureaucrats, while holding in check the conservatives, especially the really dangerous ones in the organs of repression. Gavriil Popov, the liberal mayor of Moscow wrote in December 1990 that the transition to the market required a "free régime of executive power". This freedom from direct popular control was necessary, he argued, because the Soviet people, raised under the old system, suffer from egalitarian values and the desire for social justice. Therefore, it would be ill-advised for the liberals to take power on their own, since that required popular mobilization to defeat the bureaucracy. Having thus come to power, the liberals would be prisoners of the people, who would cease to be a passive electorate (like in "Western-style democracy"), whose role is limited to casting ballots every few years for candidates who have no intention of carrying out electoral promises. Having become an active political subject capable of imposing their will, the people would be an obstacle to liberal market reform. Popov called instead for an alliance of liberal bureaucrats with "market democrats," excluding "populist democrats" and conservative bureaucrats.[14]

Not all liberals were happy with Yeltsin's "declaration of war" against Gorbachev. Many continued to insist on the necessity of a Yeltsin-Gorbachev alliance and opposed more radical, "populist" tactics. Some called quite openly for an authoritarian régime to impose the market reform.[15] However, the liberal movement had to do something. Having been elected in the the spring of 1990 to the head of a series of key soviets (including those of Russia, Leningrad, Moscow), they soon began to lose popularity in face of their inability to improve the economic situation.[16] With the "democratic" movement divided and losing popular support, Yeltsin and his colleagues decided it was time to attack Gorbachev directly. This would refocus popular anger on the centre and undoubtedly provoke a conservative counter-offensive, a time-proven means of raising the popularity of the target of conservative anger and recementing unity in the liberal camp. And the counter-offensive was swift in coming. In February, the conservative faction of the the Russian parliament called an extraordinary Congress of People's Deputies for March 28 with the avowed aim of deposing Yeltsin as chairman. The traditional Armed Forces Day parade in Moscow turned into a mass conservative rally, with numerous speakers demanding the resignation of Yeltsin and vowing to maintain the country's territorial integrity. This was immediately followed by a mass pro-Yeltsin rally.[17]

The Labour Movement on the Eve of the Strike Wave

Since their July 1989 strike, most of the collective actions of the miners had been political, or at least had a strong political accent. Already in the fall of 1989, when the Vorkuta miners struck over non-fulfillment of resolution 608 (the accord that ended the July 1989 strike), they issued an appeal to the citizenry, explaining that without a radical transformation of the political system, improvement in the economic situation would be impossible. On March 1, 1990, the miners of Donetsk oblast' (region) held a one-day strike to demand the abolition of the district and city party committees and new elections of the oblast' committee.[18]

The First Congress of Miners in June 1990 called on the government to resign, asking Gorbachev to form a new one.[19] This was followed on July 11, 1990 by a political strike in the coal mines, as well as in some non-mining enterprises, in support of these demands. The Ministry of the Coal Industry reported full or partial stoppages in 305 of its 574 mines. Besides resignation of the Union government, "incapable of carrying out the needed reforms because it does not enjoy popular confidence," the miners demanded new elections to the seats in the USSR Supreme Soviets occupied by deputies sent from the various "social organizations" (and not elected by universal suffrage), a mechanism for recalling deputies at all levels, depoliticization of state administrative and legal structures, nationalization of party and trade-union property.[20]

Two aspects of this strike are of particular note. The first is that it coincided with the 28th Congress of the CPSU, at which the party conservatives were expected (yet again) to launch an all-out offensive against Gorbachev. The strike was thus, at least in part, intended as a warning to the conservatives. The second is the consistently and radically democratic nature of the workers' demands. The liberals at this time showed no particular interest in a recall mechanism (especially not after their electoral victories in the spring) and made no serious attempts to mobilize the population to press for further democratization. On the contrary, as noted above, many of their ideologues were calling for a "strong régime" capable of introducing "harsh and unpopular measures." Liberals in high posts, like Leningrad's mayor Anatolii Sobchak, were complaining bitterly about soviet-type democracy and all the deputies who "hinder our [the executive's] work."[21] (Only a few months before, Sobchak himself had figured prominently among the "hinderers.") Yeltsin appealed on this occasion to the miners not to strike, saying they had no right to take action that would hurt the economy. (According to one report, this appeal was responsible for the decision to limit the strike to one day.)[22] The miners had good reason to be concerned with democracy. As one of them put it, "The transition to the market will entail the closure, not only of enterprises and production assocations, but of entire regions. How will the reprofiling, the retraining of workers from the closed enterprises be organized? Will they be protected? The fear exists that once again it will all be decided in ministers' offices without the miners' participation and without consideration of their interest."[23]

The Second Congress of Miners in October 1990 that founded the IMU reiterated the political demands of its predecessor, including resignation of the Union government (but still not Gorbachev). However, many observers in the months leading up to the strikes of March and April noted a deepening alienation among workers and the general population from parliamentary and electoral politics. Even the spring 1990 elections to local and republican soviets, the first under genuinely universal suffrage, were marked by a significant decline in interest and participation. Referring in February 1991 to a planned strike for that spring, a local leader from Vorkuta stated: "We would like to make political demands too, but let's be realistic. Would the miners support them?" In the latest elections to the Vorkuta city soviet, only two out of the city's nine districts had been able to elect delegates; the others failed to muster a quorum of voters.[24] Yet in 1989, the Vorkuta miners had been the most politicized cohort of strikers. A journalist who visited Chulochka, a miners' settlement in Donetsk oblast', in late February 1991, reported widespread political apathy. "In the last elections, they had to bring the urns to the houses …The miners do not care who is in power. As long they get their pennies, it might just as well be the devil himself."[25] In Volgograd, where mass demonstrations the previous year had brought down the local political bosses, an observer in February 1991 found that "the population is even more apolitical than it was ten years ago." Only pensioners turned out to meetings and demonstrations.[26]

There were several interrelated reasons for this, and first of all the accelerating economic decline, along with the newly elected soviets' inability to stop, let alone reverse, it. At the same time, doubts were eroding the initial enthusiasm aroused by the liberals' promises of a bright future from market reform. It is difficult to mobilize people who do not see attractive, credible alternatives. In a survey conducted among the delegates to the Second Miners' Congress, only 36% of the respondents said they were aware of the existence of a political movement capable of improving the situation in the country. 38% saw none, and 25% did not answer.[27] The subjects of this survey were among the most politically aware workers. There are limits to the ability to mobilize people around a purely negative programme of opposition to a common enemy. "Recently in the Ukraine," wrote on observer at the end of 1990, "the police had to defend some democrats who were trying to topple Lenin's monument from a group of miners. The miners' logic was instructive: if toppling something could bring more food to the shops, then the democrats would deserve a word of gratitude."[28]

The "market," too, was taking its toll of political interest. Mines that had been able to conclude export deals for above-plan production were importing consumer goods, including televisions, video players and even cars. "Barter is a noose around the neck of the labour movement," offered a deputy to the Komi republican soviet from Vorkuta. "Management doses it out in small portions, like bones: Fight over it and don't bark! ...They have bought the working class with this barter."[29]

When the council of the Kuzbass Union of Workers' Committees called for a general political strike on January 18, 1991 to denounce the bloodshed by troops in the Baltics and to demand, for the first time (a month before Yeltsin), the abolition of the presidency and the dissolution of the USSR Supreme Soviet, the majority of Kuzbass work collectives rejected this. Vyacheslav Golikov, one of the Council's leaders[30], attributed this to rank-and-file passivity and apathy, a view that would be belied by the strike later that year.[31] Indeed, many of the workers' committee and trade-union committee leaders, who were in closer contact with the rank-and-file, had themselves urged the council to call the strike, arguing that otherwise it would break out spontaneously. But while dissatisfaction with the "centre" and its policies was undoubtedly very strong, the grounds and the timing of the strike were off: an unlimited political strike in the middle of winter over events in far-off Lithuania, in which the centre's role was far from clear, did not make much sense to the miners. Besides, the declarations of two miners' congresses and their July political strike had yielded no real results, though their demands had been less radical.

At the same time, in the Donbass in Eastern Ukraine pressure was mounting for an economic strike. Aleksandr Sergeev, a member of the Executive Bureau of the IMU, reported on his trip there in February: "Everywhere the same question — when do we strike? ...Inflation has eaten all the wage increases won with such difficulty, ...and their income level is back to the starting point."[32]

Apart from the miners, most Soviet workers had still not experienced even their first economic, though strikes and the threat of strikes were becoming increasingly frequent as the situation deteriorated, particularly in sectors where wage rises could not be financed by jacking up prices.

Trud, the daily of the "official" trade-union federation, warned in February of an explosive situation in metallurgy and chemicals.[33] Strikes were also occurring among teachers, librarians, daycare workers, and in such Moscow enterprises as the ZIL truck factory and the Lyublinskii Mechanical-Foundry Factory (which makes parts for locomotive and railway cars), staffed largely by "limitchiki." All these are among the most vulnerable and usually docile groups of workers.[34] Conflicts with management over "creeping privatization" were also on the rise, though they remained isolated from each other, despite the recent creation of the Union of Work-Collective Councils.

The Evolution of the Strike Wave of March and April

It is not easy to present a coherent summary of the main events of this strike wave. Demands varied not only from region to region but from week to week and, to some degree, from spokesperson to spokesperson. It is not entirely clear which authorities were reponsible for the mines' administration and at whom the strikers were directing their demands. Nor do the sources allow anything approaching a precise idea of the number of striking enterprises on any particular day, since even the same source sometimes varied as to whether it included among the strikers mines that were working on the decision of the strike committees, mines that were only partially on strike, mines that were working but not shipping coal. In addition, there was at times a significant turnover among the strikers, some mines beginning to strike while others returned to work.

The Second Miners' Congress in October had mandated the IMU to negotiate a general collective agreement with the central government that would establish a minimal framework for the negotiation of local contracts. The union's proposal in the form of a draft agreement was sent to the government on November 20. Although the law requires a response within five days, it did not come until a month later and was negative. In this eventuality, the law provides for conciliation. The union requested it but received no answer. It notified the government that it was considering a strike. Again, no reply. Then the government changed, Pavlov replaced Ryzhkov as prime minister, and the IMU repeated the entire procedure. In asking to open talks, it made clear that its demands were not ultimatum. Still no answer. On February 11-13, a meeting of IMU delegates and representatives of the regional strike (workers') committees decided to prepare for a spring strike, sometime in May. Besides the government's refusal to treat with the IMU, there was also some concern about losing initiative to the mine administrations who were using the threat of a strike to pressure the government into raising coal prices.[35] Once the strike broke out in March, the view was widespread that it had been provoked by the government. This was certainly true, though it is doubtful that the provocation was a conscious one.

The "One-Day Warning Strikes"

The miners' leaders misjudged the situation and failed to grasp fully how much more difficult unified action had become as a result of the "march of republican sovereignties" and the disintegration of the "command economy." The mines in the Donbass and Western Ukraine had been transferred to the jurisdiction of the Ukrainian republic, which had earlier declared its sovereignty, at the beginning of 1991, and the miners soon after presented the republican government with demands to extend the right to retire after 25 years to all underground professions (and not only the most dangerous) and a 250% raise for miners and 200% for all other mine employees. The wage demand was based upon resolution 608, which provided for the correction of wages in correspondence with the movement of prices. While agreement was reached on pensions, the Ukrainian government said it lacked the resources to meet the wage demands. Moreover, it would be unfair to low-paid workers, such as teachers. After some hesitation, the Donbass Union of Workers' Committee on February 26 decided to call a strike on March 1. While the representatives of some towns wanted a one-day warning strike to be followed, if necessary, by an unlimited strike, others wanted the unlimited strike to begin on March 1. The decision was left to the mines. The meeting adopted a resolution that noted that the strike's economic demands were essential elements of the collective agreement the IMU was trying to negotiate. It also stated that no real improvement in the workers' economic situation would be possible without consistent and profound economic and political reform, including the constitutional enshrinement of the Ukraine's declaration of sovereignty, dissolution of the Ukrainian and Soviet Communist Parties and nationalization of their property, and new elections of the Ukrainian Supreme Soviet that summer. These, however, were not demands of the strike, which was to be economic.[36]

The March 1 economic warning strike that had been called by the Donbass strike committee against the Ukrainian government set off a chain of events that reduced the IMU's plans to nought. The response to the strike call was far from unanimous, although the situation was confused, with the first shifts in some mines returning to work upon hearing that neighbouring mines were not striking, and other mines stopping only later in the day upon receiving news that others were already striking.[37] According to the ministry, only 11 mines in the Ukraine stopped work out of a total of 248.[38] But these figures ignore the many mines that continued to work but did not ship coal. According to *Komsomol'skaya pravda*, only five of the 21 mines of the Donetsk Coal Association shipped coal on March 1.[39] It is evident, however, that a significant number of large and economically important mining enterprises did not participate. A scheduled mass rally in Donetsk was poorly attended.[40] Surprisingly, the most militant miners were located in a couple of "backwoods" mining towns, Krasnoarmeisk in the Donets oblast', where at least three of the seven mines struck, the rest not shipping coal, and Pervomaisk in Lugansk oblast'. They did not return to work on March 2 with the others, declaring their economic strike unlimited.[41]

Western Ukrainian miners did not participate in the strike. Nationalist sentiment was much stronger than in the predominantly Russian-speaking Donbass, and Rukh, the principal nationalist movement, did not support the strike, which it felt would harm the republican economy and impede the efforts of its sovereignty-minded, Communist-led government.[42]

In a related, but separate, action in Kazakhstan's Karaganda coalfield, the third largest in the Soviet Union, the regional ("official" but evidently democratized) trade-union committee, together with the regional council of workers' committees, also called a one-day strike on March 1 to support demands for higher wages, a change in the income tax laws so as not to penalize the miners for their relatively higher wages, and a republican law on indexation of wages and compensation for price rises. The Karaganda mines had also been transferred to republican jurisdiction. Participation in the strike there was much stronger than in the Donbass, reports varying from sixteen striking mines out of 26 (according to the ministry) to all but four mines, as well as some non-mining enterprises. Despite management's declared intention of prosecuting the strikers under the provisions of the Law on the

Resolution of Work Conflicts, a meeting of union delegate's decided to extend the strike until March 4.[43]

The Kuzbass in Western Siberia was quiet. At this time, delegates of the Kuzbass miners, along with representatives of the "official" Russian trade-union federation and the Russian government were in Moscow discussing the transfer of the mines to Russian jurisdiction. In the far north in Vorkuta, the miners informed the central government that they would strike if it did not agree to direct talks on their economic demands by March 7. In Rostov oblast', in southern Russia (close to the Donbass), one mine struck on March 1 and several did not ship coal. The other mines decided first to give the central government a chance to respond to their economic demands.[44]

It would take four weeks for the central government even to agree to talks. The disunity that the miners displayed on March 1 and the failure of the January 18 political strike call before it, as well as the known divisions among the miners, apparently convinced the central government that the miners' movement had lost its steam and could safely be stonewalled and scared into quiescence. It not only refused to negotiate but let it be known that this time there would be no pay for strikers. Management informed miners that they would be held legally responsible for economic losses and threatened them with loss of seniority.[45] Workers in other sectors were hurting as much as the miners, and the government feared that a more conciliatory line toward the miners would encourage the others to follow their example. It also calculated that if it could hold out long enough, the market reform and the accompanying decentralization of management would deepen the divisions among the workers and redirect their fire against their directors and local governments. Early in the strike, Pavlov told journalists that he did not intend to "play nursemaid" to the strikers. "Let the production associations and concerns sort out their own problems in conjunction with the trade unions. The government will act only as moderator, as they do abroad." *Pravda* commented that Pavlov was apparently under the illusion that the country has already made the transition to the market.[46]

But Pavlov's reasoning had some basis in reality. In Karaganda most miners returned to work after 36 hours, and by March 3 none were striking. With the USSR ministry threatening legal action and at the same time promising to open talks if the strike was suspended, the regional trade-union committee called the strike off until the end of the month. The regional council of workers' committees protested, but in Karaganda, it was the "official" trade union that the miners followed.[47] However, Pavlov failed to appreciate the depth of the miners' despair and their resentment toward the central government. The militancy of the traditionally quiescent "boondocks," who angrily rejected the admonitions of their regional leaders seeking a last-minute agreement with the Ukrainian government, might have alerted a more sensitive government. These miners told journalists that they did not want to be held hostage to failed reforms; they wanted what had been promised a year and a half ago. "Let them know that we have nothing to lose."[48] In their view, the government had tricked them in July 1989, since nothing had fundamentally changed. Reacting to the Donbass conflict as well as to the conservative political offensive in Moscow, the Kuzbass Council of Workers' Committees called a one-day strike for March 4, to be resumed on an unlimited basis a week later (when the Donbass miners were also to resume theirs) if their demands were not met: the resignation of the USSR President, of the government and Supreme Soviet and the transfer of supreme power to a "Council of the Federation" consisting of leaders of the republics. Only one central newspaper mentioned an additional, economic demand — the conclusion of a general collective agreement.[49] The political demands were more radical than those of the July 1991 strike and coincided closely with Yeltsin's, whose position the strikers undoubtedly wanted to strengthen. Although the Kuzbass leaders stated that their strike was in solidarity with the Ukrainian miners, this is far from clear: the Kuzbass strike was basically political and directed against the central government, while the Donbass strike was economic and its demands were addressed predominantly to the Ukrainian government, though the central government was involved to the extent that it still bore responsibility for resolution 608.

Unlike the failed January political strike, this time the Kuzbass miners did respond, though far from unanimously. The ministry claimed that only fourteen of the region's 101 mines were striking (and ten of these fourteen were striking only partially). Other reports put the number of striking mines at about 30, though some of these struck for only two hours. Others continued to work but made payments to a strike fund. Of eleven coal towns in the region, six worked normally. The miners that did strike — and this would be true for the entire two-month period in all regions — ensured essential coal deliveries to power and heating stations as well as to metallurgy and other continuous-process industries.[50] As in the Donbass, a few mines decided not to return to work the next day and when some of these eventually did, they were replaced by others. Surprised by this local initiative, the Kuzbass Council of Workers' Committees appealed to the working mines to support the strikers morally and materially but to remain at work themselves, unless there were reprisals against the strikers.[51]

Following the Kuzbass action, the Ukrainian strike began slowly to spread out of Pervomaisk and Kransnoarmeisk. The number of striking mines rose from nine on March 5 to twelve (half were only partially on strike) on March 6, and 30 (twelve partially) on March 7. Here too, some returned to work, while others began to strike, and a certain number out of solidarity refused to ship coal. The demands there were still economic. Pervomaisk, now with six of its eight mines striking, and Karsnoarmeisk, where all five were out, remained the stable centres of the movement. In an effort to reach a quick settlement, after first threatening criminal prosecution, the Ukrainian Prime Minister offered to transfer to Pervomaisk the resources of some other mines that he was planning to shut. The strikers rejected this out of hand, declaring that they would not accept a solution at the expense of their colleagues. They pointed out that the prime minister could not even say what the fate of the dismissed miners would be.[52]

The Donbass regional miners' leadership was a passive spectator to these developments, as it vainly sought to reopen talks in Moscow and Kiev in the hope of reaching an agreement before the deadline it had set for an unlimited strike. But both governments continued to take a hard line. Officials from the republican prosecutor's office visited the mines, warning that the strikes' instigators were liable to five years' imprisonment. Mine directors threatened to dock pay and seniority for each strike day. Coal Minister Shchadov warned the strikers not to expect him to lower plan targets after the strike to enable them to receive their bonuses, as he had done in 1989.[53]

The strike also began to expand slowly in Rostov oblast'. On March 4, four mines struck, including one employing 5000 workers. By March 8, seven were out. The others (there were 49 in the oblast') were awaiting the March 11 deadline they had set for talks. In this southern Russian region near the Donbass, the strikers combined the latter's economic demands with the political demands of the Kuzbass. But their call for the central authorities' resignation did not stop them from sending a delegation to Moscow to seek a meeting with the assistant prime minister in charge of energy. They seemed oblivious to the contradiction involved in seeking talks on economic matters with a government whose resignation they were demanding. Although they undoubtedly believed in the political demands, it is possible that they did not have much confidence they could be won. But they served to exert pressure on the conservative forces and added weight to the economic demands. But the government's position was at least as contradictory: having completely ignored the miners' requests for talks before the strike, it now insisted that it could not talk with them as long as they were on strike.[54]

The "Unlimited General Strikes"

In Vorkuta, eleven mines (of thirteen), struck on March 7, the deadline given to the government to agree to talks on wages, taxes and pensions.[55] The preceding evening, the chairman of the Komi[56] republican government had informed the miners of the USSR Prime Minister's readiness to talk if they refrained from striking. But it was too late. The miners did not trust the government. However, the smaller nearby mining centre, Inta, continued to work, except for a few partial stoppages, as did the largest and most profitable mine in Vorkuta, Vorgashorskaya. Its miners, which the others were now calling strikebreakers, had been by far the most militant in 1989. However, the mine had since obtained the right to export above-plan coal, and the miners did not want to lose their foreign contracts and the resulting "barter." The other non-striking mine in vorkuta, Severnaya, was attempting to follow the legal strike procedure.[57]

On March 11, the Kuzbass Regional Council of Workers' Committees declared an unlimited political strike. According to the regional government, 28 mines were on strike on March 14. By March 18, as many as 50 of the 101 mines may have been on strike, though even the regional council of workers' committees was not sure. It said it had adopted a relay-type tactic, with some mines always working to meet emergency coal needs. However, there were mines that remained closed for the entire duration of the strike.[58]

In the Donbass in the Eastern Ukraine, the March 11 deadline for the start of an unlimited strike was not met by an immediate upsurge in the number of strikers. About 25 mines were out on that day. In Rostov oblast', the number of striking mines rose slightly to eleven.[59] However, in a surprising move, twelve mines in Chervonograd in the Western Ukraine joined the strike. In addition to the economic demands of their colleagues in the Donbass, they called for the complete abolition of the USSR presidency and Supreme Soviet, and rejection of any Union treaty — all these, they said, were not needed by an independent Ukraine — as well as constitutional status for the Ukrainian parliament's declaration of sovereignty.[60]

On March 12, the Donbass regional strike committee met in a special session that was marked by divisons between the representatives of striking and working mines. The debate was not so much over goals, as over the means to attain them. Some were very critical of the strike, which they felt had been poorly planned and lacked clear direction. Some wanted to suspend it, since this was the government's condition for talks. But the representatives of the striking mines would hear nothing of that and reproached the representatives of certain of the towns for calling the strike and then failing to raise the miners. The meeting finally decided to appeal for an unlimited strike and called on work collectives throughout the country to support the demand for indexation of wages.[61] Over the next few days, the number of striking mines in the Ukraine gradually increased, reaching 80 (of the Ukraine's 249 mines) by March 18.[62]

On March 12, *Komsoml'skaya pravda* printed an interview with Pavel Shushpanov, chairman of the IMU, which gives some idea of the prevailing confusion. Shushpanov claimed that the miners demands were the same in all regions: primarily political — for the sovereignty of the republics — and only secondarily economic. In fact, it was only several days later that the Donbass regional strike committee joined the Kuzbass in calling for Gorbachev's resignation. The striking mines in Vorkuta had added political demands a few days earlier, explaining this by the government's refusal to negotiate and its threats of legal prosecution. But they maintained their original economic demands addressed to the central government, even while insisting that it resign. A few days later, the miners of nearby Inta joined the strike with the same demands.[63] But contrary to Shushpanov's claim, it was only the relatively small group of Western Ukrainian miners who at that time were striking, among other things, to support their republic's sovereignty. As for the Kuzbass, its leaders insisted that they were making no economic demands.

One of the strangest episodes of the strike wave began on March 13, when four Kuzbass strike committee members and Bella Denisensko, a member of the Russian parliament from the Kuzbass and assistant minister of health in Yeltsin's government, began a hunger strike outside the Kremlin. The four miners, later joined by three others, had come to Moscow on March 10 as part of a Kuzbass delegation to personally inform Gorbachev of their demand that he, his government and parliament resign. When Gorbachev, not surprisingly, refused to meet with them, the five, apparently on their own initiative, went on a hunger strike that ended ten days later on the insistence of the Kuzbass miners. Anatolii Malykhin, one of the strikers and a Kuzbass miners' leader close to Yeltsin, claimed later in an interview that the hunger strike had been completely justified. Nevertheless, one has to wonder at the intended role of such individualistic action in the midst of what was supposed to be a general strike. Its stated purpose was to support the Kuzbass miners' demands for Gorbachev's resignation in face of the latter's refusal to hear their demands directly and "if need be, [to receive] the necessary explanations," as if there was even the slightest chance Gorbachev would have accepted them.[64]

On March 19, Gorbachev met with a Kuzbass delegation led by the chairman of the regional Soviet executive committee, which was opposed to the strike. The delegation had no representatives of the miners' organizations. But while the central government insisted it would not talk with "political" strikers, Yeltsin and his prime minister, Silaev, met with a Kuzbass miners' delegation and encouraged them to demand the transfer of their mines to Russian jurisdiction. Responding to various appeals that he use his influence to persuade the miners to call off their strike, which, at least partly, was intended to support him, Yeltsin repeated that "the choice of forms of defending their interests is a matter for the labour collectives themselves." This was reiterated by the Russian Supreme Soviet that demanded Pavlov open talks with the miners. To convince the miners of the benefits of a shift to Russian jurisdiction, Silaev declared while in the Kuzbass that "the miners are perfectly correct in putting forward such high demands."[65]

The Government Agrees to Talks

On March 29, the central government suddenly dropped its refusal to negotiate with strikers and offered to begin talks on April 2. The only condition was that negotiators arrive with mandates enabling them to take binding decisions, hardly a realistic condition in view of the initiative displayed in this strike by the rank-and file miners. The government's change of heart was influenced by the stubbornness of the strike. Although the response to the call for a general coal strike was not unanimous, the partial strike showed no signs of abating and was beginning to spread to new regions and mining sectors. 169 million worker-days were lost to strikes in the USSR in March, with a total of 542 enterprises striking. Meanwhile, the economic losses were mounting, warm weather was still several weeks away, and the metallurgical sector and railways were pressing the government to settle.[66]

Izvestiya reported that 200 of the country's 580 mines were in one way or another engaged in the strike, but about the same time, a leader of the IMU stated that "almost one quarter of all the USSR's coalmining enterprises" were on strike. According to more detailed sources, from 38 to 47 of the Kuzbass's 101 mines and several shaft-sinking directorates were on strike; 45 to 55 mines in the Ukraine (about 21 in Donetsk oblast', down from a reported high of some 40), seven in Lugansk oblast' (Pervomaisk) and seventeen in the Lvov-Volynian basin of West Urkaine), that is, about one fifth of the republic's mines; ten of Vorkuta's thirteen mines and all five in Inta; and ten in Rostov oblast'.[67] On the other hand, all the mines of Karaganda were working, the miners having decided not to resume their strike after its suspension on March 3 in view of the preliminary agreement reached with the central and republican governments. Kazakhstan's President Nazarbayev promised to supervise personally the execution of the accord, which included a wage raise, a lowered seniority requirement for special pension benefits, the enterprises' right to dispose independently of 10% of the coal produced under state contracts and a licence to export.[68]

However, on March 27, the Taimir nickel mine in Norilsk struck, presenting economic and political demands similar to the coal miners'. A meeting at the mine on the eve of the special Russian Congress of People's Deputies expressed support for Yeltsin and the Russian government. The other mines and enterprises of the nickel complex were to decide whether to strike on April 3. Three months earlier, these workers had presented economic demands to the government and were still awaiting a reply.[69] On March 28, 3000 coal miners on Sakhalin Island in the Pacific struck, demanding immediate talks between the government and all the miners' collectives.[70] On April 1, four of five bauxite mines in the northern Urals also went out.[71]

On March 18, representatives of the different coalmining regions meeting in Moscow established a unified interregional coordinating council of strike committees (ICCSC). Many of its members were also leaders of the IMU. At a press conference on March 29, the council presented a set of common demands: resignation of the USSR president and cabinet, dissolution of the USSR Supreme Soviet, transfer of power to a council of the federation of sovereign republics, and the conclusion of a general collective agreement in the coal industry, and in any other branch so wishing, setting basic wages and working conditions.[72] This last demand covered, at least in general fashion, the economic demands of the Donbass and was a way of broadening the strike's support in other sectors. It was also intended to allow the IMU to regain some of the initiative it had lost since the beginning of the strike.

The difficult negotiations between the miners and the government held on April 2 and 3 resulted in a document containing the following main points: wages would be raised by stages until they doubled their present level by the first quarter of 1992, on the condition that output rose from 685 to 711 million tonnes in 1991; a collective agreement would be signed in the coal industry before mid 1991; the mines were given the right to freely dispose of 7% of their production (regardless of total volume of output) of energy coal and 5% of coking coal; wages of the highest-paid categories would be raised to offset losses due to the progressivity of the income tax; the right to a pension after 25 years of underground work was extended to all professions; extra funds would be allocated for housing and other social construction as well as for investment in production; there would be no persecution of strikers.[73]

The government was desperate for a settlement. Its initial offer to let the mines dispose of part of the coal produced had been dependent upon plan fulfillment. But when this raised a storm of protest in the hall — the miners felt that plan fulfillment depended on many factors beyond their control — the prime minister literally tore the document from his coal minister's hands and with a stroke of his pen crossed out the condition.[74] Had these concessions been offered earlier, they might well have affected the course of the strike. As it was, only 52 of the 195 present (only a part of whom were miners' delegates) signed the document.[75] The representatives of the striking mines immediately and almost unanimously rejected the accord, arguing, first of all, that the miners had not been fairly represented: only 48 of the delegates were from striking mines, even though the latter's number exceeded 100. (The Kuzbass had sent no representatives at all, explaining that its demands were strictly political.) As for the substance of the accord, they complained of the fact that wages would be raised only gradually and that even that was made conditional upon an increase in output and plan fulfillment. This was no substitute for indexation. Even more serious in their view was the fact that no return-to-work agreement had been worked out, with the consequence that the striking miners would not be able to benefit from the wage raise as they could not meet plan targets. On the contrary, their mines would go bankrupt. The declaration of the delegates of the striking mines concluded: "What has taken place demonstrates the true intentions of the Cabinet of Ministers and the President, of the whole system of power: to stop the strike at any price, to split the miners' movement, to condemn the striking enterprises to closure and their collectives to hunger and poverty."[76]

Gorbachev addressed the meeting at its conclusion and responded to the miners' political demands, insisting that the constitutional road to changing governments and parliaments had to be followed. In saying this, he glossed over the fact that the USSR Congress of People's Deputies that had enacted the constitution and appointed Gorbachev president had not been elected by universal suffrage (one third of the deputies were sent by "social organizations," including the Communist Party, the official trade unions, the Communist youth organization, the Academy of Sciences, etc.) or in an open multi-party context. Moreover, that there was still no provision for recall of deputies, this in a period of rapidly changing circumstances, attitudes and perceptions of interests. Gorbachev also defended himself against accusations that he had led perestroika into a dead-end, pointing out that the miners themselves had not yet come up with a programme for reorganizing their industry that they all found acceptable. He failed to mention that the government had never transferred its responsibility for running the industry to the miners. He also accused unnamed people of wanting "to play the miners' card" and of disorganizing the economy for political ends.

Gorbachev rejected the criticism voiced from the hall that the "criminally long silence on the part of the government [concerning the miners' demands] brought about the situation today," citing his talks with the chairman of the Kemerovo soviet executive committee. When another questioner reminded him of his promise of a broad debate and consultation before raising prices, he replied that he had been wrong to make such a promise, since consultation on a price rise leads to chaos. At the same time, he claimed that "everyone has reported": the republics had signed an agreement on the price rise, which then went to the Supreme Soviet. "Do you want everyone to consent to the prices and everyone to agree?" he asked. "That will never happen!"[77] Gorbachev had a point. But given the sad historical record of price rises in the Soviet Union and the present government's proven inability to achieve its declared aims, there was no basis here for blind trust. Besides, there was nothing to prevent a discussion of the principles of price policy. But any democratic discussion and choice of the overall orientation of the economic reform had long since been ruled out by the government. And in that, at least, it had the full support of the liberals. All in all, Gorbachev gave the miners little reason to reconsider their political demands.

The negotiations between the central government and the miners coincided with the special session of the Russian Congress of People's Deputies, that had convened on the initiative of the conservatives as part of an offensive against Yeltsin. As with all the previous conservative offensives, this one too ended in defeat: the congress established a strong executive presidency and set elections for June 11. The only unanswered question was the size of the vote that would elect Yeltsin. Soviet parliaments are not organized along real party lines, and in the confused ideological atmosphere of Soviet society and with the absence of party platforms that could orient them, the vast majority of deputies are guided by one basic principle: try always to be on the winning side. Most Russian conservatives had sensed which way the winds were blowing and were quite prepared to change sides.

The same congress voted overwhelmingly to recognize the miners' demands as just. On the joint initiative of some miners' leaders and liberal deputies, it decided to organize an interrepublican parliamentary committee of deputies and of miners representatives to work out a concrete plan for meeting the miners' demands.[78] The authors of this idea saw it as a way of circumventing the central government and even creating dual power.

The Price Rise of April 2

The failure of the government's economic concessions to satisfy the miners or even of Yeltsin's victory at the Russian Congress to affect noticeably the strike owed much to the price rise of April 2. It dealt a new, cruel blow to already falling living standards and greatly intensified popular anger with the central government. Prices of consumer goods and services in the state sector, with the exception of medicines, coffee, vodka, toys, clothes made from synthetic materials and fuel, rose 200-300%

(though such basics as rye bread, boiled salami and sausages increased by up to 400%). However, even these prices were not always observed, despite a presidential decree prohibiting the further use of so-called "contractual" (really, free) prices. The population had been led to believe that the government would compensate most of the price rise. But wage and salary earners received only a flat 60 roubles (though local governments and enterprises could supplement them), while the average wage was about 280.[79] The compensation for people on fixed incomes (stipends, pensions, social welfare), already below the poverty level, was also well below the rise in the cost of living. Savings in banks were increased by 40%.[80]

The impression among the population was that the government had robbed them of from a half to two thirds of their real income. This was supported by the chairman of the USSR General Confederation of Trade Unions, who stated that the minimum per capita subsistence level had risen from 130 to 320 rubles as a result of the price rises.[81] The immediate pain was somewhat muted, however, by the fact that many goods had long since disappeared from state shops and could only be found in the private and/or black market sector at prices even higher than the new state prices, while the purchase of more expensive consumer items could wait until the fall, when school reopened and the winter drew near. The price rise did not lead to more goods appearing in the state shops in the following weeks.

A week after the talks ended in Moscow, about 50 mines were still on strike in the Ukraine. In the Kuzbass, the number of strikers, according to the strike committees, had increased by approximately one-third: 70 mines were participating (TASS reported 50, with the coalfield working at 50% capacity) as well as three coal-enrichment factories and twelve mine-construction organizations. The workers of the "Bolshevik" mine appealed to their colleagues not to accept the government's concessions in order to avoid a split in the working class. The Kuzbass council of strike committees expressed its support for the efforts of the interparliamentary group, suggesting that it could become "the prototype for a federation council capable of creating a government of popular confidence and signing the Union treaty." One of the Kuzbass leaders, Golikov, even hinted that the strike might end once the group began constructive deliberations.[82]

By now, all the major and minor coalfields of the Russian republic had been drawn into the strike. In Rostov oblast', only one of the ten striking mines returned after the agreement. The Sakhalin Island strikes also continued, while several mines in the small southern Urals coalfield joined the movement.[83] In the Far North, twelve of Vorkuta's thirteen mines were participating in various ways and to different degrees (six were completely idle). On the other hand, on April 5, after eighteen days on strike, four of Inta's mines "suspended" their strike and were soon followed by the fifth. The Inta miners had entered the strike late, after considerable prodding by Vorkuta emissaries. They were discouraged by the divisions in the movement and decided that there was little more that could be gained. They were also sensitive to pressure from the local population, whose livelihood depended heavily on the mines.[84]

In the other mining sectors, the Taimir nickel mine suspended its strike on April 6 after the administration agreed to double wages.[85] But the Urals bauxite mines stayed out and were joined by a tungsten and molybdenum mine in Buryatiya on April 8, which declared its support for the coalminers and dissatisfaction with the government's concessions and the supply of consumer goods.[86]

But the most important development of this period was the appearance for the first time of a co-ordinated strike movement (as opposed to isolated strikes) outside of the mining sector and in a major political and administrative centre. The strike began on April 3 in Minsk, the capital of Byelorussia, when workers at the Kozlov Electrical Engineering Factory found that prices in the cafeteria had tripled. Since the administration refused to let them meet on enterprise territory, they gathered in the street, where they were soon joined by workers from the nearby tractor, automated lines and gear wheel factories. The basic slogan of the rally was "market wages for market prices." But there were also demands to abolish the 5% "presidential" tax and to reduce payments from enterprise profits to the central government. Strike committees were formed that day in numerous Minsk factories.[87]

On the morning of April 4, the strike spread to the automobile, motorcycle, engine and other factories, as huge columns of factory workers in blue overalls made their way down the main thoroughfare to the central square, where a rally with tens of thousands of participants, lasting several hours, was held. The base of Lenin's statue served as a tribune. The rally expressed its solidarity with the miners. Many of the speakers added political demands to the original economic ones: resignation of the USSR president, government, dissolution of the USSR and Byelorussian Supreme Soviets, resignation of the latter's chairman and new multiparty elections in Byelorussia. The Byelorussian prime minister was shouted down when he tried to address the crowd. The meeting elected a city-wide strike committee, headed by R. Mukhin and G. Bykov, two workers who were also members of the Byelorussian Popular Front.

That day an agreement was reached to suspend the strike until April 10 to allow the republican government time to come up with a reply to the demands. The government had also agreed to give the strike committee 15 minutes of live daily television time.[88] The same day, small rallies were held in Gomel, Grodno and Zhodino. On April fifth, except for some scattered strikes, mostly at the Soligorsk potassium mines, Byelorussia was quiet.[89]

Byelorussia had been the most politically quiescent of the European republics of the Soviet Union. Communists dominated the government and 80% of the deputies of the parliament were party members. The predominantly liberal and nationalist Popular Front had made little headway. This is why Gorbachev had chosen Minsk for a rare public sortie into the provinces in late February, where he spoke to workers at the Minsk Tractor Factory. Why then did the major protest against the price rise occur here?

Part of the answer probably lies in the fact that the state shops, where basic goods were sold at low prices, were relatively better stocked. The immediate effect of the price rise was, thus, more painfully felt here, and the sense of betrayal deeper — Gorbachev had promised "adequate compensation" during his visit. Byelorussia's numerous machine-construction giants were also particularly vulnerable to the "parade of sovereignties" and the general disintegration of traditional economic ties, since the republic had few natural resources of its own. As a result, the last few years had seen increasingly frequent disruptions of production with their depressing effect on the workers' morale and wages. Traditionally, support, or at least tolerance, of bureaucratic rule had been based upon the state's guarantee of a level of economic security. The effects of the Chernobyl' accident were also still being strongly felt in the republic.

In general, the very fact that the lid here had been kept on so much longer, meant that when the right provocation came along — and few issues are more explosive than prices in the Soviet Union — that lid would blow far. Only a few days before the price rise, a gathering of labour initiative groups from around the republic founded the Byelorussian Confederation of Labour, some of whose leaders were members of the Popular Front. The price rise would catapult them to the leadership of the new labour movement, and to a certain degree, give Popular Front goals a mass base. By contrast, the official trade unions remained in the background.[90]

A similar strike occurred on April 2 at the Bryansk Machine-Construction Factory (25,000 workers) south of Moscow, when the workers found they could no longer afford lunches at the cafeteria. Despite the administration's offer of partial compensation, the workers elected a strike committee, demanding a 200-300% wage rise, reduction of the size of the managerial staff, and removal of the party committee from factory premises. They also declared their solidarity with the miners' political demands. But the strike was suspended in the afternoon of April 3, as talks with management continued: the prospect of losing foreign currency earnings from the factory's Western clients apparently played a role in this decision. Similar protests during this period at the Bryansk Auto Factory, the Bezhitsa Steel Mill, the Baku Machine-Construction Factory and in many other places. But they were short-lived and isolated from each other. Even when they put forth political demands, as did the Bryansk factory, the strikes ended on economic concessions. The government's quick action in reducing enterprise payments to the state budget to allow the enterprises to subsidize cafeteria prices and its expansion of the list of consumer goods exempt from the 5% tax also helped to defuse the situation.[91]

The Byelorussian government also proceeded to implement measures to cushion the blow to living standards, including lowering prices on children's goods, subsidization of school and enteprise cafeterias, and gradual pay increases for industrial workers. According to the government, these measures would double its projected 1991 deficit of 3.5 billion rubles. However, they failed to satisfy the strike committee. In addition, the government reneged on its promise of air time. On April 10, a rally of delegates sent from Minsk's factories took place in the central square, although most enterprises continued to work. The strike committee demanded that the Council of Ministers open negotiations the next day. When this was rejected, it was decided to call a general strike. At a press conference, the Minsk strike committee cited the government's refusal to talk with it, declared its support for the miners' political demands, and added some of its own: "de-partization" of state administrative structures, nationalization of the property of the CPSU, equal access to the electronic media for all parties, a round-table meeting of the government, workers' representatives and opposition parties, formation of a provisional coalition government of popular confidence, resignation of the Presidium of the Byelorussian Federation of Trade Unions, and inviolability of the strikers.[92]

On April 11, according to the Minsk strike committee, 82 factories were on strike in the capital. Another huge rally took place in the central square. Preparations were being made for a republic-wide political strike. Scattered actions also occurred in other towns. An organizing committee was formed to organize elections to a republic-wide strike committee. But the strike was suspended for another ten days when the Presidium of the Supreme Soviet finally agreed to hold talks on both economic and political demands.[93]

After rejecting the central government's economic concessions and spurred on by the price rise and the reaction to it in Byelorussia, the miners in the Ukraine and Russia applied themselves more seriously to expanding the strike beyond their own sector. Most of the striking mines had been out for nearly a month, and despite contributions of food and money from around the country, the strikers' material situation was very difficult. It was clear that if the movement did not expand soon, there would be little chance of an outcome favourable to the miners.

A series of rallies in the Donbass appealed to workers in other sectors to join the strike. Teams of striking miners began to make the rounds of Donetsk factories to agitate for a citywide general strike. Small groups of miners also began to arrive in Kiev to picket the government and to try to raise the workers of the capital and the rest of the republic in support of their demands.[94] The Donbass strike committee, in conjunction with a newly formed Kiev strike committee, called for a one-day general strike and mass rally in Kiev on April 16 to coincide with the new sitting of the republican parliament. According to one of its members, this would serve as a prelude to an unlimited Ukrainian strike if the government refused to open negotiations on the miners' demands.

The strike in Kiev on April 16 was far from general. According to the strike committee, 22 enterprises struck, including some of the largest, as well as the local transport workers (the latter for economic demands). A rally of many thousands of people in the city centre declared its support for the miners and collected donations. Various speakers called for the Ukrainian government to raise salaries, cut prices on basic goods, cancel the "presidential tax" and index wages to the cost of living. Some also demanded the dissolution of the republican parliament, new elections on a multi-party basis and the rejection of any Union treaty, though most of the strikers merely wanted the declaration of Ukrainian sovereignty to be enshrined in the consititution. It was announced that a republican strike committee had been formed.[95]

It is worth noting that this strike was directed at the Ukrainian government and parliament, while the miners' demands, at least as formulated by the ICCSC at the end of March, were aimed at the central authorities. If the miners saw any inconsistency in this, there was no attempt to explain it. At the Ukrainian parliamentary session, the government outlined measures to soften the impact of the price rises. The parliament also voted a ban on political strikes, which suffered the same fate of most laws passed by the various parliaments — it was ignored.[96]

Although some Kiev workers, in decreasing numbers, continued to strike over the next few days, by April 19 all enterprises were working. According to one miner, a member of the republican strike committee: "Again our sacrifices have been in vain... The Ukraine did not support us."[97] The idea of a general strike was eventually dropped. One of the reasons was the failure of most opposition organizations actively to support a strike against the Ukrainian government and parliament. Both had Communist majorities, but they were dominated by the pro-sovereignty faction of the party. Except for the militant, but small, Ukrainian Republican Party, the main nationalist forces, Rukh and the Narodnaya Rada, did not welcome the strike movement. They preferred the threat of a strike to a real strike in order to spur on the Communist government and the parliamentary majority. A popular mobilization was something they could not easily control and it would hurt the republican economy. Nor were they very interested in the new elections that the strikers were demanding, since they had already achieved their goal of a liberal/nationalist-bureaucratic alliance. Some "democrats" even claimed that the strike was a provocation by the Moscow-oriented Communists. In Western Ukraine, Rukh openly agitated against a republican strike.[98] In July 1989 the Donbass miners had wanted nothing to do with Rukh. Now it was Rukh that was effectively rejecting the miners, frightened by their demand for popular sovereignty. Rukh's idea of sovereignty was more along the lines of "Western-style democracy" — sovereignty for the local republican élites.

The Ukrainian government, however, did open talks with the miners and mine managers on April 17. This resulted in a joint protocol on April 18 in which the government promised parliamentary discussion of a new consitution enshrining the republic's sovereignty before signing any Union treaty; a gradual increase in wages; credit on favourable terms to the mines; a guarantee against closures in 1991; compensation to the miners for lost wages during the strike; protection against claims by the mines' clients; television time for the miners' representatives; and the inviolability of the strikers. In return, the strike would be suspended within two days. This was rejected by the council of representatives of the Donbass strike committees as insufficient, since it did not deal with the miners' main political demands addressed to the central government and even condemned it as an attempt to split the movement. The council called for continuation of the strike.[99]

Parallel to these events, the Kuzbass and Vorkuta miners in Russia called for an all-Union political strike on April 17 in support of their political demands. The results were also disappointing. Except for some shops in the Kuzbass metallurgical factories, the appeal went unheeded, though on April 18, 45 metallurgical factories in the Urals staged a two-hour strike in solidarity with the miners on the call of their (official) trade-union council.[100]

As if to underline the strike's failure, on April 17, the Raspadskaya mine, the largest in the Kuzbass and USSR, returned to work after signing a protocol with the Russian government transferring the mine to the jurisdiction of the Russian government. This move was motivated less by patriotic sentiment than by the Russian government's promise to leave the mine three times as much coal as the central government was offering. The next day, a delegation of Kuzbass miners met with the Russian prime minister to discuss a general transition of the region's mines to the republic. Silaev told the miners that he did not have a lot of money but would untie the mines' hand, letting them decide the form of management and property of their mines and leaving them a significant part of their production. A commission was established to work out a procedure for the transition within ten days. According to one of the miners' representatives, the transfer would help to destroy the centre and speed up reforms. At the same time, the IMU declared that the strike would end only on the common agreement of all the regions.[101]

The strike's prospects did not look good. Unlike 1989, the strikers were not receiving wages now, although it seems that some mines paid advances to striking workers with money borrowed from the banks.[102] Miners' families survived mainly on the wages of wives, support from parents and savings.[103] Some aid was also coming from citizens and organizations sympathetic to the miners' political demands. A solidarity fund had been organized in Moscow by the IMU and the ICCSC. The Democratic Russia movement, a basically pro-Yeltsin liberal coalition, also collected aid, and food was sent from the Baltics and Georgia. Mines working at the behest of the strike committees also contributed. Even mines that refused to strike offered money, though, at least according to one report, it was rejected.[104] But this fell far short of what was needed. According to A. Sergeev, deputy chairman of the IMU executive bureau, there were half a million rubles in the union's account in the second week of April, while by the most modest estimates, the strikers required 20 million. By May 15, when the strike had ended, 2.35 million rubles had been paid out to strikers from the solidarity fund.[105]

Around this time, members of the IMU and ICCSC leadership signed an agreement with the chairman of the Union of Co-operators and Other Non-State Enterprises (UCNE) (sic) that raised a few eyebrows. This private entrepreneurs' organization recognized the strikers' political demands as necessary conditions for economic change, including the economic independence of enterprises, "de-statization" and privatization. If the strike ended in defeat, stated the document, this would have a negative effect not only on the strikers, but also on the entrepreneurial sector and all of society. The UCNE estimated that the strikers needed 100 million rubles and committed itself to giving this sum in stages, beginning with 10 million. It obviously also had its eye on the coal that the mines would be exporting and generously expressed its readiness to co-operate with the mines in creating new economic structures and in the area of foreign trade. This document is all the more curious in that it implied that the effective owners of that coal were the miners. Neither management nor the ministry took part drafting or signing it. On their part, the miners' organizations pledged to continue the strike until its political demands were won. In the end, it seems that neither side lived up to the bargain: the strike ended without winning the political demands, and a May 12 report on the state of the funds of the two miners' organizations showed total receipts from all sources at only 5.037 million rubles. Malykhin, one of the two signatories of the document on the part of the miners' organizations, in an interview published on April 23 even denied any knowledge of the 100 million, claiming that the co-operators had agreed to give a mere 100,000 rubles.[106]

Another abortive joint initiative with liberal forces was the interparliamentary committee, which some miners' leaders had been promoting vigorously in their declarations. On April 22, deputies from the parliaments of ten republics met in Moscow, but spent most of their time arguing about the relations among the future sovereign republics. Some wanted a federal structure, while others insisted on complete independence for republics, which would merely consult each other. The meeting did, however, express its support for the miners' demands and for the creation of a roundtable of political forces to create a government of national confidence for the transition to real sovereignty in the republics.[107] The very next day, Yeltsin and Gorbachev would announce their new alliance, completely undermining the interparliamentary initiative. Yeltsin had not bothered to inform the miners of his negotiations with Gorbachev.

Meanwhile, in Byelorussia, talks between the strike committee leaders and the government broke down. Some of the key economic demands had been met, incuding a salary raise, abolition of the 5% sales tax on a variety of goods, improved food for children affected by the Chernobyl' disaster, and even a cut in the government's administrative staff. But the strike committee was insisting on its political demands, in particular the convocation of a special session of parliament to consider its demands for new elections on a multi-party basis, depoliticization of state administrative and juridical structures, nationalization of Communist Party property for the benefit of victims of Chrenobyl', a law allowing private ownership of land, and enforcement of the declaration of sovereignty. The government, however, refused to convoke the parliament before its scheduled May 21 sitting, arguing that time was needed to prepare draft laws on those issues.[108]

The strike committee called for a general republican strike on April 23 to demand the convocation of a special session of the Supreme Soviet. The Minsk strike committee reported 42 fully or partially striking factories. The workers of the motor vehicle factory, who had just been granted a large pay raise, did not strike. But they hung a banner on the factory gate expressing solidarity with the strikers, which did not prevent the latter from dubbing them "sausage-eaters" (kolbasniki). Strikes also occurred in Mogilev (five factories), Vitebsk (three), Borisov (four), Liga (six), at the large truck factory in Zhodino, in Orsha, a key railroad junction, where the strike was general, and in several large factories in smaller towns. In Soligorsk, the potassium miners had been out since April 17.

On April 24, the situation grew more tense, as up to a hundred thousand people gathered in the centre of Minsk and the Orsha strike committee shut down movement on the Moscow-Brest and Leningrad-Kiev mainlines for several hours. On April 25, the strike continued in Minsk, while the Orsha strikers blockaded the railway junction for twelve hours. But the Byelorussian Supreme Soviet still did not budge. Citing the danger of the use of force against Orsha's workers and bloodshed, on the evening of April 25, the Minsk strike committee voted to suspend the strike until the scheduled meeting of the Supreme Soviet on May 21. Some Minsk enterprises, including the motor and tractor factories rejected this decision and continued to strike, complaining, not without justification, that the strike was being called off at its most decisive moment. Some spoke of a betrayal of Orsha. However, by April 27, most of the strikers were back to work.[109]

The suspension of the Byelorussian strike was merely one more indication that the striking miners could not count on their political strike spreading to other sectors, although this was happening to a very limited degree, with strikes at the Anzherskii Transport Agency in the Kuzbass, the Donetsk Textile Mill and some machine-construction plants in the Urals. But these strikes did not change the general picture of a working class that in its large majority was not prepared to follow the miners' example. Even the general, one-hour economic warning strike called by the (official) Russian trade-union federation on April 26 and endorsed by Democratic Russia fell far short of its organizers' expectations. Of 160,000 enterprises in the Russian republic, only some 200 actually held a one-hour strike. The others that participated held meetings outside of work hours.[110] In these circumstances, the miners naturally began to think of cutting their economic losses. On April 22, three mines of the Kuznetskugol' Concern followed Raspadskaya's example and left the strike. The bauxite miners in the Urals also ended their strike, citing the threat to the aluminum plants upon which the local economy heavily depended.[111]

Yet despite these defections, the economic concessions by the Ukrainian government and the fixing of the conditions for transfer of the Russian mines to republican jurisdiction, the bulk of strikers were not returning to work. On April 23, according to the Postfactum press agency, a total of 61 mines were still on strike in Ukraine, and 56 in Russia (43 in the Kuzbass).[112] The strike committees themselves put the number of striking mines on April 22 at 157: 49 in the Kuzbass, 21 in West Ukraine, 55 in the

Donbass, ten in Vorkuta, ten in the Urals, five on Sakhalin Island, five in Krasnoyarak, two at the Kizelugol' Association. TASS reported on April 25 that there were no signs of compromise on political demands in the Kuzbass.[113]

The "Accord of Ten"

A factor that greatly accelerated the end of the miners' strike and which undoubtedly played a role in the Byelorussian strike committee's decision to suspend the strike was the publication on April 24 of a joint declaration by Gorbachev and the leaders of nine republics entitled "Immediate Measures for the Stabilization of the Situation in the Country and Overcoming the Crisis." This accord, reached at secret talks outside of Moscow on April 23, marked, in effect, a restoration of the uneasy alliance between Yeltsin and Gorbachev that the latter had broken off in the fall of 1990. The declaration provided for a new union treaty within six months, which would "radically increase the role of the union republics," and a new constitution based upon that treaty, to be followed by new elections to the Soviet parliament and, presumably, to the presidency. It was left to the individual republics to decide if they wished to remain in the union, though those who chose to leave were forewarned that they would have to fend for themselves economically. In the interim, the existing laws and constitution were to be enforced; measures would be taken to soften the impact of the price increase; and a "special work régime" would be introduced into all the basic branches, as well as on the railroads and in consumer goods industries. The ten signatories called on the miners and all other strikers to return to work and to make up the losses, declaring that it was "unacceptable to try to achieve political goals by inciting to civil disobedience, strikes and appeals to overthrow the political authorities."[114]

In Vorkuta, the strike committee decided to call off the strike on April 27 after receiving word from Moscow of an agreement to transfer their mines to the Russian republic. A spokesman stated that the miners reserved the right to resume the strike if the conditions of transfer did not satisfy them and that they were not renouncing their political demands, although, in practice, of course, they were. Four mines did not agree with this decision and continued to strike.[115] Also on April 27, the miners in Mezhdurechensk, the largest coal town in the Kuzbass, ended their strike. But the Kuzbass strike committee still reported 77 mines on strike on April

29 (TASS reported 40). By then, the miners had also removed over 60 party commitees from the territory of their mines.[116] On April 26, after striking for nearly two months, the miners of Krasnoarmeisk in the Donbass returned to work, followed by seven mines in Donetsk, Makeevka, and Selidovo, and six in Western Ukraine on April 29. The Ukrainian government reported 37 mines still striking on April 30.[117] The Byelorussian potassium miners, who had been striking for over a week, also returned on April 28.[118]

The initial reaction among many of the miners' leaders to the "accord of ten" was one of shock and betrayal: they had been striking for close to two months for Gorbachev's removal, which Yeltsin himself had first demanded in February, and Yeltsin had not even informed them that he was negotiating with Gorbachev. Moreover, the "special work régime" sounded very much like martial law. "Of course, this accord can be interpeted in different ways," offered Aleksandr Kriger, co-chairman of the ICCSC, "but I think that Yeltsin betrayed us. With this step, Boris Nikolaevich has severely lowered his standing." Some leaders were saying that he had encouraged the strikes as a means to put pressure on Gorbachev in order to strengthen his own power and when he got what he wanted, without consulting the miners, he quickly shifted positions.[119] The ICCSC asked for a meeting with Yeltsin, but he chose to meet only with two Kuzbass representatives, Golikov and Malykhin, who were close to him politically. Meanwhile, telegrams began to pour in from the regions, and especially the Kuzbass, demanding an explanation of the "special labour régime" and of the agreement generally. Yeltsin finally decided to go out to the Kuzbass on April 30. When the miners' leaders in Moscow learnt of this, representatives of the Kuzbass and Rostov strike committees (but none from the Ukraine) decided to follow.[120]

Upon arriving in the Kuzbass, Yeltsin explained to the miners that they were deeply mistaken if they thought he was asking them to end their strike (though his signature figured on a document calling for just that). That was their own affair. Yes, he had called for Gorbachev's resignation in February because the latter was in practice assuming the leadership of a conservative offensive. But the opposition movement had succeeded in dissuading Gorbachev from this path. Now he should be given a last chance. Russia had gained much more from the new accord than the centre: there was recognition of its sovereignty and provision for new elections to the Soviet parliament. The centre would retain a mere three or four functions. The army, KGB and Ministry of Internal Affairs would be de-politicized. New elections would be held to the presidency. As for the "special work régime," Yeltsin declared that he had not approved any prohibition of strikes. The "special régime" should rather be directed at creating conditions for efficient work: special financing and supply arrangements, as well as guarantees of the miners' social rights, including stable living standards, but also, of course, unswerving fulfillment by the collective and the government of their respective obligations.[121]

Yeltsin knew that the miners are very practical people and that they wanted concrete results. Accordingly, he placed his main emphasis on the transfer of the coal mines to Russian jurisdiction and what it would give the miners. He had brought with him the draft document, which he presented to the regional strike committee as a great victory. Their initial reaction was less than delighted. After two days of hard negotiations, it was agreed that the mines would keep from 50 to 70% of their production to dispose of freely. The mines would receive full economic autonomy, including the right to decide the form of management and property of the enterprise. While affirming the principle of a gradual transition to market prices, the document provided for the maintainance of state purchase prices tailored to the cost of extraction in the individual mines in the interval. Instead of the Union subsidies, the mines would keep what they until now had paid into the Union budget. Subsidies to cover current expenses would be gradually phased out and replaced by the mines' earnings from exports as well as the additional money resulting from their lightened tax burden. The state's participation in the development of the coal industry was recognized as necessary but would henceforth take the form of a special system of credits rather than direct investment. The government also undertook to organize work on a collective agreement taking into account all the above changes.[122]

The End of the Strike Wave

On May 1, at a demonstration in Novokunetsk, before a crowd of 10,000, Yeltsin signed the document, declaring: "Here is recognition of the demands of the miners, of our new relations, the norms of transfer to Russia and mutual obligations. ...This is a big step, and for its sake it was worth coming out here to Novokuznetsk to be with you on May 1. This is a document of solidarity of the toilers of Russia."[123] Yeltsin's signature notwithstanding, the Kuzbass strike committee decided to wait until publication of a joint resolution by the USSR and Russian governments on the transfer that was to be signed on May 5 before raising the issue of suspending the strike. On May 5, as many as 51 Kuzbass mines were still on strike, since the document had not yet been signed. On May 8, with 30 mines still not working, it finally arrived in the Kuzbass. The strike committee decided to end the strike on May 10 with the provison that it would be resumed on July 11 (the anniversary of 1989 strike) if the "accord of ten" and the documents on the transfer were not implemented. By May 10, only one Kuzbass mine was striking, Taibinskaya in Kiselevsk, where the workers were demanding new elections of the director. In Vorkuta, where the strike had been called on April 27, it was resumed a few days later, when the strike committee decided that its earlier decision had been hasty, since the agreement between the Union and Russian governments had not yet been signed. It was only on May 10 that the strike was suspended again, though one mine continued to strike for new elections to the post of director. In the Ukraine, where there were no documents to await, all but two mines were working on May 5.[124]

On May 18, a conference of Byelorussia's strike committees discussed the demands to present to the opening of the Supreme Soviet on May 21. It was decided not to make economic demands, since truly effective changes in the economy depended primarily on changes in the political structures. But these changes should be achieved by constitutional means. Among the many demands, four were given priority: putting into practice the declaration of Byelorussian sovereignty, which should be given constitutional status, "departization" of all state administrative and legal structures on Byelorussian territory, inviolability of political strikers, and fifteen minutes daily television and radio time for strike commmittee representatives. A general strike would be called on May 22 if these items were not included in the agenda of the Supreme Soviet. If the items were included but not satisfactorily resolved, a strike would occur at the end of May.[125] Among the other demands were a law guaranteeing equal voting rights, cancellation of the 3% sales tax, wage and pension rises, full compensation for the price rises in state stores, nationalization of party property and its use for financing the resettlement of Chernobyl' victims as well as for education and health care, abolition of all privileges of members of the party and government apparatuses, an end to party control of the mass media and replacement of the head of Byelorussian television, accused of discrimination on the basis of ideology.[126]

Already on the eve of the Supreme Soviet session, the workers of the Minsk automobile factory held a one-day strike to press for the removal of the party and Komsomol cells from enterprise territory.[127] The parliament's opening was met by a demonstration of representatives of work collectives of Minsk and other cities. Although the demands were placed on the session's agenda, the strike committee complained that this was merely a *pro forma* gesture and that, in fact, the demands had been rejected. Moreover, the parliament even refused to let a representative of the strike committee address it. A strike was called.[128]

On May 22, columns of workers again marched from their enterprises to the city centre. But not all enterprises in Minsk participated, including the electrotechnical works, the motorcycle and bicycle factory and a number of others large factories. On May 23, only eleven enterprises were on strike in the republic, and none in Minsk. Moreover, these were local strikes protesting administrative reprisals. The strike committee's hesitation in April had let the moment pass. The situation had changed, and the workers were not ready now to pursue the political strike. In face of this, the strike committee suspended the strike and decided to organize a petition campaign to express non-confidence in the Supreme Soviet and demand a new law on democratic elections and the dropping of plans for a republican presidency — given the weakness of the opposition, it was feared this would lead to a dictatorship.[129]

Conclusions and Perspectives

A meeting of the Kuzbass council of strike committees on May 14 concluded that although the major political demands of the almost two-month strike had not been won, the results could nevertheless be considered satisfactory. However, the spokesmen of several city strike committees, in particular those of Kemerovo and Leninsk-Kuznetskii, complained that the strike had been poorly organized, since it had not been joined by workers of sectors in the region nor even by all the coal miners.[130]

A meeting the same day of the executive bureau of the IMU and the ICCSC drew similar conclusions. The positive results of the strike were: to have sharply accelerated the realization among the strikers and others that real improvement of the toilers socio-eocnomic situation requires "the dismantling of the existing in totalitarian state-political system, the liquidation of the monopoly on power of the Communist party from top to bottom"; to have helped to show who among the political personalities, organizations and movements are "allies of the toilers in fact, and who are only capable of loud slogans"; to have aided in the process of freeing the toilers from "paternalism, faith in the 'good Tsar', President and other such saviours of the fatherland and people." It listed among the other positive results: the creation of the interrepublican parliamentary group, partial satisfaction of economic demands and recognition of the need for a collective agreement, acceleration of the process of the transfer of power from the centre to the republics on the basis of the transfer of enterprises to the jurisdiction of the republics, acceleration of the process of transfer of the miners from the "state union" to the IMU, and the further consolidation of the labour movement, its moving beyond a branch framework.[131]

Even if much of this is true, it does not alter the fact that the miners' leaders declared over and over during the strike that "we warn with all seriousness that economic questions alone, without political, will not resolve the problems either of the coal sector or of the country as a whole. The striking collectives...insist on the fullfilment of their political demands."[132] It was possible to argue that the strike's political demands had been achieved in an indirect manner, since the "accord of ten" provides for a new constitution to be signed within six months and for new elections to the USSR Supreme Soviet to follow. The strike did play an important role, as Yeltsin had claimed, in Gorbachev's shift away from the conservatives. On the other hand, the new constitution and the elections are still only promises. Moreover, they are made by the leader of a government in whom the miners have expressed total lack of confidence. This discredited government will be negotiating the union treaty on behalf of the Soviet people as a whole. There is no guarantee that this fundamental law of the Soviet state will be the outcome of a democratic process. Much can, and undoubtedly will, happen in the interval. If the promises are not kept, will the miners be capable of mobilizing again?

In the end, the most concrete gains of the strikes, including those in Byelorussia, were economic. Yet the emphasis on political demands had been based upon the workers' realization that economic progress is not possible without fundamental political change. This was the conclusion the miners had drawn from their experience with resolution 608 after the July 1989 strike. Among the main economic gains of the 1991 strike was the state's recognition of the principle of a branch-wide collective agreement, which will now, apparently, have to be negotiated separately in each republic. But is there reason to believe that the provisions of these agreements will be carried out more faithfully than resolution 608? Many strikers seem to feel that the republican governments are, or potentially could be with new elections, more responsive to the popular will than the central government.

But even if the will is there, will the republican governments be able to satisfy the strikers' basic economic demand for a guaranteed, decent living standard? Economists are predicting that the economic concessions made to the miners will not prevent the continued deterioration of their situation and new strikes.[133] An editorial in the liberal *Literaturnaya gazeta* suggested that the transfer of the Kuzbass mines to Russia would probably keep things quiet until the Russian presidential elections, scheduled for June 1991, but that it might turn out to be a time bomb for Yeltsin.[134] For the mines, the transfer boils down to greater autonomy and, in particular, the retention of a greater part of their revenues. It is assumed that prices will be raised, perhaps eventually freed, so that mines currently working at a loss will have revenues.

These are highly inflationary measures that will also deprive the government of needed revenues for restructuring of the economy. Many liberal economists are critical of demands for higher wages, indexation and lower taxes, arguing that they exacerbate shortages and drive the inflationary spiral.[135] Analyzing the situation after the strike, economist L. Popova called on liberals to educate the miners to a more sober view of the market, which they tend to see in the same terms as they once viewed communism: a radiant future, justice for all. She went on to argue that particularly in the base industries, like coal, which cannot live without state subsidies, workers should not expect immediate improvements. The miners should press to accelerate the market reform, "but not for their own sake, or that of their shop, mine or sector, but for the economy as a whole."[136] These words are strongly reminiscent of what the Communist bureaucrats had been telling workers for over 60 years. Coming from one of the liberal economists, who have spent the last few years castigating collectivism and "levelling," they make a strange impression indeed.

All the foregoing points to the conclusion that the strikers were right to concentrate on political, democratic demands, since only popular control of the reform process will ensure that it will not be carried out at the workers' expense, as has generally been the case in the past. The results of the strikes, therefore, should be judged first of all by the degree to which they strengthened popular democratic forces, as the joint resolution of the IMU and the ICCSC tried to do, although the objectivity of these organization is somewhat tainted by their desire to put the best face on things. The real picture is rather mixed. On the one hand, the strike, even if it did not end in a clear victory, did not end in defeat either. The strikers forced the central and republican governments to retreat on a number of important issues and this over the long run will probably strengthen the workers' sense of political efficacy, as the resolution argues. The fatigue that had been noted among the miners before the strike turned out to be fatigue not with politics as such, but with electoral and parliamentary politics, which they saw as talk fests and personal power trips in which their concerns and interests were not reflected.

Another positive result of the strike also noted in the resolution was the spread of the organized labour movement out of the coalmining sector. But though many workers declared their sympathy and solidarity with the strikers' goals, the movement failed to embrace the largest Soviet cities, and the miners' attempts to expand the movement in their own regions met with very limited success. "We showed that we are not afraid of the government," explained a member of the Makeevka strike committee in the Donbass, "and that we have our own opinion concerning the standard of living. We thought that the workers of the other branches, who are being robbed by the state in the same manner, would support us, but nothing of the kind happened. Morally, they are all with us, but they did not decide to strike... We have understood that we won't achieve anything until we consolidate our forces."[137]

Moreover, the strike revealed serious divisions along republican, regional and enterprise (market) lines among the coalminers themselves. The conditions of transfer of the mines to the Russian republic will probably deepen these, unless the miners take specific measures aimed at strengthening their solidarity as their most basic economic and political resource. The unity of July 1989 and the months that followed was still very much an artifact of the "command system." With that system fast crumbling, unity will have to be rebuilt on a new basis.

In this context, the strikers' support for republican sovereignty merits some comment. Except in a minority of cases, mostly in the Western Ukraine, this demand should not be equated with "blind," affective nationalism. It is not very likely that Russian-speaking Donbass miners, who until recently have shown little interest (not to say hostility) for

Ukrainian independence, should suddenly becomes converts to Ukrainian nationalism. A similar argument can be made for the workers of Russia, who have traditionally shown little inclination to nationalism. Even many West Ukrainian miners saw fit to strike against their republican government, ignoring the advice and reproaches of nationalist politicians who accused them of hurting Ukrainian interests. For the most part, workers' support for republican sovereignty arises directly from their deep-rooted democratic sentiments. The March referendum on the future of the Union showed that a majority of the population of Russia and the Ukraine want to maintain the union, but at the same time they want republican sovereignty.[138] In other words, the union must be a voluntary one, built from below, the centre wielding only those powers that the republics decide to give it. The existing central government is seen by the workers, and not without reason, as undemocratic, a tool of the bureaucratic dictatorship. In effect, the strikers' demands for republican sovereignty and for the resignation of the central authorities are different sides of the same coin. There is little danger at present that nationalism will become a substitute for democracy in these republics. (The situation is rather different in the predominantly non-Slavic republics.) This, of course, does not mean that the process of disintegration of the old union does not pose very serious problems for the Soviet labour movement.

Another development of the strike was the closer co-operation between the miners and liberal movements. But this too was not without its ambiguities. Liberals were obviously delighted to have the miners' support in their campaign against Gorbachev. Nevethless, many recognized that this is a double-edged sword that makes them and Yeltsin more dependent upon the labour movement, the only organized popular political force, and so less able to take the "harsh, unpopular measures" called for by their reform. A closer look at the workers' demands and at the economic concessions they won reveals important areas of conflict with the liberal programme. In the first place, the miners see themselves as the collective managers of their mines. This is implicit in the very conditions of their transfer to republican jurisdiction (it is the miners who will decide how to spend the additional revenues left with the enterprise, its form of management and ownership) and explicit in the draft collective agreement drawn up by the IMU which states that, regardless of the form of property, "the government and the union will by all means facilitate the development and productive work of workers' self-management of the enterprises."[139] It will also be recalled that several mines continued to strike after the others had returned because they wanted to elect new directors.

The draft collective agreement also states that privatization should be accomplished through the transfer of the enterprises to the collectives, either as the collective's property or in leasehold. In cases where the collective refuses to take over the enterprise, the latter remains state property.[140] The miners' leaders who favour full enterprise autonomy under the market mean by this "the free economic entrepreneurship of the mine collectives."[141] Miners typically talk of their "right to dispose freely of their product."[142] The draft agreement also pledges that the union will decisively fight against job losses. In principle, of course, self-management can be compatible with a market-driven economy. But, in practice, will workers agree to fire each other or themselves? Will they allow the bankruptcy or sale of their enterprises?

Yeltsin, as a populist leader, is careful not to contradict openly these aspirations. Speaking on national television a few days after his trip to the Kuzbass, he was lavish in his praise of the miners, refuting accusations that their strike disorganized the economy. On the contrary, he stated, the strikers prevented its collapse during the strike by organizing measures to maintain the mines in working order. And he continued: "It is possible that this is in fact a prototype for self-management. We are looking for ways of doing this and have not yet managed to find them in theory. But in practice, life prompts us to believe that this will probably be the best self-management system in the collective, or in some organization [sic]."[143] It is instructive to compare this what Yeltsin's prime minister had to say to US businessmen in New York a week earlier: "We have begun promoting entrepreneurship and believe that the entrepreneur will save Russia. To achieve this we are seeking legislative and constitutional rights that would create a favourable atmosphere and protect the Russian entrepreneur from negative influence."[144] For liberal reformers (as Eastern European experience also attests), workers self-management is high on the list of these negative influences.

The issue of enterprise autonomy is also far from clear. For the miners, this means above all the free disposition of a larger part of their product so that they can do away with subsidies. This is primarily a reaction against the mines' dependence on the ministry, which was — and still is — not subject to popular control. On the other hand, the agreement on transfer of the Kuzbass mines to Russian jurisdiction lets the mines decide if they want to be autonomous and makes specific provision for individualized, i.e. non-market, prices based upon the cost of extraction. True, these are said to be temporary, until market prices can be introduced, but these may just turn out to be rather permanent transitional measures, since market prices mean mass closures and dismissals. The miners are committed to maintaining employment. The IMU's draft collective agreement allows closures only with the agreement of both sides and calls for job guarantees for those who are dismissed and generous state support between jobs. Since these conditions are not likely to be fulfilled, it is hard to see miners accepting real enterprise autonomy and market prices that would inevitably mean mass closures, and not only in the Donbass. Even in the Kuzbass not all mines would be profitable. As for Vorkuta, some economists have argued that the entire economy of that far-northern city, developed during the war to offset the loss of Ukrainian coal, is artificial.[145]

Even in the Kuzbass, where liberal influence is strong, some of the miners' leaders are concerned that these concessions might turn out to be poisoned candy. In this context, it is worth quoting at length from an interview with A. Sergeev, co-chairman of the ICCSC and member of the executive bureau of the IMU, who was asked if the new arrangements might not divide the miners:

> I can answer as one of the leaders of the trade union. I consider this measure that Yeltsin is proposing to be populistic. It may well turn out that he will take into Russian jurisdiction only the profitable mines and leave the others. We have to see. But the threat of closure is real in Russia too, including the Kuzbass. So this matter of Russia taking the mines into its jurisdiction and giving them autonomy has to be closely examined first.
>
> In general, I am categorically opposed to such blanket recipes. In the 1930s, there was mass collectivization. Now they want to conduct mass privatization at full speed, without any economic analyses or studies of the situation in the coal industry as a whole. What will the unprofitable mines do? We need time to study these questions. They are holding out to the miners the prospect of becoming

owners and masters. But what will happen after that, no one knows.

I told the representatives of the Raspadksaya mine: Two and a half years ago they offered you a leasing arrangement to persuade you to abandon the strike. Two years later, in 1991, you struck again, and they let you become a joint stock company to end the strike. What will you strike for next time? You haven't even understood the first stage and already you are jumping into another. They are throwing you bones. These are pure slogans without any economic basis...

This is my personal opinion and that of some of my colleagues, for which, by the way, we are sometimes harshly criticized. They tell us: You're wrong! How can you talk like that!

[...Among the rank and file] opinions are also divided. This is a complicated question. ...A person who has spent six hours at physical labour and then has to think about how to get food naturally is not worried about these things. They are told: Here's your chance to become master; until now you have been working without being master. And so he thinks to himself: Hey, maybe that really is true! Who the hell knows?

While some of the miners' leaders, like Golikov, have clearly hitched their wagon to Yeltsin (Golikov has told the miners that their function is to be "battering rams" for the "democrats"[146]), most share Sergeev's emphasis on the independence of the labour movement:

...We are now in practice going through a period of self-education... We take one point of view, then another, and we try to compare them and draw our own conclusions. But always...we start from the principles of our trade union: it was created to defend the workers' interests in the areas of employment, wages, health and safety. All I can say is that none of the programmes, neither that of Pavlov nor that of

Silaev, takes these problems into consideration. They don't even mention them. In principle, that is correct, since that's what a government exists for: in order to get out of the crisis, you have to cut off the ends, do anything that will keep the ship afloat. But we can't adopt such a view.[147]

A leader of the IMU in the Western Ukraine, when asked if his union was among the radical organizations, told the Berlin newspaper *Neues Deutschland*: "That should not be the issue. It is probably closer to the people because all of us come from the mines. I myself worked eight years on site. We do not support any specific politicians. We represent the grass-roots demands toward any politician in power."[148] As noted, many West Ukrainian miners refused to follow Rukh and the elected nationalist local officials who opposed the strike.

This independent outlook on relations with the existing political parties and movements is widespread among Soviet workers. The support they have given to liberals is conditional and owes much to the absence of other credible alternatives to the conservatives. On April 26, ten shops of the Lenin Machine-Construction Factory in Perm' conducted a four-hour political warning strike. In their declaration, the workers stated that they "did not want to strike under the leadership of the trade unions or of Democratic Russia and adopted these demands independently":

1) a 200-300% wage rise, with the money to be found in the funds of the enterprises, or alternatively

2) the reduction of retail prices to the previous level through subsidies paid by the city's enterprises;

3) workers' control of the financial resources of the enterprises, and, in the first place, of the accounts of private enterprises that receive payments from factories. To this end, the organs of workers' self-management should be restored in the enterprises and given the right of ownership of profits, of the means of production and of the product;

4) modification of collective agreements to limit the average annual salary of directors to double the average wage of workers;

5) "In connection with the failure of deputies of all political orientations to fulfill their promises, conduct new elections to the soviets at all levels, including the Supreme Soviet of the USSR, and hold general elections of the president."[149]

These demands were formulated with the help of the Perm' Union of Workers, which has about 70 members (workers and intellectuals) and is part of a larger network of worker-oriented, socialist organizations in the industrial towns of the Urals. They illustrate the type of demands that can result from collaboration between workers and socialist activists. But such collaboration is still very rare.

Some miner activists expressed doubts about the entire course of the strike on the grounds that the miners were being used by alien interests. A. Aver'yanov of the Zasyad'ko mine in the Donbass, which did not strike, resigned from the Donetsk city strike committee. He told a journalist that he did not feel that the miners were fundamentally split over goals, only over tactics. He did not see the strike as advancing the miners' goals: "I do not wish to be a political prostitute. The strike began for one set of issues and ended on others. Someone is turning us like a weather-cock."[150]

Aver'yanov's evaluation of the strike may seem overly harsh. The workers do share certain interests with the liberals in opposing bureaucratic power, though as noted earlier, in this area most liberals are far from the radicals they present themselves to be. But the labour movement, so long as it does not develop its own programme of socio-economic and political transformation, is condemned to be a political weathercock, or, worse, a battering ram for interests that are fundamentally hostile to it. Yet, none of the miners' leaders cited above, including Aver'yanov, seems to envision the possibility of the workers themselves (the vast majority of the population) forming the government through their own political representatives organized in a party.

Asked how he saw the relationship between the miners' movement and the liberal Democratic Russia movement, Sergeev replied:

Out trade union adheres to a purely trade-unionist principle, that is the trade union, for now at least, should not support any political party. That is in principle. But we have to look at the situation... To put it briefly, a struggle is taking place today between — this might seem crude and abstract — the boyars [artistocrats in feudal Russia], the Communist boyars, and the new bourgeoisie that used to serve the boyars but has grown tired of that role. They now want to rise to the top themselves... These are enterprising people, whose capital for now is knowledge. They worked for the boyars a long time, servicing their ideology. [... These are] the intelligentsia, economists, and the like. ...For us, the workers and the workers' movement, it makes more sense to support this boursgeoisie, because for 70 years the Communists' idea that everything belongs to everyone and to me, "everything belongs to the Kolkhoz," has shown its unsoundness. This is in general, although in principle some degree of centralization and planning are necessary. It is a question of what is rational.

The new bourgeoisie is proposing a system that gives the worker a chance to sell his labour power according to the amount agreed upon, that is: "You, too, are a person, and we give everyone a chance" — although that is really open to debate, here, as well as in the West. In any case, they are proposing a concept of a normal society in which everyone will have a chance — though I repeat, the validity of this claim is far from obvious. So while this struggle is going on, we naturally support the new bourgeoisie. Because the Communists' foggy, orthodox idea, that is, the idea of a radiant future, is not based upon concrete reality and concrete forces.

But we must never forget that when the new bourgeoisie comes to power — and this is an inevitable process, for either they will share power with the boyars and live with them in peaceful coexistence or they will come to power on their own — those whose capital is knowledge will want to transform it into material capital [...and] they will want to exploit us. That is part of their system. So, while supporting at present the movement of democrats — though we know that they are really a bourgeoisie, in principle, a social-democratic orientation, if you judge them from the point of view of world experience — we must never forget that sooner or later we will clash with them. We are already clashing over a number of issues.

Sergeev does not feel that the workers are ready yet for their own party. They must first define themselves politically. But he did note the "stratification" that was taking place in soviet society, the creeping, illicit privatization. "In essense, capital is being accumulated." Will not the workers revolt against this? "I don't at all deny that. It's at that point that the possibility of a workers party will be real."

Sergeev may be right. Nevertheless, for socialists, and indeed for anyone who identifies with popular interests in the Soviet Union, it is hard to avoid a sense of urgency. In principle, expropriators can always be expropriated. But one cannot ignore the divisive effects on the workers of the market and the accompanying disintegration of the Union. On the other hand, these same conditions have given rise to a workers' self-management movement, which has forged links with the miners and is quickly growing disillusioned with the liberals. The independent spirit of both wings of the labour movement is encouraging, as is the movement's profound politicization, sometimes almost despite itself.

The "accord of ten" has opened a new phase in the "post-stagnation" period of Soviet history. The coming months are likely to see attempts to accelerate the transition to capitalism. All that can be predicted with reasonable certainty is that a period of socio-political struggles lies ahead that will make the last seven stormy years seem almost tranquil.

June 1991

NOTES

1. See *Izvestiya*, May 5, 1991. The rank-and-file, too, were abandoning the party. At the Vorgashorskaya mine in Vorkuta, party membership had fallen from 500 in July 1989 to 100 in February 1991. (*Moskovskie novosti*, no. 8, 1991, p. 5) Many of the miners leaders had joined the party in the early years of perestroika, seeing the party as a force for progressive change. (See, for example, *Kuranty*, Mar. 29, 1991.) This, of course, is not to characterize the Communist Party's orientation as anti-liberal. To the degree that its leadership had any orientation, it, too, was essentially liberal in the area of economic reform. But in the popular consciousness, the Communist Party came to be identified with the Centre's inability or unwillingess to carry out effective reforms of any kind.
2. V. Kirichenko, "Otrezvlyayushchie tsifry," *Pravitel'stvennyi vestnik*, no. 1, 1991, p.2; *International Herald Tribune*, May 11-12, 1991; *Manchester Guardian Weekly*, Mar. 24, 1991.
3. For example, in 1990, at the AZLK auto factory in Moscow, these sales amounted, curiously enough, to more than the total yearly wage fund. (*Moskvich* (Moscow), February 27, 1991). Of course, employees in smaller, poorer or less important enterprises would not have access to anything approaching these quantities of goods.
4. *Trud*, Feb. 5, 1991.
5. In a survey conducted by the State Statistical Agency in the summer of 1990, one-third of the respondents said that private sector food prices were inaccessible, while 40% could allow themselves to purchase only a few selected goods. *Pravitel'stvennyi vestnik*, no. 39, 1990, p. 5.
6. *Komsomol'skaya pravda*, Feb. 5, 1991; *Trud*, Feb. 5, 1991.
7. *Trud*, Feb. 27, 1991.
8. *Trud*, Feb. 2, 1991.
9. Ibid.
10. *Moskovskie novosti*, no. 8, 1991, p. 5.
11. Ibid.
12. *Komsomol'skaya pravda*, Feb. 22, 1991.
13. *Vechernyaya Moskva*, Oct. 7, 1990.
14. G. Popov, "Perspektivy i realii," *Ogonek*, no. 50, pp. 6-8 and no. 51, pp. 5-8, 1990.
15. In February, writing in the pages of a liberal newspaper, economist S. Sugushev, cited the "Chilean model" as relevant for the Soviet Union and called for a bloc of "real entrepreneurs" and the military. Pinochet was totalitarian in politics, he explained, but not in economics. And he was competent: he had even graduated from a leading U.S. business school. (*Komsomol'skaya pravda*, Feb. 2, 1991.) Compare this with the statement of Politburo member Yu. Prokofiev that in the Soviet Union, like Japan, South Korea, Spain, "and I would not be afraid to name even Chile," centralized authoritarian state structures are needed to create a market and its structures in a brief time and in an organized manner. (*Financial Times* (London), Feb. 22, 1991)
16. An all-Union survey conducted in January and March 1991 asked people whose ideas they identified with more closely, Gorbachev's or Yeltsin's. In January, 22% chose Gorbachev, 44% — Yeltsin, 18 — neither, and 14 did not answer. In March, 22%

still chose Gorbachev, but Yeltsin's supporters had declined to 36% and the proportion that did not find their views reflected in either leader rose to 30%. (12% did not answer.) (*Moskovskie novosti,* Apr. 21, 1991, p. 5)
17. *Gazette (Montreal),* Feb. 24, p. A-6 and Feb 25, p. B-4.
18. *Moskovskie novosti,* Mar. 11, 1990, p. 5.
19. *Moskovskie novosti,* June 24, 1990, p. 4; *Gazette,* 15 June 1990, p. A-10.
20. *Trud,* July 13, 1991.
21. B. Ikhlov, "The Elites No Longer Can, and the Masses No Longer Want To," in *Socialist Alternatives* (Montreal), no. 1, fall 1991.
22. *Sobesednik,* no. 29, 90, p.3.
23. Ibid.
24. *Moskovskie novosti,* Feb. 24, 1991, p.5.
25. *Komsomol'skaya pravda,* Mar. 5, 1991.
26. *Komsomol'skaya pravda,* Feb. 7, 1991. See also Dec. 22, 1990.
27. Unpublished opinion survey conducted by L. Gordon, A. Nazimova and others in Donetsk on October 22, 1990.
28. Ikhlov, "The Elites No Longer Can..." In the Soviet Union today, "democrats" means economic and/or political liberals.
29. *Moskovskie novosti,* Feb. 21. 1991, p. 5.
30. The Kuzbass Union of Workers' Committees grew out of the miners' strike committees of July 1989. Until that strike, Golikov had been a mineworker. At present, he is a member of the Russian parliament and since December 1990 a member of Yelstin's "brain trust".
31. *Rabochaya tribuna,* Jan 17, 1991.
32. *Rabochaya tribuna,* Feb. 26, 1991.
33. *Trud,* Feb. 5 and 6 1991.
34. *Moskovskie novosti,* May 5, 1991, p.8; *Kuranty,* Feb. 20, 1991; *Komsomol'skaya pravda,* Feb. 16, 1991. "Limitchiki" are workers residing in the large cities on temporary work permits. They have little recourse against the administration.
35. Interview with A. Sergeev; *Rabochaya tribuna,* Mar. 26, 1991; *Komsomol'skaya pravda,* June 6, 1991.
36. Unpublished resolution of the Regional Council of Strike Committees of the Donbass, Feb,. 26, 1991; *Rabochaya tribuna,* Feb. 20, 1991, *Trud,* Mar. 1, 1991, and unpublished interview with A. Sergeev.
37. *Komsomol'skaya pravda,* Mar. 2, 1991.
38. *Rabochaya tribuna,* Mar. 5 and 7, 1991.
39. *Komsomol'skaya pravda,* Mar. 2, 1991.
40. *Komsomol'skaya pravda,* Mar. 2 and Apr. 4, 1991; *Trud,* Mar. 3, 1991. According to one report, the demonstration did not take place because of a mine accident in one of the town's mines. But this would seem all the more reason to protest.
41. *Trud,* Mar. 2, 1991; *Sobesednik,* no. 12, 1991, p. 7.
42. *Nezavisimaya gazeta,* Apr. 20, 1991.
43. *Trud,* Mar. 2, 1991; *Komsomol'skaya pravda,* Mar. 2, 1991; *Rabochaya tribuna,* Mar. 5, 1991.
44. *Komsomol'skaya pravda,* Mar. 2, 1991; *Trud,* Mar. 2 and 5, 1991; *Rabochaya tribuna,* Mar. 5, 1991.

45. *Izvestiya*, Apr. 10, 1991. In the first, and apparently only, case to come to trial, the Karaganda regional court ruled that the strike had not been illegal since it was essentially political in nature and the law covered only economic conflicts. The USSR Supreme Soviet later outlawed political strikes. This law, like so many others, will probably go ignored.
46. *Pravda*, Mar. 18, 1991.
47. *Komsomol'skaya pravda*, Mar. 5, 1991.
48. *Sobesednik*, no. 12, 1991, p. 7. See also *Komsomol'skaya pravda*, Mar. 5, 1991.
49. *Komsomol'skaya pravda*, Mar. 5, 1991.
50. Ibid.; *Rabochaya tribuna*, Mar. 6, 1991; Moscow Central Televsion, Mar. 5, 1991, reported in *Daily Report on the USSR* (henceforth DR) Mar. 5, 1991, p. 41.
51. *Izvestiya*, Mar. 8, 1991.
52. *Rabochaya tribuna*, Mar. 7, 1991; *Trud*, Mar. 8, 1991; *Kontinent* (Naberezhnye chelny), no. 3, 1991.
53. *Komosmol'skaya pravda*, Mar. 12, 1991; Moscow Central Television, Mar. 5, 1991, reported in DR, Mar. 5, 1991, p. 39.
54. *Komsomol'skaya pravda*, Mar. 7 and 12, 1991; *Trud*, Mar. 7, 1991.
55. *Trud*, Mar. 5, 1991; *Komsomol'skaya pravda*, Mar. 5, 1991.
56. Vorkuta is located in the former Komi Autonomous Republic of the Russian Federation. In 1990, it declared its sovereignty and changed its name to the Komi Republic, though in practice little had changed by the time of this strike.
57. *Komsomol'skaya pravda*, Mar. 7 and 28, 1991; *Trud*, Mar. 8 and 15, 1991; Moscow Domestic Radio Mar. 7, 1991, reported in DR, Mar. 8, 1991, p. 58; *Nedelya*, no. 21, 1991, p. 3.
58. *Komsomol'skaya pravda*, Mar. 16, 1991; *Financial Times*, Mar. 11, 1991; *Trud*, Mar. 15, 1991; *Ravochaya tribua*, Mar. 13, 1991; *Manchester Guardian Weekly*, Mar. 24, 1991, p. 4.
59. *Komsomol'skaya pravda*, Mar. 12, 1991.
60. Moscow Central Television, reported in DR, Mar. 13, 1991, p. 39.
61. *Trud*, Mar. 14, 1991; *Financial Times*, Mar. 13, 1991, p. 5; *Komsomol'skaya pravda*, Apr. 4, 1991.
62. *Manchester Guardian Weekly*, Mar. 24, 1991, p. 8.
63. *Trud*, Mar. 15, 1991; *Nedelya*, no. 21, p. 3.
64. *Komsomol'skaya pravda*, Mar. 19, 1991; *Rabochaya tribuna*, Apr. 23, 1991; *Izvestiya* Mar. 21, 1991; I. Zhuravskaya, "Zalozhniki", *Ogonek*, no. 14, 1991. p. 2; Radio Rossii, Mar. 18, 1991, reported in DR, Mar. 19, 1991, p. 43.
65. Komsomol'skaya pravda, Apr. 4, 1991; *Pravda*, Mar. 15, 1991; TASS, Apr. 9, 1991, reported in DR, Apr. 10. 1991, p. 43.
66. *Pravda*, Mar. 29, 1991; TASS, Apr. 16, 1991, reported in DR, Apr. 17, 1991, p. 53.
67. *Izvestiya*, Mar. 26, 1991; TASS, Apr. 2, 1991, in DR, Apr. 3, 1991, p. 36; *New York Times*, Mar. 28, 1991; *Sobesednik*, no. 14, 1991, p.2; Moscow All-Union Radio, Mar. 28, 1991, Mayak Radio, Mar. 29; Moscow Central Television, Mar. 28, 1991, in DR, Mar. 29, 1991, p. 35; *Trud*, Apr. 6, 1991.
68. *Komsomol'skaya pravda*, Mar. 19, 21 and Apr. 16, 1991.
69. *Rabochaya tribuna*, Apr. 5, 1991; Moscow Radio, Apr. 3, 1991, in DR, Apr. 5, 1991, p. 29; *Izvestiya*, Mar. 30, 1991.
70. *Sobesednik*, no. 14, 1991, p. 2.

71. *Izvestiya*, Apr. 23, 1991; TASS, Apr. 1, 1991, in DR, Apr. 2, 1991, p. 45.
72. *Izvestiya*, Apr. 30, 1991.
73. *Pravitel'stvennyi vestnik*, no. 15, 1991, p. 4.
74. *Trud*, Apr. 4, 1991.
75. *Moskovskie novosti*, Apr. 5, 1991, p. 7.
76. Unpublished declaration of the delegates from striking enterprises to the talks with the government on Apr. 2 and 3, Apr. 4, 1991;*Rabochaya tribuna*, Apr. 9, 1991; *Trud*, Apr. 6, 1991.
77. Central television, Apr. 4, 1991, reported in DR, Apr. 5, 1991, pp. 36-37.
78. TASS, Apr. 9, 1991, reported in DR, Apr. 10, 1991, p. 43; *Komsomol'skaya pravda*, Apr. 5, 1991.
79. *Komsomol'skaya pravda*, Apr. 3, 1991.
80. *Komsomol'skaya pravda*, Apr. 2, 1991; *Pravitel'stvennyi vestnik*, no. 10, 1991.
81. Central Television, Apr. 13, 1991, reported in DR, Apr. 15, 1991, p. 30.
82. *Izvestiya*, Apr. 11, 1991; *Komsomol'skaya pravda*, Apr. 9, 1991.
83. *Trud*, Apr. 6, 1991; *Moskovskie novosti*, no.18, 1991. p.6; *Pravda*, Apr. 5, 1991; TASS, Apr. 12, 1991, reported in DR, Apr. 15, 1991, p. 26.
84. *Izvestiya*, Apr. 8, 1991; *Pravda*, Apr. 8, 1991; *Komsomol'skaya pravda*, Apr. 9, 1991; TASS, Apr. 8, 1991, reported in DR, Apr. 8, 1991, p. 63; TASS, Apr. 9, 1991, reported in DR, Apr. 10, 1991, p. 41; Moscow Radio, Apr. 9, 1991, ibid. p. 42; *Nedelya*, no. 21, 1991, p.3.
85. *Rabochaya tribuna*, Apr. 6, 1991.
86. *Izvestiya*, Apr. 23, 1991; Mayak Radio, Apr. 5, 1991, reported in DR, Apr. 8, 1991, p. 46.
87. *Trud*, Apr. 4, 1991.
88. *Izvestiya*, Apr. 5 and 14, 1991; *Pravda*, Apr. 5, 1991; *Rabochaya tribuna*, Apr. 4, 1991; *Komsomol'skaya pravda*, Apr. 5, 1991; K. Mihalisko, "The Workers' Rebellion in Byelorussia," *Report on the USSR*, Apr. 26, 1991, pp. 21-5.
89. *Argumenty i fakty*, no. 19, 1991, p. 2.
90. *Izvestiya*, Apr. 15, 1991; *Rabochaya tribuna*, Apr. 6, 1991; *Moskovskie novosti*, No. 15, 1991, p. 6 and no. 17, 1991, p. 4; *Nezavisimaya gazeta*, Apr. 20, 1991; Mihalisko, "The Workers' Rebellion..." p. 22.
91. *Trud*, Apr. 5, 1991; Central television, Apr. 5, 1991, reported in DR, Apr. 8, 1991, p. 48.
92. *Izvestiya*, Apr. 11, 1991; TASS, Apr. 10, 1991 and Radio Mayak, Apr. 11, 1991, reported in DR, Apr. 11, 1991, p. 44-5.
93. *Izvestiya*, Apr. 12, 1991; *Pravda*, Apr. 12, 1991; *Moskovskie novosti*, no. 16, 1991, p. 11; Radio Mayak, Apr. 12, 1991, reported in DR, Apr. 12, 1991, p. 68.
94. *Pravda*, Apr. 13, 1991; *Moskovskie novosti*, no. 17, 1991.
95. *Report on the USSR*, Apr. 26, 1991, p. 29-30; *Moskovskie novosti*, no. 17, 1991; *Izvestiya*, Apr. 18, 1991; *Gazette*, (Montreal) Apr. 17, 1991, p. A-10; TASS, Apr. 16, 1991, reported in DR, Apr. 17, 1991, p. 82; TASS, Apr. 18, 1991, in DR, Apr. 19, 1991, p. 62; AFP, Apr. 16, 1991, in DR, Apr. 18, 1991, p. 45.
96. *Pravda*, Apr. 17, 1991.
97. *Moskovskie novosti*, no. 17, 1991, p. 3.
98. *Nezavisizmaya gazeta*, Apr. 20 and 25, 1991; *Moskovskie novosti*, no. 17, 1991.
99. *Pravda*, Apr. 19, 1991, Kiev International Service, reported in DR, Apr. 22, 1991, p. 86; AFP, Apr. 19, 1991, in DR, Apr. 19, 1991, p. 35; *Nezavisimaya gazeta*, Apr. 20 and 23, 1991.

100. *Komsomol'skaya pravda*, Apr. 16, 1991; *Nezavisimaya gazeta*, Apr. 20, 1991; *Pravda*, Apr. 25, 1991.
101. *Nezavisimaya gazeta*, Apr. 20, 1991; *Moskovksie novosti*, no. 17, 1991, p. 10.
102. Central television, Apr. 30, 1991, in DR, May 1, 1991, p. 55.
103. *Trud*, May 1, 1991.
104. I. Zhuravskaya, "Zalozhniki"; *Komsomol'skaya pravda*, Apr. 9 and June 1, 1991; *Izvestiya*, Apr. 11, 1991.
105. *Izvestiya*, Apr. 11; unpublished document of IMU revision commission, May 12, 1991.
106. *Rabochaya tribuna*, Apr. 23, 1991; unpublished documents; Radio Rossii, Apr. 15, 1991, reported in DR, Apr. 16, 1991, p. 31.
107. *Report on the USSR*, May 13, 1991, p. 30; TASS, Apr. 22, 1991, reported in DR, Apr. 23, 1991, pp. 44-5.
108. *Moskovskie novosti*, No. 16, 1991, p. 11; *Nezavisimaya gazeta*, Apr. 17 and 23, 1991; *Izvestiya*, Apr. 23, 1991.
109. *Nezavisimaya gazeta*, Apr. 25 and 30, 1991; *Izvetsiya*, Apr. 30, 1991; TASS and Radio Rossii, Apr. 23, 1991, reported in DR, Apr. 24, 1991, pp. 52-3; Minsk Radio, in DR, Apr. 25, 1991, p. 64; Minsk Radio, Apr. 25 and 26, 1991, in DR, Apr. 26, 1991, pp. 50-1; TASS, Apr. 26, 1991, in DR, Apr. 29, 1991, p. 52. .
110. *Nezvisimaya gazeta*, Apr. 20, 1991.
111. *Izvetsiya*, Apr. 23, 1991.
112. *Izvestiya*, Apr. 23, 1991; Radio Mayak, Apr. 23, 1991, in DR, Apr. 23, 1991, p. 49.
113. TASS, reported in DR, Apr. 25, 1991, p. 37.
114. *Pravda*, Apr. 24, 1991.
115. *Komsomol'skaya pravda*, Apr. 27, 1991; Radio Mayak, Apr. 25, 1991, reported in DR, Apr. 29, 1991, p. 34; Radio Mayak, Apr. 27, in DR, Apr. 29, 1991, p. 39.
116. AFP, Apr. 30, 1991, in DR, May 1, 1991, p. 35; TASS, Apr. 27, 1991, in DR, Apr. 29, 1991, p. 39.
117. Radio Kiev, Apr. 30, 1991, in DR, May 1, 1991, p. 36; TASS, Apr. 29 and 30, 1991, in DR, Apr. 30, 1991, p. 36.
118. Minsk Radio, Apr. 28, 1991, in DR, May 1, 1991, p. 36.
119. *Nezavisimaya gazeta*, Apr. 30, 1991.
120. Interview with A. Sergeev.
121. *Vechernyaya Moskva*, Apr. 30, 1991; *Nezvisimaya gazeta*, Apr. 30, 1991; *Izvestiya*, Apr. 30, 1991; Radio Rossii, Apr. 30, in DR. May 1, 1991, p. 54.
122. *Kommersant*, Apr. 29-May 6, 1991, p. 2; Radio Rossii, May 4, 1991, in DR, May 6, 1991, p. 53.
123. *Sovetskaya Rossiya*, May 2, 1991.
124. *Izvestiya*, May 6 and 9, 1991; TASS, May 10, 1991, reported in DR, May 13, 1991, p. 43; TASS, May 13, 1991, in DR, May 14, 1991, p.45.
125. Izvestiya, May 20, 1991.
126. *Znamya yunosti* (Minsk), May 15, 1991.
127. Interfax, May 20, 1991, in DR, May 21, 1991.
128. *Izvestiya*, May 23, 1991; TASS and Interfax, May 22, 1991, in DR May 23, 1991, p. 71.
129. Interfax, May 23, 1991, in DR, May 24, 1991, pp. 68-9.
130. Interfax May 14, 1991, in DR, May 16, 1991, p. 40.

131. Unpublished joint resolution of the executive bureau of the IMU and the ICCSC, May 14, 1991.
132. From an unpublished joint declaration of delegates of the IMU and representatives of the striking regions (n.d.).
133. Radio Moscow, May 13, 191, DR. May 14, 1991, p. 45.
134. *Literaturnaya gazeta*, May 1, 1991.
135. *Komsomol'skaya pravda*, Apr. 26, 1991; *Izvestiya*, May 7, 1991.
136. *Moskovskie novosti*, no. 18, 1991, p. 7.
137. *Trud*, May 7, 1991.
138. *New York Times*, Mar. 20, 1991; *Manchester Guardian Weekly*, Mar. 24, 1991.
139. *General'noe tipovoe tarifnoe soglashenie rabotnikov gornyatskikh pregdriyatii SSSR*, Donetsk, Oct. 1990, p. 4.
140. *General'noe tipovoe...*, p. 7.
141. *Trud*, Apr. 6, 1991.
142. *Rabochaya tribuna*, May 1, 1990.
143. Central Television, May 4, 1991, in DR, May 6, 1991, p. 50.
144. TASS, Apr. 27, 1991, in DR, Apr. 30, 1991, p. 53.
145. *Sovetskaya Rossiya*, May 1, 1991.
146. B. Ikhlov, "When the Elites No Longer Can..."
147. Interview with Sergeev.
148. *Neues Deutschland*, Apr. 8, 1991.
149. From a leaflet of the Perm' Workers' Union, May 1, 1991.
150. *Komsomol'skaya pravda*, June 6, 1991.

BLACK ROSE BOOKS
has also published the following titles:

IMAGINING THE MIDDLE EAST, *by Thierry Hentsch*
THE MYTH OF THE MARKET, *by Jeremy Seabrook*
THE NEW WORLD ORDER AND THE THIRD WORLD, *edited by Dave Broad and Lori Foster*
GERMANY EAST: Dissent and Opposition, *by Bruce Allen*
RACE, GENDER AND WORK: A Multicultural Economic History of Women in the United States, *by Teresa Amott and Julie Matthaei*
WORDS OF A REBEL, *by Peter Kropotkin, Introduction by George Woodcock*
IN RUSSIAN & FRENCH PRISONS, *by Peter Kropotkin, Introduction by George Woodcock*
MEMOIRS OF A REVOLUTIONIST, *by Peter Kropotkin, Introduction by George Woodcock*
MUTUAL AID, *by Peter Kropotkin, Introduction by George Woodcock*
THE GREAT FRENCH REVOLUTION, *by Peter Kropotkin, Introduction by George Woodcock*
THE CONQUEST OF BREAD, *by Peter Kropotkin, Introduction by George Woodcock*
PETER KROPOTKIN: From Prince to Rebel, *by George Woodcock and Ivan Avakumovick*
BANKERS, BAGMEN AND BANDITS: Business and Politics in the Age of Greed, *by R.T. Naylor*
THE DECLINE OF THE AMERICAN ECONOMY, *by Bertrand Bellon and Jorge Niosi*
THE LIFE AND WORK OF KARL POLANYI, *edited by Kari Polanyi-Levitt*
PARTNERS IN ENTERPRISE: The Worker Ownership Phenomenon, *edited by Jack Quarter and George Melnyk*
THE ANARCHIST COLLECTIVES: Workers' Self-Management in Spain 1936-39, *edited by Sam Dolgoff*
THE KRONSTADT UPRISING, *by Ida Mett*
THE UNKNOWN REVOLUTION, *by Voline*
DEMOCRACY AND THE WORK PLACE, *by Harold B. Wilson*
THE HISTORY OF THE LABOUR MOVEMENT IN QUEBEC, *by the Education Committees of the CSN and CEQ*
THE TRADE UNIONS AND THE STATE, *by Walter Johnson*

send for our complete catalogue of books:
BLACK ROSE BOOKS
P.O. Box 1258, Succ. Place du Parc
Montréal, Québec H2W 2R3 Canada

Printed by
the workers of
Ateliers Graphiques Marc Veilleux Inc.
Cap-Saint-Ignace, Qué.
for
Black Rose Books Ltd.